ROOSEVELT'S BLUES

ROOSEVELT'S BLUES

African-American Blues and Gospel Songs on FDR

Guido van Rijn

University Press of Mississippi Jackson

Library of Congress Cataloging-in-Publication Data

Van Rijn, Guido.
    Roosevelt's blues : African-American blues and gospel songs on FDR / Guido van
Rijn.
        p.   cm.
    Includes bibliographical references (p.   ), discography, and index.
    ISBN 0-87805-937-7 (cloth : alk. paper).—ISBN 0-87805-938-5 (paper : alk. paper)
    1. Roosevelt, Franklin D. (Franklin Delano), 1882–1945—Songs and music—History
and criticism.   2. Blues (Music)—Texts—History and criticism.   3. Gospel music—
Texts—History and criticism.   I. Title.
ML3521.V36   1996
782.42'16431599—dc20   96-24693
                                                                                   CIP
                                                                                   MN

British Library Cataloging-in-Publication data available

In memory of

my father

CONTENTS

FOREWORD

"It is interesting to speculate on what southern history would have been if the Negro had not been a singing race," reflected Guy B. Johnson in 1934. He did not develop the speculation in his essay "Negro Folk Songs" in the 1934 collection *Culture in the South*. But he noted how a black composer "borrowed from the storehouse of folk blues, shaped up his 'blues hits' and turned them back to the folk with interest. It is all a bit confusing to the folk-song collector who tries to keep origins and paths of diffusion straight, but to the folk it makes no difference. The phonograph and radio blues are rapidly becoming at home in the folk tradition."

In the "veritable flood of literature on Negro songs" which was published after World War I, there were several works that noted blues, though generally the emphasis was on ballads and spirituals. Conventional folk-song scholarship, combined with uncertainty as to the authenticity of blues that had "become the basis for commercial exploitation," resulted in a growing disregard of the idiom at the very time when it was exceptionally revealing of black attitudes and experience.

Opportunities for research on popular African-American values were present even in the depths of the depression era. Narratives from black interviewees were gathered in seventeen states, mainly in the South, for the Writers' Unit of the Library of Congress; from these, two thousand "slave narratives" were selected and published. Important as they were, sixty years later one can only regret that complementary narratives of life in the segregated South were not gathered at the same time. Yet some studies of rural black culture based on field research were written by, for example, Carter Woodson, Arthur Raper, and Charles S. Johnson. The latter, in particular, cited extracts from the personal narratives of those from whom he gathered data.

Quite the most extensive study of blacks between the world wars was undertaken by a thirty-person team led by the Swedish economist Gunnar Myrdal. Substantially funded by the Carnegie Foundation, it provided a solid socio-economic base for black studies and assessed white and black "beliefs," "valuations" and expressed "opinions." Although an unrivaled work, *An American Dilemma* spared a mere eight of its more than fourteen hundred pages for "Negro achievements" in business, literature, sports, dance, theater, popular entertainment and the visual arts. In this disregard for African-American culture it reflected the work of black sociologists E. Franklin Frazier, J. G. St. Clair Drake, Horace Cayton and others who were members of the team. Yet blues was mentioned, even if "Negroes have contributed such popular music forms as ragtime, jazz, the blues, swing and boogie-woogie" was all they had to say on the subject.

Song collecting was the province of the Archive of Folk Song of the Library of Congress, and the invaluable location recordings of John A. Lomax, Alan Lomax and other field workers such as Zora Neale Hurston and John W. Work give us insights into the work song, ballad and folk song traditions that survived in the South. A decade later John A. Lomax described the circumstances of his field recordings, in which, however, the blues played little part. A dozen blues songs were included in the Lomaxes' 1936 collection, *Negro Folk Songs as Sung by Leadbelly*, which related to the singer's past life.

In spite of the fact that many thousands of blues records representing hundreds of individual titles were on general sale in the 1930s, whether in country stores and chain stores, from tailgates or by mail order, they were rarely accorded more than a passing word in the social literature of the period. There was no recognition that they could be significant indicators of the spirit and suffering of the African-American poor, or that blues singers expressed the feelings and attitudes of those who shared their color, class and culture.

In order to ascertain the impact on the black community of the depression, the implementation of the New Deal and the involvement of the United States in World War II, Guido van Rijn's book *Roosevelt's Blues* analyzes, in depth for the first time, the content of the blues of that period. Some may argue that the blues is not reliable as an indicator, but, as noted above, there are few, if any, others. As the author shows, some singers were particularly concerned with social issues, but a significant proportion of all blues and gospel titles were sociopolitical in content or implication. That many of these referred directly to President Roosevelt may seem surprising, but the nature of the presidency in American politics is such as to personify government.

Analysts will continue to assess the depth of the crisis, the efficacy of the administration, and the measure of recovery. But postmortem analyses, though revealing and necessary, seldom reflect the perceptions of the times. Echoing Guy B. Johnson, we may find it interesting to speculate on what we would know of black southern feelings and opinions in the interwar years if African-Americans "had not been a [blues] singing race," and had not been recorded for the phonograph, or if Guido van Rijn had not undertaken so rigorously and sympathetically the formidable task of transcribing and analyzing the content of large numbers of those records and placing them so precisely in their historical, social and political contexts.

Sometimes with impassiveness and resignation, frequently in anger or frustration, often with irony or scepticism, and always with simplicity and economy of expression, the blues songs transcribed and explained in this important book open windows on the inner lives and emotions of African-Americans in the depression, giving human dimensions to the raw statistical data of 1930s sociological surveys.

Paul Oliver
Oxford Brookes University

ACKNOWLEDGMENTS

My lifelong involvement with the blues began in the first form of Pius X Lyceum in Amsterdam in 1962, when my music teacher, Nico Hermans, played a record called "Pinetop's Boogie Woogie" to the class.

In the latter half of the sixties, the American Folk Blues Festival tours of Europe visited the Netherlands annually, and I had my first chance to meet some of my heroes and heroines in the flesh. Arend Jan Heerma van Voss had already led me to the Dutch magazine *Jazz Wereld* (1965–1973) and later to the British journal *Blues Unlimited* (1963–1987).

In 1970, Martin van Olderen and I founded the Dutch Blues and Boogie Organisation, and together we arranged the first concerts by American blues artists. Especially influential on my thinking about blues in those early years were Leo Bruin, Herman Engelbart, Rob Hoeke and Wim Verbei. In 1978 I started the Agram Blues label, and have since produced sixteen albums reissuing 78s. My friends Hans Vergeer and Cor van Sliedregt have been closely associated with this project and have further influenced my thinking on blues. The late Max Vreede became a respected friend, and the many evenings I spent with the treasure trove of his collection of 78 rpm records did much to deepen my understanding of the blues.

When I decided to embark on a book-length study, I chose a subject that had first been suggested by Karl Gert zur Heide in the late seventies: blues and gospel songs about the American presidents. In 1991 and 1992 I wrote draft chapters on all the presidents dealt with by blues singers, from Wilson to Clinton. These were scrutinized by John Newman, who provided me with many valuable lessons and insights. I decided to concentrate on President Franklin Roosevelt and make a deeper analysis of songs specifically relating to him and his presidency. At this stage Chris Smith took over from Newman, and his influence is felt throughout the present work, both in the analysis of the songs and in the accuracy of their transcription. As always, Hans Vergeer was an important source of discussion and ideas.

The progress of the Roosevelt manuscript was supervised by the departments of history and English at Leiden University. The idea for this book was born during the lectures of Professor Theo D'Haen on black American literature. But the greatest debt goes to my "promotor," Roosevelt expert Professor Alfons Lammers, who taught me much about FDR, about Leiden University and about life itself. His visionary thoughtfulness prepared the way.

Regarding the ethnomusicological aspects of the book, Professor David Evans of the University of Memphis provided invaluable guidance, advice and insights. The manuscript was also read in its entirety by F. Jack Hurley, Robert McElvaine, Dave Moore, John Newman, Kees van Rijn (my father), Jan Spoelder, Guus Stevens, and Hans Wijnberg. Some chapters were read by John Cowley and Roger Misiewicz.

A number of other people contributed ideas and information, and I extend my thanks to Rolf von Arx, Ray Astbury, Alan Balfour, Eduard van de Bilt, Tony Burke, Paul Duvivié, Bob Eagle, Mel van Elteren, Daniel Gugolz, Robert Javors, Tom Kelly, Klaus Kilian, Rob Kroes, Robert Laughton, Kip Lornell, Ron Meis, Marianne Mout, Paul Oliver, Freddy de Paepe, Johnny Parth, Mark Phillips, Chris Quispel, Tony Russell, Robert Sacré, Neil Slaven, Steven Tracy, Pete Whelan and Rien Wisse.

Much research was done in libraries and/or by librarians at my request, and I would especially like to thank Ingeborg Schwalbe of the Kennedy Institute of the Freie Universität in Berlin; the Amerika Instituut of the Gemeentelijke Universiteit, Amsterdam; the library of the Vrije Universiteit, Amsterdam; Leiden University Library; M. G. de Kievit of the Koninklijke Bibliotheek, The Hague; Hans Krabbendam of the Roosevelt Study Center, Middelburg; Marja Lynne Mueller, reference librarian, Special Collections, Mitchell Memorial Library of Mississippi State University; Mary Bess Paluzzi, archivist of the public library, Columbus, Mississippi; and Jim Baggett, assistant archivist of the public library, Birmingham, Alabama.

Finally I must thank my wife, Nelleke, and my children, Paul and Emily, who have been a constant support. Without them this book, whose creation has been a presence in their lives for so long, would never have become a reality.

INTRODUCTION

Many elements of black culture remain to be explored through an analysis
of black music. Only when the codes are cracked and diverse signals are received will a more comprehensive view of the United States be available. The
blues historian can lead the way. The call of this music should be heard and
acknowledged.

For outsiders the blues is often merely entertainment, but, especially for
the African-American working classes, the music is a social ritual that creates a
sense of order in life. Blues and gospel music is a social mirror whose reflection
has become obscured by the lack of scholarly attention. By ignoring these oral
sources historians have silenced the voice of the black population.

Blues lyrics usually deal with experiences common to the singer and his or
her audience. Although the lyrics are frequently imaginative, they are often
based on personal events and thus imitate reality. For the artists and their
audiences the songs can be an escape from hardship through a glorifying of the
joy of love. The blues is rich in sexual imagery. The man-woman relationship is
subject to the many changes in people's lives. Political decisions and historical
events, which can cause disruption of everyday life, may ultimately even break up
a love relationship.

Blues songs with political comment are very rare; they may have been infre-
quently recorded because of the singers' fear of possible consequences. Blues
is not usually about racial discrimination itself but instead analyzes the consequences. Unconsciously the blues singers may have chosen a metaphorical way
of expressing their feelings about this situation.

Still, there are some noteworthy blues recordings and a smaller number of
gospel recordings that contain intriguing comment on the presidents of the
United States in office at the time. Of the approximately 25,000 blues and

gospel songs recorded in the period from 1902 to 1945, only 349 with relatively direct political references were considered suitable for the purpose of this study. This amounts to only about 1.4 percent of the total store available.

In the early twenties Lawrence Gellert (1896–1980), a son of Hungarian immigrants, moved from New York to Tryon, North Carolina, because of ill health. He lived with a black woman in the black section of the town, and became part of her community. The gospel music in the church his partner belonged to made such a lasting impression on him that he decided to start recording black music in Georgia and the Carolinas. In all, Gellert made five hundred acetate and aluminium recordings between 1924 and 1937. His politics were left-wing, and his ultimate aim was to expose the conditions of the black people among whom he was living. Half the songs he collected contained outspoken political protest, a surprising number compared to the mere 5 percent of protest songs in the Library of Congress recordings collected by John and Alan Lomax[1] and the even smaller percentage on commercial recordings.

Lawrence Gellert no doubt asked for outspoken lyrics, and certainly promised protection by giving complete anonymity to the artists. Gellert did not even record the artists' names in his field notes, and we are consequently at a loss with regard to identification. Fortunately Gellert did make notes of the recording locations and the years in which the songs were collected. The unique Lawrence Gellert recordings now rest in the Archives of Traditional Music at Indiana University. Only three long-play albums have so far been issued of his material, making a mere fifty-eight of his five hundred recordings available.[2]

John A. Lomax (1875–1948) was a pioneer folk song collector. Even President Theodore Roosevelt had encouraged him and had written a letter to plead for research grants.[3] Lomax acquired a professional portable recording machine and together with his son Alan roamed the country in search of original folk song artists from 1933 on. All discs were deposited at the Library of Congress, which now houses a vast collection of unique recordings from an intriguing past. In his memoirs, *The Land Where the Blues Began,* Alan Lomax describes black artists' reluctance to record outspoken social comment: "Even after months of living with and being interviewed by me, Leadbelly never spoke of these things to me. Try as I might, I was unable to move into this forbidden territory until I came into the Delta with a partly black crew and worked with Lewis Jones, the best of Southern fieldworkers. Even then, black censorship held firm. And it wasn't till I talked to blacks who had moved North and then returned South after the Supreme Court had ruled against segregation that I was able to record truly candid accounts from black workers of the Deep South."[4]

When Dr. George H. Gallup, founder of the American Institute of Public Opinion, began to interview the public in late 1935, the first questions were about President Roosevelt's voter appeal. Franklin Delano Roosevelt was seeking a second term, and in so-called "trial heats" several groups of American citizens were asked, "Which candidate do you prefer for president?" For the first time Negroes were asked this question too. The remarkably accurate results of this poll, conducted from 24 to 29 August 1936, were only published as late as 11 October 1936: "Sixty-nine per cent said that they preferred Roosevelt. Roosevelt is especially popular among Negroes in New York State, where he receives 80%."[5] When the stupendous results of the election proper became clear on 3 November, it was found that 81 percent of the voters in the black New York districts had indeed chosen FDR.

To the black population the Republican Party had always been their party. Had not Abraham Lincoln abolished slavery? In 1936 Roosevelt gained 60 to 250 percent more votes in the black neighborhoods of the big cities than in 1932.[6] Why had the black electorate forsaken the Republican Party so massively? Had the relief measures of the New Deal made so big an impression? Several studies on the major American cities have failed to support this hypothesis. In *A New Deal for Blacks* Harvard Sitkoff puts it this way: "No one knows for sure. Given the absence of in-depth interviewing at the time and the scarcity of evidence in the preferences of lower-, middle-, or upper-class African Americans, all conclusions remain speculative."[7]

Ever since Roosevelt's successful reelection this question has intrigued and puzzled historians, not least because the voice of black people can hardly be heard. Many of them were illiterate or barely literate, and in the thirties there was not sufficient interest in them to generate in-depth interviews.

There is, however, one important exception. In 1935 Federal Project One of the WPA included a writers' project. B. A. Botkin, head of the folklore unit, argued that "[h]istory must study the inarticulate many as well as the articulate few."[8] Former slaves were asked to tell their stories; in other interviews the results of the depression for the common black man and woman were also analyzed. But it was an exceptional project. Black opinion remained largely ignored, in spite of the black newspapers in which the educated elite conveyed opinions that more often than not also reflected the opinions of the masses.

The lack of interest by whites does not mean that black people had not raised their voices. Since the early twenties thousands of blues and gospel songs had been recorded on 78 rpm discs. Although these important sources have seldom been used by historians, an evaluation of black music is an important way to try to understand black consciousness.

In this book I will try to find answers to the question of why Roosevelt was so popular among blacks. Sources will be used that have been neglected by historians: the many blues and gospel lyrics that contain more or less direct political comment on the Roosevelt era. The blues and gospel records can all be dated quite accurately, most of them to the exact day, some at least to the month of recording. A thorough discographical study leaves no doubt about the vast majority of recording locations. Even the origins of most singers can be es-tablished by biographical research. However, careful attention should be paid to the circumstances under which the recordings took place, and which may have led to self-censorship. Sometimes words are swallowed and the guitar replaces the line. Some artists refrain from mentioning the name of President Hoover.

Bearing all this in mind, an attempt will be made to answer the following questions: what did the blues and gospel singers have to say about FDR and his predecessors? Did the origin and gender of the singer, the recording location and the commercial or noncommercial aspect of the recording influence the nature of the political comment? How did the blues and gospel singers learn about political news? What political subjects were sung about and how did the singers react to them? How did the singers handle topical themes and relate them to personal concerns? Do the blues and gospel songs discussed represent political thought? What effects did the Roosevelt style, his New Deal measures, his leadership in the Second World War and his tragic death have on his popularity among blacks?

After a brief discussion of political comment in blues and gospel lyrics in the pre-Roosevelt period, the fourteen main topics found in recordings from the Roosevelt era will be examined chronologically. This approach will reveal much about the meanings of the songs and their relation to history.

The lyrics will be presented in their complete form, although repetition of lines will be omitted for reasons of space. The utmost attention has been given to a painstaking transcription. As the full emotional impact of their messages is communicated when the songs are heard, careful attention has been paid to discographical detail, including information on long-play album and compact disc reissues.

Few blues historians have analyzed political topics in these lyrics. Many years ago Paul Oliver led the way with his *Blues Fell This Morning* (1960), *Screening the Blues* (1968), and *Songsters & Saints* (1984). His example was followed by writers like William Barlow, John Cowley, Bob Groom and Giles Oakley. These writers told the story of the blues or dealt with one particular subject; although several lines might be quoted to sustain an argument, the whole text of the blues song was seldom presented.

The present work is different. Complete lyrics are given so that a discrete historical period can be examined from the perspective of the blues and gospel singers. The chronological approach allows a day-to-day following of events. As all available songs have been studied, this book presents the first comprehensive approach to this subject.

ROOSEVELT'S BLUES

THE PRESIDENT, SITTIN' ON HIS THRONE

In order to understand the implications of the blues and gospel songs that comment on the Franklin Roosevelt era, it is necessary to study what was sung about his predecessors. Apart from the occasional reference to George Washington or Abraham Lincoln, the earliest American presidents mentioned by black singers are Grover Cleveland, who served two terms (1885–1889 and 1893–1897) and William McKinley, who served from 1988 to 1901.[1]

The Republican McKinley was assassinated in 1901 and succeeded by his vice president, Theodore Roosevelt (1858–1919; president 1901–1909). Countless black male babies, including no fewer than fourteen future blues and gospel artists, were named after Roosevelt.[2] He advanced Negro rights in many respects, but an important part of his success with the black population was due to his receiving the prominent African-American leader Booker T. Washington at the White House. On 16 October 1901 Washington was invited to dinner by the then-new Republican president. Their meeting was severely criticized, even resulting in threats against the lives of both Roosevelt and Washington. The memory of these events was still vivid when Mississippi banjoist Gus Cannon (1883–1979) sang his "Can You Blame the Colored Man" about it twenty-six years later.

Booker T. Washington and President Theodore Roosevelt at White House dinner, 17 October 1901. Lithograph by C. H. Thomas and P. H. Lacey, 1903.

Now, Booker T., he left Tuskegee,
To the White House he went one day.
He was goin' to call on the president,
In a quiet and a sociable way,
Was in his car, was feelin' fine.

Now, when Booker knocked on the president's door,
Old Booker he began to grin.
Now, he almost changed his color,
When Roosevelt said to "Come in,
We'll have some dinner, in a little while."

chorus: *Now, could you blame the colored man,*
           For making them goo-goo eyes?
           And when he sat down at the president's table,
           He began to smile.
           Eatin' lamb, ham, veal an' roast,

Chicken, turkey, quail on toast,
Now, could you blame the colored man, for makin' . . . ?

Now, Booker was so delighted,
At the social was given to him,
Well, he hired him a horse and carriage,
And he taken the whole town in,
Just drunk on wine, he was a-feelin' fine.

Washington had established the Tuskegee Institute, a coeducational college for African Americans, in Alabama in 1881. The song was taught to Cannon by an old Delta musician at the beginning of the century. A phrase like "goo-goo eyes" also points to an earlier minstrel-show time of origin.[3] The song incorporates stereotypes of black gluttony, drunkenness and subservience ("Old Booker he began to grin"). Often songs like this function on two levels: as apparent acceptance and as ironic comment on race relations.

Because of the mythical proportions the visit assumed, historians have taken great trouble to find out if a real dinner took place. White southerners preferred to refer to a "sandwich during a business meeting," but historians concluded that it had been a real dinner to which Washington had been officially invited.[4] For that matter the mystification was increased by the obscure reactions to the meeting of both the president and the African-American leader. Washington was never again invited to the White House, and Theodore Roosevelt does not even mention him in his memoirs.[5] Nevertheless, the popularity of Theodore Roosevelt among blacks may have paved the way for Franklin Roosevelt's popularity. In the thirties every black person knew someone named Roosevelt. In a sense "Roosevelt" was already the poor man's friend.

Apparently no songs were devoted to president William Howard Taft (1857–1930; president 1909–1913), but with his successor, the Democrat Woodrow Wilson, who led his country in the Great War, things were different.

The Kaiser and Uncle Sam

As Wilson (1856–1924; president 1913–1921) was a devout Christian, many blacks had hoped that the president's social conscience would encompass "all of God's children." After all, had he not promised during his 1912 campaign to raise his voice against lynching and to treat black Americans with equality? But the southerner Wilson was not free from prejudice against African Americans and felt he could not afford to estrange himself from his white southern electorate. He refused to appear in the company of Negroes, he refused to have the race issue studied by a national commission, he resented the appointment of black officials in the South and he did not speak out against lynching. As a result the clock was put back, and segregation once again reigned supreme in Washington, D. C. Harvard Sitkoff even calls Wilson's presidency "the most Southern-dominated, anti-Negro, national administration since the 1850's."[6]

When war in Europe broke out in 1914, Wilson desperately attempted to remain neutral. After the German declaration of unlimited submarine warfare and the publication on 1 March 1917 of the infamous Zimmermann telegram, which showed that Germany was a real threat to the Western Hemisphere, Wilson finally had to give in. On 2 April 1917, less than a month after his second inauguration, he delivered a speech before both houses of Congress in which he asked for a declaration of war on Germany. Congress acceded and all "able-bodied" men between the ages of twenty-one and thirty-one were drafted, by means of the Selective Service Act. On 5 July 1917, 371,710 black soldiers were selected for service, 31 percent of those drafted. Because of discrimination, it was easier for white men to escape the draft, and only 26 percent of them were eventually selected. Whereas only 2.6 percent of the American army was black at the outbreak of war in 1914, more than one-third of the American soldiers fighting in Europe were black.[7]

As many black soldiers were sent overseas after America's intervention in World War I, there are several songs about the events of 1917 and 1918. Blues recordings by black artists were not made until the twenties, and all these songs were recorded in the period from 1927 to 1961, many years after the actual events. The question arises, however, as to whether the blues artists who still sang these old war songs after so long a time had themselves seen service overseas.

In 1917 black songwriter Maceo Pinkard (1897–1962) composed a topical song called "Those Draftin' Blues."[8] In 1940, when the Second World War had broken out, world-famous jazz and blues singer Jimmy Rushing (1902–1972) sang it accompanied by the Count Basie Big Band.[9] Two months later the song was also recorded by Yack Taylor.[10] An even later version exists by Mississippi country blues artist Joe Calicott (1900–1969).[11]

At least two singers served in France: John (Big Nig) Bray and "Kingfish"
Bill Tomlin. Bray recorded a "Trench Blues"[12] in which the number of soldiers
mentioned is forty thousand. There were in fact fifty thousand black soldiers in
Europe. The important black leader W. E. B. Du Bois had strongly supported
the participation of black soldiers, and it was widely hoped and believed in black
circles that a brave war record would be beneficial to blacks in their postwar
position at home. "Kingfish" Bill Tomlin recorded an "Army Blues"[13] about his
days in Belgium. To these early blues artists the kaiser was the personification
of German evil. The kaiser, as would later be the case with Hitler and Mussolini,
was the only white person who could be insulted with impunity.

One example of the myths surrounding the kaiser is found in Pink Anderson's
1961 song "The Boys of Your Uncle Sam."[14] Here the kaiser suffers from a
fictional heart disease, and he asks President Wilson to "put a pad in between
my knees." Anderson concludes a second version of his song with the observation that the German soldiers could not withstand the combined powers of
the "Dixie Boys" and the "Yankees."[15] The origin of Anderson's World War I
song is to be found in recorded white country music performances by Henry
Whitter, Ernest V. Stoneman and Charlie Oaks.[16]

In 1931 Kid Coley, an obscure Louisville artist who may originally have hailed
from Cincinnati,[17] sang a "War Dream Blues."[18] It is the song of a black American who stayed at home during the war and felt the effects of the war effort.
Kid Coley complained of "all the beer and liquor, shipped way 'cross the deep
blue sea."

Accompanying themselves on guitar and tambourine, William and Versey
Smith made four Chicago recordings in 1927. Their songs may derive from
printed lyrics, although no source for their song "Everybody Help the Boys
Come Home"[19] has been found so far. Black gospel singer William Smith was
quite cynical about the white world leaders. To him Woodrow Wilson was a
king sitting on a throne and making laws. When a version of this song, called
"When the War Was On," was recorded by Blind Willie Johnson two years
later, the same image was used to level harsher, though self-censored, criticism
against the president:

chorus: *Everybody, well, when the war was on, (3x)*
         Well, they registered everybody, when the war was on.

         Well, it's just about a few years, and some months ago,
         United States come and voted for war.

Sammy called the men from the East and the West:
"Get ready boys, we got to do our best."

Well, President Wilson, sittin' on his throne,
Makin' laws for everyone.
Didn't call the black man, to lay by the white,
[guitar replaces words].

Price on the letter, began to raise,
Gettin' no better, but the same old thing.
Eight cents on the dollar, ride the train,
Freight's gettin' cheaper, take a ride again.

Yes, you measure your boiler, measure your wheat,
Half a pound of sugar per person a week.
Folks didn't like it, they blamed Uncle Sam,
Have got to save the sugar for the boys in France.

Well, boys whupped the Germans, home at last,
Would have brought the kaiser, but he run too fast.
Couldn't blame the kaiser for a-leavin' the land,
Uncle Sammy had the greatest share of muscle and man.

Tax gettin' heavy, have to pay,
Help the boys, over across the sea.
Mud and water up to their knees,
Faced the kaiser for you and me.

"President Wilson, sittin' on his throne, makin' laws for everyone, didn't call the black man to lay by the white," Johnson sang, perhaps not daring to finish his phrase. One could criticize the kaiser without risking a lynching, but not the president of the United States. Black men and white men were sent to Europe, but the segregation Wilson defended in the United States was even more strictly adhered to on the battlefields of Belgium and France. In a secret memorandum General Pershing made it clear to the French army command that the Negro was regarded as an inferior human being whose vices (especially rape) were a constant menace.[20]

In 1931, thirteen years after the end of the war, gospel singer Sister Cally Fancy reminded her countrymen and -women what they had promised God in the war: "If he would save your land, you would change your lives, and live for Christ." Now man was sinning again, and such promises had been forgotten, the result being that "Death is riding through the land, he's bringing vengeance on beast and man." "Presidents, your life is in God's hand, this message is for you too," she sang in her "Death Is Riding Through the Land."[21]

Woodrow Wilson, although mentioned by name in only two songs, was the first American president whose office is reflected upon in some detail by the blues and gospel singers. Black American participation in the First World War was felt to be a national necessity. The songs are quite patriotic but mixed with some serious resentment. After an ocean voyage of a fortnight the soldiers lived in the trenches, with "the muddy water up to their knees," were drilled up on the firing line and liberated Belgium and France. The kaiser is the personification of German evil. Myth surrounds him, as can be concluded from the fantasy surrounding his defeat.

Back home the return of "the boys" was eagerly awaited. Heartfelt prayers were heard everywhere. The taxes levied to pay for the war effort were felt by everyone. Special mention is made of postage rates and train tickets. There was a shortage of sugar and fuel, which were sent overseas. After the war people soon forgot and thought that this had been the war to end all wars. Some were more realistic and uttered warnings.

President Wilson was seen as an unapproachable king on a throne. He drafted both white and black, but humiliated the brave black soldiers through a strict system of segregation. In his biography of Woodrow Wilson, Jan Willem Schulte Nordholt analyzed Wilson's attitude towards the black population: "Woodrow Wilson, we would conclude, was not a fanatic, a 'racist' in the extreme sense of that overworked word. His blindness was the blindness of his time and even more of his region. Yet it was a fault that grates unpleasantly when measured by the religious sublimity of his idealism."[22]

Them White Folks' Business

On 22 September 1924 a Louisville jug band recorded a "Jail House Blues." Its leader, Kentucky-born guitarist Buford Threlkeld (1894–c. 1937), also played the nose whistle and recorded as Whistler and His Jug Band. The song, a favorite of the medicine show performers, referred to the "last election, when the white folks was in action, tryin' to get a man for president." The song has been traced back to at least 1917,[23] but the use of the abusive term "coon" in the lyrics may point to an earlier origin, perhaps around the turn of the century.[24]

The lyrics emphasize that the presidential elections were felt to be a "white folks' action." Some black people, like "the great promoter, brother Moses," were allowed to vote, but apparently misapplied their legal rights by voting twice.

Earl McDonald's Original Louisville Jug Band recorded the song in March of 1927.[25] The lyrics are very similar to the 1924 version but interestingly the phrase "the white folks was in action" was replaced by "our folks was in action," although later recordings again used "white folks."

Some months later, old-time medicine show performers Blind Blake and Jim Jackson both recorded "Jail House Blues." In Jackson's version the election references have disappeared.[26] However, Blind Blake's recording of "He's in the Jailhouse Now" with Gus Cannon on banjo and Blake himself on guitar, is of interest here because it mentions a specific black politician for the first time:

> Remember last election,
> Everybody was in action,
> Trying to find themselves a president?
> There was a man named Lawson,
> From New York, down to Boston,
> Representin' the colored peoples we had sent.
>
> My brother was a voter,
> Also a great promoter,
> Goin' 'round giving advice,
> Says, "Go down to the poll and vote,"
> 'Stead of voting once, he voted twice.
>
> He's in the jailhouse now, (2x)
> We got him downtown in jail,
> No one to go his bail,
> He's in the jailhouse now.
>
> I went downtown last Friday,
> I met a gal named Lidy,
> I thought she was the swellest gal in town.

She started to call me "honey,"
I started to spendin' money,
We went into a cafe and sat down.

I thought that I was in it,
Buyin' a drink a minute,
Buyin' wine, champagne by the doz'.
When I went to pay that man,
I found that lady's hand,
In my pocket where my money was!

spoken: *They got her!*

She's in the graveyard now, (2x)
When I went to pay that man,
I found that old gal's hand,
She's in the jailhouse now.

Who was "Lawson"? The reference probably was not in the original song, but was an addition by Blake. Is there a historical "Lawson"? He represented the "colored peoples" in the election. Which election? Why from New York to Boston? Some more information may be gained from a much later version. Both in 1950 and in 1961 another old-time medicine show performer, Pink Anderson (1900–1974), recorded "He's in the Jailhouse Now."[27] The song must have belonged to Anderson's standard repertoire since his medicine show days and had probably not undergone many textual changes over the course of the years. "Lawson" is now "Bill Austin," and he walked from New York to Boston "just to find a colored settlement" (i.e., sentiment). There is a possibility that the song refers to Alderman William L. "Fred" Dawson, who was born in Albany, Georgia, in 1886 and studied law in Chicago. He was a close ally of Oscar DePriest, the black Republican who was elected to Congress from Chicago in 1928 and who became a member of the Chicago City Council in 1933. In 1939 Dawson switched to the Democratic Party because of Roosevelt's New Deal, and became second ward committeeman.[28]

Bill Dawson was trying to get elected to Congress when Blind Blake first sang about "a man named Lawson," but he was defeated by DePriest's predecessor, Martin Madden.[29] More research needs to be done on Dawson, who died in 1970, to provide conclusive evidence.[30] Unwittingly Pink Anderson might also refer to Rev. J. C. Austin of Chicago's Pilgrim Baptist Church. In the reminiscence quoted in chapter 3, Mahalia Jackson mentions both Dawson and Austin.

White medicine show performers were not slow to pick up the song either. Country music celebrity Jimmie Rodgers (1897–1933), who worked as a black-face artist in medicine shows, recorded "In the Jailhouse Now" in 1928,[31] in the wake of the Blind Blake version. The song was such a success that the discography in Rodgers's biography lists no fewer than seven 78s on which it was issued.[32] In 1930 "He's in the Jailhouse Now"[33] was also recorded by the Memphis Jug Band, another group with experience in the medicine shows. This version tells about black people who got in trouble with the law because of the sale of bootleg liquor, and how a political friend influences a corrupt judge so that the sentence will be suspended.

In 1936 an obscure Fats Waller-influenced piano player, Billy Mitchell, re-corded "In the Jailhouse Now" in Chicago.[34] Mitchell's version contains stanzas found in the recordings by Whistler and His Jug Band and Jim Jackson, although he may have been working straight from sheet music as well.

A black songster, John Jackson, still sings "He's in the Jailhouse Now." John Jackson was born in Virginia in 1924 and recorded the song in 1982.[35] He learned the white hit version by Jimmie Rodgers from one of the 78s his par-ents played when he was a boy.

"He's in the Jailhouse Now" is a very important song with a long history. It probably had its origins in black vaudeville, and formed a convenient lyrical frame that provided ample opportunity for inventive adaptations by a variety of musicians. Besides the now-obscure reference to a certain Bill Austin/Lawson, it emphasizes the accurate perception that elections were still very much the "white folks' business" in the 1920s.

Blacks had been disenfranchised in large numbers, and their apparent apathy in response often led white voters to believe that suffrage could be taken away without repercussions. Most whites would probably have agreed with Missis-sippi Secretary of State J. L. Power when he claimed that "[i]n State or local matters blacks manifest little or no concern, and so long as white folks pay the taxes, and they [blacks] enjoy the schools and churches, and get plenty of work, they are more than willing to let the white folks do the voting and hold the offices."[36] The bitter reality of 1920 can be read in the private letters that the NAACP received that year from people like C. E. Johnson, a black man from Mississippi: "We want only one thing, primarily, that is the ballot. Ballot everywhere. My people cannot vote down here. . . . We want the damnable

Paramount advertisement for "No Job
Blues" by Ramblin' Thomas, *Chicago
Defender*, 31 March 1928

curse of disfranchisement in primary elections [re]moved in every form of state
government."[37] Segregation and unemployment forced thousands of poor black
people to travel to "the promised land," the industrial north.

Goin' To Chicago

The harsher side of the massive migration that was taking place from the
South to the industrial cities of the North was reflected in blues lyrics. In 1928
Louisiana blues singer Willard "Ramblin'" Thomas (1902–c. 1945) sang a "No
Job Blues" for Paramount Recordings. The unemployed singer was arrested
for vagrancy while trying to find a job. The leasing of convicts to business was

outlawed by Congress in 1887, but continued, especially in the Alabama coal
mines, until 1928, and Ramblin' Thomas may well have rambled to that state and
fallen foul of the system.[38]

> I been walking all day, and all night too,
> 'Cause my meal-ticket woman have quit me, and I can't find no work to do.
>
> I pickin' up the newspaper, and I look-ed pickin' in the ads,
> And the policeman came along, and he arrested me for vag.

spoken: Now, boys, y'all ought to see me in my black and white suit. It won't do!
>   Asked the judge, "Judge, what may be my fine?"
>   He said, "Get you a pick and shovel, and get deep down and mine."
>
>   I'm a poor vag prisoner, working in the ice and snow,
>   I got to get me another meal-ticket woman, so I won't have to work no more.

It is difficult to give national unemployment figures for the Coolidge era
(1923–1929). Statistics were simply not compiled on the subject. Estimates
vary from 5.2 to 13 percent.[39] Obviously figures for the black population were
dramatically worse. President Calvin Coolidge did nothing to assist blacks.
During Coolidge's presidency manufacturing output per person-hour increased
by almost 32 percent. In the same period wages increased by only 8 percent.[40]
The gap between rich and poor became wider and wider.

To southern field workers the North was the Promised Land. The low cotton prices and the voracity of the boll weevil had weakened the economy of
the South. The industrialization of agriculture resulted in unemployment and the
lure of the factories in the North became irresistible. An example of a blues
singer who had migrated to a northern city is Bertha "Chippie" Hill (1905–
1950). When she was only fourteen years of age she left her family (she had
fifteen siblings) in Charleston, South Carolina, for New York City and found
work as a dancer. She subsequently moved to Chicago, where she made her
first recordings with Louis Armstrong in 1925. Two years later Chippie Hill
recorded the song "Hard Time Blues," with Lonnie Johnson on guitar, but this
session is unissued.[41] When she rerecorded "Hard Time Blues" with Tampa
Red and Georgia Tom as accompanists in 1928, she explained her move to the
"Windy City":

> Hard times, hard times, what makes you stay so long?
> You see the snow is falling, many people have no home.

It's cold, cold, no matter where you go,
Some people's shoes are thin that their feet are wet with snow.

spoken: *Cry down on it, Mr. Tampa! Look like them hard times blues are 'bout to ruin you!*
Sound of them blues 'bout to ruin you too, ain't they, over there!

I'm goin' to Chicago, that's the best place to be,
Hard times, hard times, sure don't worry me!

Few people saw what was coming. The poor were starving among an abundance of commodities, while the rich were speculating on the stock market. In the wings Secretary of Commerce Herbert Hoover was getting ready to take over from Calvin Coolidge.

HARD TIME IN HOOVERVILLE

Hard Times

Herbert Hoover (1874–1964; president 1929–1933) did his best to drive blacks from the Republican Party. He segregated blacks[1] and refused to be photographed with Negro leaders. In fact he did his best to ignore them altogether. Although the twenties saw the rise (and fall) of Marcus Garvey and his Universal Negro Improvement Association (UNIA) and the flowering of the Harlem Renaissance, it was not a decade known for a great amount of black protest. Even A. Philip Randolph's Brotherhood of Sleeping Car Porters lay dormant during Hoover's presidency.

After the 1928 elections disappointment soon set in. The blacks who were allowed to vote were mostly from the northern states, and they had preferred Hoover to the Democratic candidate Alfred Smith. Hoover's party, the Grand Old Party of Abraham Lincoln who had freed them from slavery, was still their party, but Hoover's complete disregard of blacks began to open their eyes.
In his 1933 autobiography the writer James Weldon Johnson mourns the disappearance of the "Black Cabinet," a group of black intellectuals available for consultation by the government: "The Cabinet no longer exists, and for the reason that Presidents since Taft have adopted a policy of appointing fewer and

fewer Negroes to important positions; the lowest mark, close to zero, being reached in President Hoover's administration."[2]

It is evident from the blues lyrics that the black population ignored Hoover as much as he did them. Several "hard time" blues were recorded from 1929 to 1933, but President Herbert Hoover's name is mentioned only sporadically, and then in a circumstantial manner. Hoover's name was used as late as 1966 in a blues nominally about Chesterfield cigarettes, which were held up as an example of luxuries that had to be foregone in hard times. The singer was Georgia blues guitarist Eugene "Buddy" Moss (1906–1984), who had sung the blues in Atlanta when Hoover was president:

chorus: *Chesterfield, these days, boys, is hard to find,*
Smoke one in the morning, one at night,
Choke my duck[3] and hold the other two tight,
Chesterfield, these days, boys, is hard to find,

Our father, who art in Washington, Hoover will be his name,
Took me off my good Chesterfield, and stuck me on Golden Grain.
Now, I rave,
Yes, I crave 'bout the ducks I should have saved.

I begin to wonder why Chesterfield is gone so high.[4]

For this song the wording of the Lord's Prayer was parodied, a daring gimmick that would not have been appreciated by everybody. As this would certainly have been unacceptable in the thirties, no original recording from the time when Moss probably first sang the song exists. "Golden Grain" was "powder," a cheap rolling tobacco.[5]

Hoover was in charge of the Red Cross relief effort in 1927 and promoted the Red Cross as the relief agency in the 1930–31 drought. A separate chapter will be devoted to the many versions of the blues song about the "Red Cross store" and its implications. However, one version should be quoted here because of its rare references to Hoover. It was sung by guitarist Brownie McGhee, who, like Franklin D. Roosevelt, was a victim of polio. McGhee's "The Red Cross Store" dates from 1942, but was only issued as late as 1994. As a field recording it was not so subject to censorship.

spoken: *Sonny boy, did you ever hear about those hardships*
way back in the year of twenty-nine, when Hoover was in force?
Took us off-a Camel cigarettes and put us on Golden Grain.

Brownie McGhee at the NBBO Blues Festival, Amstelveen, 18 May 1974. Photo by Hans ten Have, from the collection of the author.

I wanna tell you a little about the Red Cross store,
the hardship that I had to go through with:

Me and my girl talked last night, talked for 'bout an hour:
"Brownie, go to the Red Cross store, to get a sack of Red Cross flour."

Said, "No, baby, I don't wanna go,
Lord, I'll rob a bank for you, woman, but I won't go to that Red Cross store."

spoken: *Why?*

Them old Red Cross people, sure do treat you mean,
One can of tomatoes, two or three cans of beans.

I said, "No, baby, I don't wanna go,"
spoken: *(Why, Brownie?)*
"Lord, I'll rob a bank or stop a train, but I won't go to that Red Cross store."

Now, you can go down in the morning, they'll ask you: "How do you feel?"
They'll give you a bag of tomatoes, a peck of bolted meal.

I said, "No, little girl, Brownie don't wanna go,
I'll do anything in the world for you, but I won't go to that welfare store."

Now, you know, that man who was in, President Hoover was his name,
Took me off-a Camel cigarettes, and put me on Golden Grain.

I said, "No, Lord, I don't wanna go,"
Well, I say, "I'll quit smoking, 'fore I'll go to the Red Cross store."

There ain't no need of me working so hard,
Sonny, I got a girl in the white folks' yard.

Ah, she told me, "No, Brownie, you don't have to go,"
spoken: (Why?)
"I'll bring your meal from the kitchen, stay away from that Red Cross store."

spoken: Play it for Brownie and see how she say talking! She said, "No!" . . .

Now Hoover, he once told us, he's gonna make things all right,
Give us one can of chipped beef, and two or three cans of kraut.

I told him, "No, no, well, you know I don't wanna go,"
Said, "I'd do anything for you, baby, I won't go to the Red Cross store."

Sonny, I done found me another girl, said she'd gonna get herself a job,
Take care of me, while these doggone times are hard.

I told her, "Yes, yes, well, you know I don't wanna go,
When you get your money, get your check cashed, I'll stay from that Red Cross
store."

Although Prohibition had started in 1920, Herbert Hoover and Prohibition were synonymous. One of the worst mistakes ever made in American social policy, Prohibition meant that "$2,000,000,000 worth of business was simply transferred from brewers and barkeepers to bootleggers and gangsters, who worked in close cooperation with the policemen and politicians they corrupted. Blackmail, protection rackets and gangland murders became all too common, and no one was punished."[6] Prohibition did not mean that liquor was not to be had. That it was easily obtainable for people with money is evident from a song by a famous Atlanta partner of Buddy Moss in the Hoover days. Robert "Barbecue Bob" Hicks recorded his "We Sure Got Hard Times" in 1930:

Got a song to sing you, and it's no excuse,
And it sure is the devil, I believe he's got a-loose.

When you want a drink o' liquor, you think it's awful nice,
You put your hand in your pocket, and you ain't got the price.

You heard about a job, now you is on your way,
Twenty mens after the same job, all in the same old day.

chorus: *Hard times, hard times, we got hard times now,*
Just think and think about it, we got hard times now.

You started in moochin', but your moochin's in vain,
Be careful with yourself, you'll get a ball and chain.

Lard and bacon, gone to a dollar a pound,
Cotton have started to sellin', but it keeps goin' down and down.

Just before election, you was talkin' how you was goin' to vote,
And after election was over, your head down like a billy goat.

People who are starving can sometimes see no other escape than survival through dishonesty. As Barbecue Bob sings, the next step after this "moochin'"[7] often meant the "ball and chain" for the poor black. Sometimes prison was the very last resort for starving people. In some cases getting locked up deliberately was the only way the poor could be clothed and fed. The sentence could also mean a break for their relatives, who could eat with the convicts on "visitin' Sunday," as a member of Rev. J. M. Gates's congregation explains in "These Hard Times Are Tight Like That," a 1930 conversation between Gates and his church members:

I want to talk to you about these hard times: these hard times are tight like that.
When I say that, I'm talkin' 'bout the times you're livin' in now.
  Mmm.
You haven't got the money to throw away like you used to have.
  Ain't got none.
Ah, your house rent is due,
  Amen.
And nothing to pay with.
  Can't pay neither. True.
And not only your house rent is due, but you have nothing to eat.
  Yeah.

It's tight like that.

It's tighter than that.

Yeah, notes past due.

I ain't got no notes.

Mmm, and grocery bills is unpaid.

I ain't got no grocery bills, brother pastor, I goes and get groceries or done went an' got 'em rather. And if he wanna make a bill out, he just have to make it, 'cause it's, it's, it's done got tight like that with me. Amen!

Yes, and the bossman is driving his own car. No chauffeur now.

Amen.

Mmm?

Amen, yes sir, brother pastor, it's tight like that with me 'cause the other day I started runnin' up against the police, knock him down, so he could lock me up, so I could get something to eat, 'cause times is tight.

Yeah, but I tell you: when the times is tight like this, and you run up against the police, he more naturally have to wrap you up somewhere in some grave; you better let the police run against you.

Yes sir, times is tight, though, brother pastor, I want somewhere to eat. I ain't got nowhere to eat, ain't a thing at home. My shoes is 'bout done gone.

Well, I realize that's true.

Well, child, runnin' up against the police to get locked up, now, that ain't bad, 'cause any time you lay in the station house all day, you done got at least two hots. That's right.

Yeah, and if times continue like this, you talk about gettin' too hot. You gonna get one cold and somebody's gonna bury you. It's tight like that.

Let me tell you-all peoples, one thing: I've got a cousin on the chain gang. I'm just as glad when the visitin' Sunday comes so I can go out there and eat with them convicts. It's tight!

Yeah, I tell you: that's what I call a prodigal son. Whenever you get free, he always talkin' 'bout the country's free, you can wear shoes or go barefooted, and now you goin' out on the convict camp, eatin' with the convicts. It must be tight like that.

I'm not wearin' any shoes, got on some old raggedy shoes and stockin's. Never had had to do that before, you know times is tight like that.

Mmm, I thought he's talkin' about me, child, when he say you can go barefooted or wear shoes: I know I can go barefooted too.

Yeah, everybody's doin' their own cookin' and washin' now. And I see a lot of people used to have a good job. And they out of the job now. It's tight like that.

Yes, sir, there's one thing though, I tell you, brother pastor, I'm a little bit proud
of: 'cause they got a breadline here and they don't have to pay but two cents,
but the Lord know sometimes I ain't got that two cents to pay.
Mmm. That's right.
And the luck I'm in, I ain't even able to find the place where you can buy the
two cent a day's meal.
Yeah.
Well, I haven't tried to find it, because they told me they didn't feed peoples
without they's crippled, or blind, or somethin' had to be wrong with them, you
know that's tight and I'm hungry.
Yeah, yes, I know it is, but it's gonna be tighter than that.
Amen!

In the prewar period about 750 sermons by black preachers were recorded, and were often tremendous sellers in the black community. The Rev. J. M. Gates (c. 1884–c. 1942) from Atlanta, Georgia, whose sermon is quoted above, was one of the most prolific of the recorded preachers. From 1926 to 1941 he recorded no fewer than 215 sermons. Some of these are topical and will consequently be analyzed in this study.

Gates was so enormously popular because of his knack for using examples from everyday life. He was also a master of words; his puns are original and ad rem. When the congregation members discuss the advantages of letting oneself be locked up, they argue that one will at least get two hots (i. e., hot meals) in jail. Immediately Gates warns about "gettin' too hot," because then "you gonna get one cold [i.e., an illness] and somebody's gonna bury you." The very title of the "sermon" is a daring pun on "It's Tight Like That," Tampa Red and Georgia Tom's sexual blues hit of 1928.

Another preacher who recorded a sermon on the depression in 1931 was Rev. Dr. J. Gordon McPherson of New Orleans (1869–1936), who made six titles for Paramount under the pseudonym "Black Billy Sunday." He adapted his nickname from a very popular white baseball-playing evangelist who used many baseball metaphors in his sermons. "This Old World's in a Hell of a Fix" is a "fire and brimstone" sermon if ever there was one. In an album review that features a fine photo of Reverend McPherson, Keith Summers called him "a highly respected, if controversial veteran of the old-time revivalist tent circuit, a campaigner for social and moral purity and a famous faith healer."[8]

chorus: *God's gonna set this world on fire (4x), some of these days.*

Housing in a Negro district of Atlanta, Georgia, March 1936. Photo by Walker Evans, from the collections of the Library of Congress.

spoken: *Amen! Glory! Amen!*
My sisters and my brothers, my subject for this evening is: "The world is in a hell of a fix." In a hell of a fix, amidst this world-wide depression, and already this old world has gone away from God, and it's in a hell of a fix.
The almighty God is thunderin' at the hearts and conscience of men and women. They endeavoring to stop them in their heedless rush, and to realize that now is . . . We're living in perilous times. And the supreme need of the world, today, amidst the crime wave that is sweeping everything like a mighty cyclone, is the forces which will make for character, shall control the forces which make for eternity. And the one great force which makes for moral character is Christianity, because this old world is in a hell of a fix. We are living in perilous times. We are living in times when the racketeers, and the bandits, and the bootleggers and the false pretenders, and the hypocrites in the amen corner have got this old world in a hell of a fix. Men have turned their backs on God. God is calling. God is calling. The world is upside down. Yet, I say to you, my brothers and my sisters: These hard times that we're having in the world, with millions out of work, with worldwide depression, unrest is because this old world is in a hell of a fix, and you better get right with God.

You better get right, my brothers and my sisters, because we're living in the last days, we're living in these perilous times, when men desire more pleasure than they do more God.

I say to you today, my brothers and my sisters: Let me warn you: Get right with God! For this old world, this old world, this, I say, this world, this very world that you're living in, this town, is in a hell of a fix and you'd better get right with God, because this old world is in a hell of a fix.

Do you hear me?

It's in a hell of a fix and you'd better get right with God. Get right!

There are many blues and gospel songs about the depression, but only one such recording may have been made in 1929, the year of the Wall Street crash. On 2 December, only a month after 29 October 1929 (Black Tuesday), Texas gospel singer Washington Phillips, who accompanied himself on a dolceola (a zither with a keyboard attached to it), recorded a two-part "The World Is in a Bad Fix Everywhere."[9] However, this recording, which, judging from its title might deal with the depression, is unissued.

The only time Hoover's name was mentioned in a prewar blues recording, albeit obliquely, was when Mississippi-born J. D. Short (1902–1962) recorded his classic "It's Hard Time" in 1933. The song was issued under the name "Joe Stone," one of Short's several pseudonyms that were probably used to avoid contractual difficulties.

It is hard time here, hard time everywhere,
Well, it's hard time here, baby, it's hard time everywhere.

I went down to the factory, where I worked three years ago,
And the bossman told me, "Man, I ain't hirin' here no more."

Now we have a little city, that they call "down in Hooverville,"
Times have got so hard, people ain't got no place (to live).

Don't the moon look pretty, baby, shinin' down through the trees?
I can see my fair brown, swear to God that she can't see me.

Sun rose this mornin', I was lyin' out on my floor,
Lord, I didn't have no cheap faro, baby, have no place to go.

I'm gonna sing this song, baby, I ain't gonna sing it no mo',
'Cause my baby keep on callin' me, baby, and I believe I had better go.

And I hate to hear, my faro call my name,
She don't call so lonesome, but she call so nice and plain.[10]

J. D. Short had come to St. Louis from Clarksdale, Mississippi, on 16 April 1923. A friend of his, who had been working at the Commonwealth steel plant in St. Louis, had told him that he made a dollar an hour: "big money!"[11] Short did find a job in St. Louis, at Mueller's brass foundry, and played his blues on the weekends. If the second stanza of "It's Hard Time" is autobiographical, which is quite likely, he lost his job at the St. Louis factory in 1930.

Having lost his job, Short may also have lost his home, the fate of many of the 13 million unemployed people of his day. To survive, they built "Hoovervilles," an ironic name in which the posh suffix "ville" was used to mock the Hoover administration. In his study *Franklin D. Roosevelt and the New Deal*, historian William E. Leuchtenburg described the Hoovervilles and identified the one Short sang about: "On the outskirts of town or in empty lots in the big cities, homeless men threw together makeshift shacks of boxes and scrap metal. St. Louis had the largest 'Hooverville', a settlement of more than a thousand souls, but there was scarcely a city that did not harbor at least one."[12]

In some depression blues "Starvation" or "Depression" is personified. Like Death itself he knocks at doors and comes to get his unfortunate victims. A good example of this poetic personification is found in Charley Jordan's 1931 "Starvation Blues":

> Lord, Lord, Starvation is at my door,
> Well, it ain't no need of running, because I ain't got no place to go.
>
> The grass is all dying, the rivers all dropping low,
> Do you know what is the matter? Starvation is at my door.
>
> Well, I used to eat cake, baby, but now I have to eat hard cornbread,
> And now I would rather be sleeping somewhere in the graveyard dead.

spoken: *Fiddle it, boy!*

> There's more women standin' begging, that never had to beg before,
> The Starvation times, have drove them from their door.
>
> Now, I almost had a square meal the other day,
> But the garbage man come, and he moved the can away.
>
> Now, I remember one time, when I had a-plenty to eat,
> But now the time has come, and I can't find no place to sleep.

As a result of the economic crisis many record companies were forced to stop the production of blues records. In 1931 the Columbia 14000-D and the

Brunswick 7000 "race" series were discontinued. The next year the Vocalion 1000 and the Paramount 12000 series came to a halt. In 1933 it was Victor 23250's turn and in 1934 the OKeh 8000 and Perfect 100 series followed suit. From 1927 to 1930 some five hundred blues records had been issued each year, but the number dropped to four hundred in 1931, two hundred in 1932 and only a hundred and fifty in 1933.[13]

In the midst of this crisis in the blues recording industry Charley Jordan (c. 1890–1954) kept making recordings. As one of the premier commentators on the hardships of the depression, he recorded fourteen titles in 1930, fifteen in 1931, six in 1932 and six in 1934. Jordan was born in Mabelvale, in Pulaski County, Arkansas, around 1890. After military service in World War I and years of wandering around in Memphis, Kansas City and the Mississippi Delta, Jordan had come to St. Louis in 1925.[14]

Jordan's "Starvation Blues" eloquently voices the hardships of the depression. The consequences of the crisis are felt to be unnatural: the grass is dying and the river is "dropping low." Nature itself is dying.

In Charlie Spand's 1931 "Hard Time Blues" the birds refuse to sing:

> Well, the time is so hard, the birds refuse to sing,
> And no matter how I try, I can't get a doggone thing.
>
> Lord, I walked, and I walked, but I cannot find no job,
> Lord, I can't 'ford to borrow no money, and I sure don't wanna rob.
>
> Lord, my woman is hard to get along with, as a sitting hen,
> And she ain't cooked me a square meal, honey, in God knows when.
>
> Everybody cryin': "depression," I just found out what it means,
> It means a man ain't got no money, he can't find no big money tree.

Pianist Charlie Spand remains an obscure artist, in spite of some serious research.[15] According to the Columbia files his "Hard Time Blues" was originally called "Depression Blues," a title that guitarist Tampa Red used for another Chicago recording, made one month later. The depression is personified, being referred to as "Old Man Depression."

> If I could tell my trouble, it may would give my poor heart ease,
> But Depression has got me, somebody help me, please.
>
> If I don't feel no better tomorrow, than I feel today,
> I'm gonna pack my few clothes, and make my getaway.

I've begged and borrowed, till my friends don't want me 'round,
I'll take Old Man Depression, and leave this no good town.

Depression's here, they tell me it's everywhere,
So I'm going back to Florida, and see if Depression's there.

Oh, how it would help me, if I could just only explain,
But Depression has got me, it's 'bout to drive me insane.

As his nickname indicates, Hudson "Tampa Red" Woodbridge (1904–1981) hailed from Tampa, Florida. "Old Man Depression" now forces him to leave Chicago, the big city where he had been since 1925, and to return to his native Florida. The Great Migration to the big cities must have seemed a serious mistake to the starving poor, who often dreamed of going back to the country. In this song Tampa Red must have voiced the hard times of the people who listened to his records.

Identification with the bluesmen's lyrics must have been easy. But how could the black American in the depression hear these records? A 1935 WPA study about consumer purchases showed that phonographs and radios were familiar items in some black homes. Only 2 to 5 percent of the black farming population of Georgia, Mississippi and the Carolinas owned a radio, whereas this percentage rose to 46 percent in a city like Atlanta, Georgia. In the same rural areas, however, the phonograph was owned by 17 to 30 percent of the black population. Blacks had more phonographs and whites more radios. Ownership bore little relation to income.[16]

A 78 rpm record cost seventy-five cents, not something everyone could easily afford. People who could not buy a radio or a gramophone at all would no doubt have gathered around a neighbor's machine or would have gone to the bars that did own a gramophone or a radio.

The Panic Is On

A phrase sometimes used in blues lyrics to describe the depression is "the panic is on." In his *Songsters and Saints* Paul Oliver explains how the term had already been used for crises in 1893 and 1908–1909.[17] Memphis blues guitarist Furry Lewis (1893–1981) recorded "The Panic's On" for an unissued 1927 recording when the Wall Street crash was still two years away.[18] The following

year the phrase occurred in Barbecue Bob's "Bad Time Blues."[19] The first time
the term was found in a postcrash recording was when guitarist Hezekiah
Jenkins recorded "The Panic Is On" in January 1931. Sales were probably very
low indeed as the initial manufacture order was only 649.

> What this country is coming to,
> I sure would like to know.
> If they don't do something by and by,
> The rich will live and the poor will die.

refrain: Doggone, I mean the panic is on!

> Can't get no work, can't draw no pay,
> Unemployment gettin' worser every day.
> Nothing to eat, no place to sleep,
> All night long, folks walkin' the street.

> Saw a man this mornin', walkin' down the street,
> In his B.V.D.'s, no shoes on his feet.
> You ought to seen the women curvin' (?) in their flat,
> I could hear 'em saying: "What kind of man is that?"

> All the landlords done raised the rent,
> Folks that ain't broke is badly bent.
> Where they get dough from, goodness knows,
> But if they don't produce it, in the street they goes.

> Some play the numbers, some read your mind,
> They all got a racket of some kind.
> Some trimmin' corns off-a people's feet,
> They got to do somethin' to make ends meet.

> Some women are sellin' apples, some sellin' pies,
> Some sellin' gin and rye.
> Some sellin' socks to support their man,
> In fact, some are sellin' everything they can.

> I pawned my clothes and everything,
> Pawned my jewelry, watch and my ring.
> Pawned my razor and my gun,
> So, if luck don't change, there'll be some stealin' done.

Old Prohibition ruined everything,
That's why I'm forced to sing.
Here's one thing I want you all to hear:
Until they bring back light wine, gin and beer.

The same feeling was expressed in Charlie "Specks/Black Patch" McFadden's 1933 "Times Are So Tight": "I never saw times so tight before, and what's caused this panic, Lord, I sure don't know."[20] (McFadden's nicknames referred to his loss of the sight in one eye, which led him to wear spectacles with one black lens.) In 1936 Mack Rhinehart and Brownie Stubblefield recorded an unissued "The Panic Is On."[21] In 1954 Jimmy McCracklin sang "The Panic's On,"[22] with different lyrics but harking back to the depression years: "The panic's on, wonder what we are going to do, Lord it remind me of, nineteen and thirty-two." Louisiana blues singer L. V. Conerly even recorded the phrase as late as 1966: "That's when the panic caught me, that was in nineteen thirty-four. Well, I got so hungry one time, I took all of my children, I had to go."[23]

Nineteen thirty-two was another election year. The odds were against Herbert Hoover, who had not understood the political game. It was time for some drastic change. On election day 15,750,000 people voted for Hoover, and 22,800,000 for the governor of New York, Franklin D. Roosevelt. Hoover and the Republicans had suffered a humiliating defeat.[24]

FDR AND BLACKS

From Hyde Park to the White House

The black population, 50 percent of which was unemployed by 1932, voted for Hoover by more than two-thirds. Who, after all, was his Democratic opponent, Franklin Roosevelt? Had he, as governor of New York, appointed blacks to important positions? Had he spoken out on African-American issues during his 1932 campaign? Had he ever known a black who was not a servant?

Franklin Delano Roosevelt was born on 29 January 1882 in Hyde Park, New York, in his parents' large old country house ninety miles north of New York City. His mother, Sara Delano Roosevelt, the daughter of a China trader, saw to his education in the overprotected surroundings of the family home. Not until Franklin had turned fifteen was he sent to the fashionable New England boarding school, Groton, where his talent for debating matured. His father, retired businessman James Roosevelt, died in 1900. From then on, a dominating mother could turn all her attention to her only son. Franklin was spoiled, and the future politician had a tendency to avoid the whole truth when his own image was at stake.[1]

Roosevelt married his distant cousin Eleanor in 1904. Eleanor was given away by her uncle, Theodore Roosevelt, who was by then the twenty-sixth president of the United States. "Uncle Teddy" was Franklin's example, and he was to follow in the older man's footsteps, first as a Harvard graduate (1900), then by going into politics. Franklin chose the Democratic Party, however, and not the Republican Party of his uncle. After having served in the New York State Senate, he became assistant secretary of the navy in the Wilson administration in 1913. In 1920 the Democratic convention nominated Franklin Roosevelt for the vice presidency. He campaigned strenuously along with Democratic presidential candidate James Cox. However, Cox and Roosevelt never stood a chance against the GOP. After his defeat Roosevelt returned to law practice. In 1921 he was stricken with poliomyelitis (infantile paralysis). The disease and its consequences (Roosevelt was never to walk again) had such a profound influence on his character development that a "new" FDR began to emerge.

Coincidentally, one of the artists whose work is studied here, blues guitarist Brownie McGhee (1915–1996) contracted polio one year before Franklin Roosevelt did. In a 1971 interview McGhee compared his plight to Roosevelt's:

> When I was a boy I was stricken with polio—what they called at that time infantile paralysis. What little money my father had saved, why he spent it all trying to rid me of that infantile paralysis, which was never successful. So, today, I'm a man with a short leg, but I had crutches and a cane until I was 18 or 19 years old. Then I met up with a fabulous lady out of Texas, Mrs. Fulbright. She was the nurse of the negro schools at the time, and she figured I could be helped and get rid of the crutches and cane, which she did. She met a German doctor at the time of Roosevelt's administration when the March of Dimes was started (he was a victim of polio too), and she said, "Brownie, I think I can help you. Would you like to walk without crutches or a cane?" I said, "Yes, I would love that." So, my case was taken, and this German doctor operated on me around '35 or '36, and today instead of having my foot five inches from the ground it's an inch and a quarter. No crutch and no cane, pretty good. But anyway I never quit, and that's when I really fell in love with the guitar, when I felt I could carry it with me.[2]

Roosevelt was not that lucky, although up to 1928 he had tried everything to regain the use of his legs. The illness caused him to view life more seriously. It also taught him, as his wife explained in an interview, "to have a greater sympathy and understanding of the problems of mankind."[3]

However, FDR had never spoken out on behalf of the black cause before being elected president of the United States in 1932. Neither in that campaign nor as governor of New York (1929–1933) had he paid much attention to the black population. It is not surprising, therefore, that more than two-thirds of the black electorate voted Republican in 1932, staying with the party of Lincoln. Although Mahalia Jackson had already campaigned for Roosevelt, to the majority of African Americans Roosevelt was still unknown.

The new president was inaugurated on 4 March 1933. On 12 March 1933 this announcement was made on the radio: "The President wants to come into your home and sit at your fireside for a little fireside chat." Then a warm, comforting voice spoke to 20 million Americans: "I can assure you, my friends, that it is safer to keep your money in a reopened bank than it is to keep it under the mattress."[4] Because of Roosevelt's energetic personality and a new willingness to act in Washington, D. C., confidence returned. In the following months the Dow Jones index rose 65 percent, a twentieth-century record for a period of time after a presidential election. Not until 1984, when Ronald Reagan was elected for a second term, was this record broken.[5]

The new president radiated hope. When asked in a 1976 BBC interview what he thought of President Roosevelt, blues guitarist Big Joe Williams (1903–1982) from Crawford, Mississippi, said: "Well, I liked everything, most he did. I think he one of the greatest presidents we had. President Roosevelt, he brought the dead to life, it's worth saying, a way of speaking. Because when he taken over there, the country was in a bad shape. Hoover left it tied all up, you know what I mean? People were starving, he come and helped the jobless: that's the man you want."[6]

The New Deal aimed to restore people's faith in the effectiveness of democratic politics. Roosevelt defended himself against Republican opposition by drawing attention to the fact that democracy had already disappeared in a number of countries. He argued that the most serious threat to democracy was unemployment, and that unemployed people sometimes sacrificed their liberty in despair.

Blacks in the White House

Franklin D. Roosevelt was the first president to increase the number of blacks in the White House as a deliberate policy. There were more black servants, Mrs. Roosevelt invited black leaders into the White House and black musicians performed there. In a 1978 interview C. R. Smith, president of American

Airlines in the Roosevelt era, remembered that "the place was running over with blacks—you never saw so many blacks in your life. And I said to Mrs. Eleanor, I said, 'Looks like we're entertaining most of the blacks in the country tonight.' She said, 'Well, C. R., you must remember that the President is their President also.' "[7]

White opposition to the increasing presence of blacks in the White House was often vilely hostile.[8] Roosevelt had to act sensibly. By subtly introducing blacks into the executive mansion he gained many black voters, but he took special care not to estrange himself from the white electorate. Thus, photos of the president with blacks are extremely scarce. The best-known exceptions are the shots taken of the president conversing genially with famed scientist George Washington Carver during a visit to Tuskegee Institute in 1939.[9] Other examples are the photos taken of Roosevelt with six leaders of the black fraternal order of the Elks[10] and the photo with white film star Bette Davis and black accordionist Graham Jackson taken at a benefit dinner at Warm Springs in 1944.[11]

A number of black blues and gospel artists performed for President Roosevelt. The Tuskegee choir sang at Roosevelt's mother's birthday celebration in January 1933, and the president asked them to sing for him in the White House. The story rated a banner front-page headline in the *Afro-American*, 21 January 1933.[12]

When he visited Nashville, the president spent fifteen minutes listening to the Fisk University glee club sing Negro spirituals. It was estimated that twenty-five thousand blacks came there to see their national leader.[13] The Fisk Jubilee Singers, or Fisk University Quartette, had made recordings from 1909 onwards.[14] As early as 1882 they had performed for President Arthur at the White House.[15] However, theirs was a music mainly aimed at white audiences, and their spirituals were altered accordingly. As they admitted themselves, they had "purged the songs of all ungainly africanism."[16]

Some black artists even campaigned for the candidate of their choice. Gospel singer Mahalia Jackson (1911–1972) sang for Roosevelt in the 1932 campaign. Her biographer, Laurraine Goreau, writes about Jackson's work in the Roosevelt campaign: "With August, she had another big enthusiasm: Franklin Delano Roosevelt was nominated for President at the convention in Chicago. 'I worked hard for Roosevelt. I went around all the different districts for him, because he said he'd put meat on the table. You know, the Second Ward used to be dead Republican, and Dawson started out Republican too, but he must have seen the way the thing was going, because he switched to Democrat and turned the

Renowned scientist George Washington Carver meets FDR at Tuskegee Institute. Reproduced from the collections of the Library of Congress.

whole ward.' Their very own Dr. Austin from Pilgrim Baptist was on Roosevelt's committee to speak all over the country. Big politics."

"Dawson" was Alderman William L. "Fred" Dawson, who was running for Congress with Mahalia Jackson's support. Jackson would sing, "Dawson has brought us all the way, and he carries our burdens. Oh, he's such a wonderful leader, we always got to vote and keep him . . . Dawson has brought us a long way. And baby, all the politicians would go crazy!"[17]

During the 1936 presidential campaign the Republicans showed many three-minute films in Negro theaters. Some featured black entertainers, such as Mamie Smith and the Beale Street Boys, who sang "Oh, Susannah" and made pitches for the GOP.[18] Mamie Smith is recognized as the first black singer to record a vocal blues ("Crazy Blues," OKeh 4169, 10 August 1920). She was born in Cincinnati, Ohio, in 1883 and died in New York City in 1946. A pioneering entertainer, she worked with her own Beale Street Boys in the Town Casino in New York City, 1936, according to Sheldon Harris's biographical dictionary of blues singers.[19] Campaigning for the Republican candidate, Alfred M. Landon, Mamie Smith and athlete Jesse Owens must have been exceptions in 1936, as the African-American population was making a massive shift from the party of Lincoln to that of Roosevelt in this election year.

Replacing regular vocalist Helen Humes, New Jersey singer Viola Wells performed with the Count Basie Orchestra at Roosevelt's inaugural ball, in Washington, D. C., in 1941.[20] Viola Wells, better known as "Miss Rhapsody" (1902–1984), toured Europe in the Second World War on a USO (United Service Organization) package show working military bases. She started her recording career in 1944. The Golden Gate Quartet (see chapter 14) also performed at Roosevelt's inauguration ceremony on 20 January 1941.[21]

Guitarist Josh(ua) White (1915–1969) "frequently entertained for President Roosevelt at White House Concerts, Washington, D. C., in the early forties. . . . Worked President Franklin D. Roosevelt Inaugural Ball, Washington, D. C., 1945."[22] Eleanor Roosevelt later fondly remembered Josh White:

One of my younger friends is Josh White. I met Josh at a concert at which he was singing, and asked him if he would come to Hyde Park to sing at a Christmas party for the children from Wiltwyck School. I, also, invited his son, little Josh [Joshua Donald White was born in 1940], because he sings too. They both came and we became friends.

Two of my best friends are Mrs. Alice Freeman and Willie White. They run my house at Hyde Park and I would be lost without them. Alice has been with me for fourteen years and of course I rely on her completely.

My son told Josh that I was looking for a man to stay in the house as I did not think it a good idea for women to stay in the country without a man around the house. Josh surprised him by his answer. He said, "I think my brother William would like to see your mother." At first I did not think William would like it too well. He had been in the entertainment world with Josh a long time I knew. One day without announcement, William appeared. We shook hands and he sat down and I interviewed him.

I said to him: "It will be very difficult for you to do housework or to drive a car." William said, "No, Mrs. Roosevelt, since the war I don't feel like singing any more." That was three years ago [1949?], and he has been with me ever since. I have an affectionate feeling for William and I hope he has an affectionate feeling for me.

Some of my negro friends thought that I was creating what they call a social problem by having one brother as a rather frequent guest and another brother as a servant, more or less. I never saw that as a problem. Each has a dignified, necessary contribution to make.

Sometimes, when Josh comes, William will come in and sing with his brother, but I always have to persuade him. Sometimes I cannot persuade him, so Josh sings alone, unless Elliott or one of the other boys joins in.

> There are many times when Josh comes, and I don't know anything about it. He simply drops in to see his brother. Then he and William eat together. Sometimes, when Josh comes as a guest, he says, "I'd rather eat with William." And he does. Other times he eats with us and William serves us. It seems most reasonable to me, and I have never had the slightest difficulty from the arrangement and never expect any. Perhaps, that is because I never saw anything unusual about it.[23]

The story is characteristic of Mrs. Roosevelt's unremitting zeal in the subtle introduction of blacks into the White House and Hyde Park. Her breakthrough integration efforts endeared her to the black population, so that the nearly total absence of blues and gospel songs devoted to her is all the more remarkable. Although her husband is the subject of many songs, Mrs. Roosevelt only gets two passing references.[24]

A news item in the arts column of the July 1933 issue of the NAACP's *Crisis* is headlined "At the White House" and reads: "At the close of the state banquet in honor of former Premier Edouard Herriot of France, the Glee Club of Hampton Institute entertained guests of the President and Mrs. Roosevelt. The young singers under the direction of Clarence Cameron White were received with much pleasure and applause."[25] In 1936 the Hampton Quartet was touring New York State in "The Roosevelt-Lehman Caravan" for the committee for the reelection of President Roosevelt and Governor Lehman.[26] On 23 and 24 April 1941 the Hampton Institute Quartet, an unaccompanied male vocal quartet whose first Musicraft recordings date from 1939, made some recordings for RCA Victor in New York City. The resultant Victor album of 78s, "Swing Low," was presented to the first lady by Lorenzo White of the Hampton Institute staff in 1942. Their leader, baritone singer Charles Flax, had acted as narrator of a film about Hampton Institute shown at Hyde Park.[27] Following the example of the Fisk Jubilee Singers, Hampton Institute (now University) had nurtured a vocal quartet since about 1885. Sponsorship continued until as late as 1960.

The three blacks whom Roosevelt knew best were the accordionist Graham Jackson and Irvin and Lizzie McDuffie, his valet and maid.[28] Graham Jackson often performed for the president at the "Little" White House in Warm Springs, Georgia, and at the "Big" White House in Washington, D. C., during the thirties and forties. Jackson was born in Portsmouth, Virginia, on 22 February 1903. He played the piano and the accordion. Jackson's mother was a singer, and he had gained fame as a child prodigy.[29] He made two recordings with his own band, the Seminole Syncopators, in Richmond, Indiana, on 15 August 1930, but as the

Graham Jackson, accordion
player and friend of FDR.
Jackson played often for
Roosevelt at Warm Springs and
in Washington. He also played
at FDR's funeral.

session was rejected by Gennett we do not even know the instrumentation. However, as early as 1924 he had recorded "Blue Grass Blues" and "Sailing on Lake Pontchartrain" under his band's name.[30] Jackson also taught music at the Booker T. Washington School and at Morris Brown College in Atlanta. In his autobiography famous big band leader Count Basie (1904–1984) remembered Jackson playing organ in Atlanta in 1926.[31] Basie was obviously impressed by Jackson's skills. Graham Jackson started out on the piano, later mastered the organ and finally, in the Roosevelt era, switched to the accordion. Roosevelt's black maid, Lizzie McDuffie, remembered Roosevelt's fondness for Graham Jackson: "He liked simple folk melodies, such as he would have accordion-ist Graham Jackson play for him. Jackson gave 24 'command performances' for the President at Warm Springs. Once Mr. Roosevelt astonished everyone, including Mrs. Roosevelt, by announcing that he and Jackson had composed a new song. The song, 'How Sweet Is the Air,' is frequently played today by Jackson on his programs, and he has built a symphony around it."[32] Another source gives the FDR composition as "How Free Is the Air" and claims that a disc of the recording is in the Library of Congress in Washington.[33] In a 1977

John Dyson, a former slave and a Farm Security Administration client, playing the accordion, St. Mary's County, Maryland, September 1940. Reproduced from the collections of the Library of Congress.

interview Graham W. Jackson said that he never discussed racial issues with Roosevelt.[34]

In *F.D.R. My Boss* Grace Tully, who was Roosevelt's secretary for nearly seventeen years, vividly remembered a heartbroken Graham Jackson when Roosevelt's body was carried from Warm Springs: "As the cortege drew into the drive and halted, the sad strains of an accordion played 'Going Home.' It was Graham Jackson, a Negro, who had played many times for F.D.R. and the hundreds of others there. Bareheaded and with tears running down both sides of his face, he stood in front of the group and paid his last homage. And as the cars started again slowly, driving around the semicircular drive and on toward the station, Jackson swung into one of the President's favorite hymns, 'Nearer, My God, To Thee.'"[35]

Lizzie McDuffie advised the president about black artists who might perform at the White House. On 31 October 1936 an article appeared in the *Afro-American* entitled: "Wife of F.D.'s [sic] valet campaigns: Gives intimate glimpses of White House, where 28 colored servants are employed." Mrs. McDuffie also intervened on behalf of famous contralto Marian Anderson. Anderson had performed in the White House on at least two occasions before her historic concert from the steps of the Lincoln Memorial in 1939. (Mrs. Roosevelt had intervened when Anderson was barred from a white high school auditorium in her own capital.)

Another vocal group that appeared several times before FDR was the Morehouse College Quartet. This unaccompanied quartet had recorded for OKeh in Atlanta, Georgia, in June 1923. In the 10 June 1933 issue of the *Chicago Defender* their photograph was published on page nine. The caption reads: "The Morehouse college quartet of Atlanta, Ga., was presented at the White House a few weeks ago and sang several numbers for President Roosevelt. In the picture, left to right, are: Simon C. Clements, Edward R. Rodriguez, Kenneth R. Williams and Wilson P. Hubert." One month later the July 1933 issue of *Crisis* said on page 160: "For the second time this spring the Morehouse College Glee Club gave a program of songs and spirituals for President Roosevelt. The quartet known throughout the south features weekly broadcasts over station WSB in Atlanta." Next the 7 December 1935 issue of *The New York Age* presented a news item under the heading "70th anniversary of Atlanta University celebrated on radio," which read: "College singers who have appeared three times for President Roosevelt, once at the White House, were heard on the Columbia network from New York on December 1, at 10:30 p.m. Eastern Standard Time. They were the Morehouse College male quartet that appeared in a dramatic sketch on Negro education 'from slave ship to Leadership' entitled 'Forever Free', produced by Atlanta University, of Atlanta." We may conclude that the Morehouse Quartet performed for Roosevelt at least three times. They were presented at the White House around May of 1933 and gave a second performance, probably at a different location (Warm Springs?), the next month. The third concert is as yet unidentified.

A special favorite of the president was famous black tap dancer Bill "Bojangles" Robinson. In Jim Haskins's and N. R. Mitgang's *The Biography of Bill Robinson* Rae Samuels remembers: "Roosevelt was crazy about him, and Bill was playing at some big newspaper thing that was being held in Washington. They brought Roosevelt in there, in the chair. (Bob) Hope and everybody else was there, and they were going up to Roosevelt and shaking hands. Roosevelt said: 'Where's Bill? Go get Bill. I want to see him.' So Bill came down and bowed to the president, saying, 'Yes sir, yes sir, Mr. President. How are you today?' He knew how to put it on for him. Then he said, 'By the way, Mr. President, I see you got some kind of New Deal going. Just remember, Mr. President, when you shuffle those cards, just don't overlook those spades.' That's the truth. He really did say that."[36]

There were of course a great many white artists who performed for FDR. A fifty-seven-second film of one of these shows has recently been issued on video. It shows Roosevelt in Warm Springs, Georgia, on 26 January 1933. Bun Wright's fiddle band honors his request, "Soldier's Joy." The governor is shown seated among the musicians, talking to his daughter Anna.[37] This unique film vividly captures the informal way in which Roosevelt liked to surround himself with musicians for relaxation.

But what kind of black artists performed for the Roosevelts? In her book *Music at the White House* Elise Kirk writes that the Sedelia Quartet from South Carolina sang on 17 May 1933. On 27 September 1938 Arenia Mallory appeared with six black singers from the Industrial and Literary School of Lexington, Mississippi. Kirk also mentions performances by the Colored Group of Detroit.[38] Others, as we have seen, included groups from Tuskegee, Fisk, Hampton and Morehouse universities, singing hymns in a polished fashion; singers Josh White and Viola Wells, who had the knack of adapting to white tastes; classical contralto Marian Anderson; popular tap dancer Bill Robinson and accordionist Graham Jackson, the record holder with his twenty-four performances of "simple folk melodies." There were no down-to-earth blues artists and few hard-core gospel shouters. However, the Mississippi Sheiks, a stringband whose members were used to white audiences, performed for Roosevelt at Warm Springs, Georgia,[39] and the gospel group the Soul Stirrers sang on the White House lawn for President Roosevelt and Winston Churchill in 1945.[40] Black artists were there. Urged on by his wife, Roosevelt began to enjoy their performances. Later he encouraged black musicians himself. To help introduce blacks on board ships, the president suggested to Secretary of the Navy Frank Knox: "Why not put a colored band on some of these ships? Because they're darned good at it. . . . Look, to increase the opportunity, that's what we're after."[41] Although this statement has a patronizing ring, it may show FDR's cautious approach and his understanding of what whites would accept.

FDR Jones

Although most blues artists called "Roosevelt" were named after Theodore Roosevelt, a younger one like Mississippi guitarist Roosevelt "Booba" Barnes

(1936–1996), born in the year of FDR's triumphant reelection, was probably named after Franklin Delano Roosevelt, "the poor man's friend." Through
his New Deal program Roosevelt became an idol for most blacks, and many
of them named their babies after him. Birth records of Harlem Hospital for
the period from 1933 to 1938 show records for "Franklin Delano Wilford,
Franklin Delano Kulscar, Donald Roosevelt Evans, Roosevelt Little, and dozens
of Eleanors, Franklins, and Delanos besides."[42]

White composer Harold J. Rome satirized the situation in his "F.D.R. Jones,"
a song he composed for the 1938 Broadway revue *Sing Out the News*. The
musical, which was strongly pro-FDR, lasted only three months, although the
reviews had been favorable.[43] Rome wrote the hit of the show, he told Nancy
Weiss, "because we wanted to say Hurrah for F.D.R. . . . Since blacks seemed to
name their children after famous men they admired, this was a good way to do
it . . . During the run of the show I received quite a few birth announcements
of new F.D.R.s."[44] The patronizing, if well-meant, song was recorded by black
artists who were popular with the white audience. The first one to record the
song in 1938 was jazz vocalist Ella Fitzgerald:

> *I hear tell: There's a stranger in the Jones' house, folks!*
> *Yes, siree, yes, siree! That's what I'm told.*
> *I hear tell: There's a new arrival six days old,*
> *Yes, siree, yes, siree!*
> *Worth his weight in gold.*
> *Come right in and meet the son,*
> *Christening's done,*
> *Time to have some fun.*
> *Yes, siree, yes, siree, yes, siree!*
> *Yes, siree, yes, siree!*
>
> *It's a big holiday,*
> *Every way,*
> *For the Jones family has a brand new heir.*
> *He's a joy, heaven sent,*
> *And they proudly present:*
> *Mr. Franklin D. Roosevelt Jones!*
>
> *When he grows up he never will stray,*
> *With a name like the one that he's got today.*
> *As he walks down the street,*

Folks will say, "Pleased to meet,
Mr. Franklin D. Roosevelt Jones."

What a smile, and how he shows it,
He'll keep happy all day long.
What a name, I'll bet he knows it,
With that handle, how can he go wrong?
And the folks in the town all agree,
He'll be famous, as famous as he can be.
How can he be a dud, or a stick in the mud,
When he's Franklin D. Roosevelt Jones?
    Yes, siree, yes, siree, yes, siree!
'Cause he's Franklin D. Roosevelt Jones!

"He never will stray, with a name like the one that he's got today"; with such a celebrated man as patron saint, happiness was assured. The message caught on, as did the tune, and the song became a big hit. Within a year no fewer than sixteen cover versions of "F.D.R. Jones" were recorded by American and British artists.[45]

The most outrageous version was recorded as late as January 1942 by Charlie and His Orchestra, a Nazi propaganda orchestra that made cover versions of famous American and British tunes. The themes for these were outlined by the Reichspropagandaministerium and worked out by special lyricists.[46] After the war the identity of "Charlie" was revealed; he was a crooner called Karl Schwedler and was responsible for this "F.D.R. Jones." It was a vile anti-Semitic attack on Franklin Roosevelt, whose enemies sometimes labelled him a Jew, claiming that his real name was Rosenfeld.[47] Imitating a Jewish accent Schwedler now sang in English: "It's a Hebrew holiday everywhere, for the Jewish family has a brand new heir. . . ."[48] German propagandists used these attacks to mobilize anti-Semites against the president of the United States.

The ironic comment on the world of difference that lay between "F.D.R. Jones" and FDR, president of the United States, raised a question foremost in blacks' minds: would a black man ever occupy the White House? Would there be a time for a black president?

I GOT TO GO TO THAT RED CROSS STORE

The winter of 1926–27 had been very wet, and when it kept raining in the spring the level of the Mississippi River rose to such an extent that the levees broke in 145 places, causing an area of 16 million acres to be flooded.[1] The American Red Cross collected $17 million to be distributed among the victims; President Coolidge appointed Secretary of Commerce Herbert Hoover as head of operations.

In *Blues Fell This Morning* Paul Oliver explains how "discreditable" Hoover's conducting of the relief effort was. Blacks were required to pay for services and food that should have been given free of charge. As many of them had seen their few possessions washed away by the mighty flood, they simply had no money and were often left to starve. White landowners were afraid their black sharecroppers would not return. The Red Cross kept lists of the sharecroppers, who were sometimes put in barbed wire concentration camps overseen by National Guardsmen. Some blacks were used for forced labor, and Oliver states that many even feared they would be conscripted into the army.

Black criticism was rampant, and although Hoover denied all the accusations, the pressure generated by people such as the journalist Walter White was so great that Hoover was forced to ask the president of Tuskegee Institute, Dr. Robert Russa Moton, to investigate conditions in the camps. Immediately the situation improved, but the resultant (unpublished!) survey still "makes distressing reading."[2] In *Dark Journey* Neil R. McMillen argues that "even some native whites reported that the guard kept blacks inside the camps and labor agents out, thus assuring Delta landlords that when the waters receded their workers would return to the plantations. The guardsmen were guilty of acts which profoundly and justly made the Negroes fear them."[3] The Red Cross felt that "while a number of recommendations were made for improvements, it was absolved of any conscious racial discrimination."[4] Many blues were recorded that grippingly illustrate the situation at the time of the 1927 Mississippi floods.[5] There are also blues recordings about the great southern drought of 1930– 31. Again violations of relief administration regulations occurred; for instance, rations were used to pay men to clear lands for farmers in Humble, Tennessee.[6] In view of these sad episodes, it is not hard to understand black reluctance "to go down to the Red Cross store." You never knew what would happen once you had entered!

The 1932 annual report of the Jefferson County chapter of the American National Red Cross devoted a page to the origins of its food stores in Birmingham, Alabama:

> Our first three neighborhood stores were opened in 1931 in order to distribute the large quantities of vegetables canned during the Food Conservation Campaign of that year. The winter brought a great amount of donated food stuff and "gifts" in kind pledged to the Chest which were handled through these stores. Economic necessity and the problem of distribution of Red Cross flour caused three more to be established during 1932. They are placed in the most thickly populated areas of the City and outlying territory. Property owners have given the use of the buildings without rent. Every man employed in the stores needed work. Since a large percentage of money is saved in this method, the stores will continue in operation. Every effort is made to have these stores run as any grocery stores in town. They are attractive, clean, and well managed. Visit them yourselves. You will be pleased. The head of the department is an expert who does all the buying, thereby assuring excellent quality of all foodstuffs. He and the Supervisor of stores furnish efficient management of stores and an appreciable saving of money.

This official Red Cross report is in strong contrast to the reality of everyday life as voiced by the blues singers. They complain of molded tripe, whereas the Red Cross proudly mentions the "excellent quality of all foodstuffs." The "efficient management" is attacked by the blues singers for discriminatory practices.

That "The Red Cross Blues" was already a local hit can be concluded from an article by Roberta Morgan, former director of the Birmingham relief agencies:

> Many Negroes, however, seemed to regard work relief as a "job" and went to the workers as to their employers with their problems. Some of them composed a work song, "The Red Cross Blues" and regularly spoke of "being on The Cross." Their good humor and optimism sustained them to a remarkable degree. Their anxieties were evident in different ways. They came to the relief offices day after day. Sometimes more than 1,000 persons were interviewed in the five or six offices in a day. One could sometimes hear the Negroes singing in a chorus while they waited. When questioned as to why they came to the office so often, a man replied: "To see what the Red Cross is puttin' out." So, in a sense, it was their stock market.[7]

On 17 July 1933 thirty-six-year-old Birmingham, Alabama, blues singer Lucille Bogan (1897–1948) was in a New York City studio. With piano accompaniment by Walter Roland, she recorded the first version of "Red Cross Blues," entitled "Red Cross Man."

> If anybody don't believe, I got a Red Cross man,
> Go out in my backyard, look at my Red Cross can.

chorus: Oh, baby, don't you want to go?
> Go with me and my man, down to the Red Cross store.

> Red Cross gives my man, three days a week,
> Sack of Red Cross flour, hunk of old white meat.

> If my man had-a-listened to me years ago,
> He wouldn't had to go to the Red Cross store.

> Oh, baby, now you've got to go,
> You can't go to no Hill, you got to go to the Red Cross store.

> Wonder what them people, standin' talkin' so?
> I believe they are talkin', 'bout a Red Cross store.

> My man worked up on the mountain, his shirt got soakin' wet,
> Say, he don't want no stuff, 'bout his Red Cross check.

> Oh, baby, don't you want to go?
> You can go with my man, down to the Red Cross store.

Lucille Bogan, contemporary record
advertisement, from the collection
of the author.

Hitherto, relief stations had often distributed food instead of money. Cash,
it was feared, would not be put to good use. Popular prejudice held that the
welfare recipient would spend his dollars on liquor instead of food and clothing.
As a consequence the unemployed worker was treated like a little child.

Bogan's song voices the determination of a woman who urges her man to go
to the Red Cross store to get flour and meat. Evidently the man is reluctant to
go and she warns him that he cannot go to "no Hill." In 1934 James B. Hill and
Nelson P. Hill were the presidents of a very large Birmingham grocery chain. It
had presumably been established some years earlier and was later bought out by
another chain.[8]

Advertisements in the Birmingham News ("The South's Greatest Newspaper")
show that Hill Stores ("Birmingham's Favorite Food Stores") were part of the
Piggly Wiggly chain of grocery stores.[9] Piggly Wiggly was founded in 1916,
as the first "cash and carry" grocery store. You took your "groceries from
the shelf" and paid at the check-out counter. Two days after her recording of
"Red Cross Man" Lucille Bogan sang "Groceries on the Shelf," a song about

the Piggly Wiggly stores in which self-service became a metaphor for sexual availability.[10]

On the same day that Lucille Bogan recorded "Red Cross Man," her pianist, the bricklayer Walter Roland, recorded his own version of "Red Cross Blues."

> Said, me and my good girl talked last night, we done talked for an hour,
> She wanted me to go to the Red Cross store, and get a sack of that Red Cross
> > flour.
>
> I told her, "No, Great Lord," said, "Woman, I sure don't wanna go,
> Do I have to go to Hill's?[11] 'Cause I got to go to that Red Cross store."
>
> Said, you know, them Red Cross folks, said, they sure do treat you mean,
> Don't wanna give you nothing but two-three cans of beans.
>
> And I told her, "No, Great Lord, girl," says, "I don't wanna go,"
> I say, "You know I cannot go to Hill, I've got to go yonder to that Red Cross store."
>
> But, you know, the government done taken it in charge now, said they gonna treat
> > everybody right,
> They gonna give 'em two cans of beans now, and one little can of tripe.
>
> And I told 'em, "No, Great Lord, girl," says, "I don't want to go,
> I think I'd better wait till I get a job and go to Hill, 'cause I've got to go to that Red
> > Cross store."
>
> Said, you go up there early in the morning, say, they ask you, "Boy, how you feel?"
> Gettin' ready to give you a nickel's worth of rice and a bag of that bolted meal.
>
> And I told 'em, "No, Great Lord, girl," said, "I don't wanna go,"
> Said, "You know I cannot go to Hill, I've got to go yonder to that Red Cross store."
>
> But, you know, say, I got a girl now, say she gonna get herself a job,
> She gon' take care of me now, while the time is hard.
>
> And I told her, "Yes, Great Lord, then I won't have to go,"
> I said, "When you get paid off, we'll go to Hill, I won't have to go to that Red Cross
> > store."
>
> But you know, say, a girl told me this morning, that she loved me 'cause I worked
> > two days a week,
> I told her I worked for the Red Cross, didn't get nothing but something to eat.

> She told me, "No, Great Lord," said, "Man, I don't wanna go,"
> She said, "Buddy, you will carry me to Hill," said, I said, "I'll take you to that Red
> Cross store."

This song was a great hit, and the recording was issued on no fewer than seven 78 rpm labels. Pseudonyms like "Alabama Sam" or "Mose Jackson" were used on all issues in preference to Roland's real name. This initial version of Walter Roland's "Red Cross Blues" proved to be so influential that, from 1933 to 1971, it was recorded by several performers, including Frank James,[12] Sonny Boy Williamson, the Washboard Trio, Brownie McGhee, Forrest City Joe, John Henry "Bubba" Brown and Thomas Shaw.[13]

In 1941 a "washboard trio" from Alabama, the Mobile Washboard Band, made two unissued recordings for the Library of Congress in Selma, Alabama. The three artists, Sidney Dawson, Virgil Perkins and George Scott, accompany themselves on kazoo, washboard and guitar. Their version of "Red Cross Blues" borrows four stanzas from the first Walter Roland version, but they add three interesting stanzas:

> Now, me and my wife talked last night, I think we talked about a' hour,
> She said, "Man, get up and go to the Red Cross store and get a sack of that Red
> Cross flour."

chorus: And I told her, "No, great God, babe, I don't wanna go,"
> But I couldn't go to Hill, and I had to ease back to that Red Cross store.

> Now, when you walk in the Red Cross store in the morning, the man'll say, "Boy,
> how you feel?"
> And he'll look round on the shelf and hand you a pack of that bolted meal.

chorus: And I hollered, "No, Great God, man, I don't wanna go,"
> But I didn't have no money in my pocket and I had to ease back to that Red Cross
> store.

> Now, the Red Cross people say that they were goin' to treat everybody right,
> They'll hand you one little can of beans and one little can of tripe.

> Now, grandma, she shouted, and grandpa preached a while,
> Before they got a sack of that Red Cross flour, both of 'em were sanctified.

> Now, the Red Cross people, they have studied out a plan,
> If you don't work for the WPA, they won't give you a thing.

Now, the Red Cross people, they sure can treat you mean,
Sometimes they give you a streak o'lean and . . .

So, I got up this morning, with something on my mind,
I went by the Red Cross store, just to see what I could find.[14]

In the second chorus the singer expresses his reluctance to accept charity, but having no money to buy food, has to go to the Red Cross anyway. The fourth stanza suggests that grandpa and grandma had to shout and preach (i.e., put on a show) before they were given their sack of flour. The fifth stanza refers to a Red Cross policy of requiring people who get handouts to be working for the Works Progress Administration (an early example of "workfare").

John Henry "Bubba" Brown, born in Brandon, Mississippi, in 1902, was a fine guitarist and a labor activist who wrote prize-winning poems. His first recordings were not made until 1967 when he was discovered by David Evans. One of the unissued songs that Evans recorded by him was "The Red Cross Store," which Brown claimed to have composed in 1932.[15]

I went home last night, argued 'bout an hour,
She wanted me to go downtown and get her a sack of Red Cross flour.

chorus: *And I told her, "No, you know I don't want to go,*
I'd rather plow me a mule from sunup to sundown,
'Cause I don't want to go down to that Red Cross store."

When those biscuits got cold, they smelled just like a plum,
Me and those children put on those biscuits just like you put on some chewing gum.

It's one thing that I want to tell you, people, it ain't no mistake,
I've seen a Red Cross biscuit give a hog the stomach ache.

Another thing I'm going to tell you, a thing sure is true,
Eating a Red Cross biscuit goes mighty hard with you.

Brown taught the song to his fellow Mississippian, "Boogie" Bill Webb, a younger artist (1924–1990), who recorded three versions of the song.[16] In spite of Bubba Brown's claim, the Webb versions are again based on the first Walter Roland version, although Webb's 1986 recording also uses the original Bubba Brown stanzas about the Red Cross biscuits.

Thomas Shaw, a Texas blues singer who only began to record as late as 1969 at the age of sixty-three, re-created Walter Roland's "Red Cross Blues" as "Richard Nixon's Welfare Blues" in 1971. Shaw, who used stanzas from the versions Walter Roland and Sonny Scott recorded, had settled in San Diego, California, in 1934 and lived there ever since. Consequently, Ronald Reagan had been his governor since 1966. Shaw's blues is the first to mention Reagan. In the blues singer's dream his governor and his president are in the welfare store themselves:

> Now, I had a dream last night, I never dreamt before,
> I dreamed I saw Mr. Nixon, standin' in the welfare store.

chorus:
> I said, "No, welfare, I don't wanna go,
> I don't wanna go out on the hill, little girl, I don't wanna go to the welfare store."

> Well, now, welfare people sure do treat you mean,
> Give you two cans of kraut, one can of beans.

> Now, I said I had a dream last night, never dreamed before,
> I saw Mr. Reagan, standin' in the welfare store.

> Now, me and my little gal, would talk, man, talk for a hour,
> She wants me to go to welfare, get a sack of that old welfare flour.

> Now, I wants a nickel's worth of sugar, dime's worth of lard,
> Big sack of flour, you know the work ain't hard.

> Now, ain't no use talking, 'bout the time being long,
> Know, Mr. Nixon, got his time and gone.

> Now, you see two women, walkin' hand in hand,
> I bet you, one got the other's man.

Evidently Thomas Shaw did not understand what "Hill" originally referred to. He consequently sang, "I don't wanna go out on the hill." Even Speckled Red had already sung, "I'd rather go to the hills and plow" in his 1938 "Welfare Blues."

Walter Roland recorded two versions of "Red Cross Blues" in 1933 and cut frequent sessions over the next two years. It has been commonly assumed that Roland composed this song, but in 1975 blues collector Don Kent found and interviewed relatives of the then-recently deceased blues guitarist Marshall Owens (c. 1880–1974).[17] Owens, who like Walter Roland hailed from Birmingham, Alabama, had made four ultra rare recordings in 1932, only two of which have ever been found. Owens died forgotten, but his relatives claimed he had written "Red Cross Store" and "spoke bitterly of its being stolen from him."

The record company must have felt that the topical song had the potential to become a hit. Why else should they have let Walter Roland record the sequel, "Red Cross Blues No. 2," that same day in 1933? For his accompaniment Roland switched from the piano to his guitar.

> *Say, you know, I had a dream last night, that I had never dreamt before,*
> *I dreamt about that head clerk, down in the Red Cross store.*

chorus: *And I told her, "No, Great Lord," said, "Girl, I can't go,"*
> *Says, "I cannot go to Hill, but I can go to the Red Cross store."*

> *Said, you know, that woman I got now, you know she won't treat me right,*
> *Every time I go home now, she wanna fuss and fight.*

> *Said, you know, they give you something to eat at the Red Cross, you have to go get*
> *it 'fore eleven,*
> *They done moved up on Seventeen Street, to Third Avenue, thirteen-o-seven.*

> *Says, I done told you once, now, says, I'm sure gonna tell you twice,*
> *Says, I know you'll keep arguin' with me about the Red Cross rice.*

> *Say, you know I'm gonna sing this here verse, now and I soon ain't gonna sing no*
> *more,*
> *'Cause my wife and children is hungry, and I 'spect I'm gonna have to go.*

> *And holler, "Oh, Great Lord, I'm gonna have to go,"*
> *Said you know, I just as well go home and get my crocus sack, go up yonder to that*
> *Red Cross store.*

> *But, you know, there's one thing that's certain, that all these people see,*
> *The Red Cross don't give you everything you want, they'll give you something you*
> *need.*

The lyrics of Roland's second version were not as influential as those of the first, although echoes of them can be heard in the first and third stanzas of Thomas Shaw's adaptation, in the third stanza of Sonny Scott's "Red Cross Blues No. 2," and in the 1972 "Red Cross Store" by Georgia guitarist Roy Dunn (1922–1988).[18]

Roland's second version gives some interesting details about a welfare station and a Hill's shop in Birmingham, Alabama. The 1934 city directory shows that there was a Hill's at 1718 3rd Avenue North.[19] Roland sings about a Red Cross store which could only be visited before eleven o'clock and which had "moved up on Seventeenth Street, to Third Avenue, 1307." From a list of Red Cross stores in the 1932 report of the Jefferson County Red Cross branch we learn that there was a Red Cross store at 1707 - 3rd Ave. North (downtown). As 1307 was an open lot at the time, Roland must have made an error in one digit of the address.[20] The Red Cross store was probably across the street from the Hill store.

A third Alabama artist, guitarist Sonny Scott, also recorded two versions of "Red Cross Blues" later that week in July 1933. Gayle Dean Wardlow interviewed singer Gress Barnett, who claimed to have known Sonny Scott when he lived in Quitman, Mississippi, in the early thirties.[21] In his first version of "Red Cross Blues" Sonny Scott mentions the same Red Cross store address Walter Roland gave in his second version:

> Let me tell you one thing, what the Red Cross people will do,
> Moved on Seventeenth Street, down on Third Avenue.

chorus: I told 'em, "No, Great God, Lord, I don't wanna go,
> Know I can't go down to Hill, but I got to go to the Red Cross store."

> Go to Red Cross in the morning, baby, go up there at night,
> Woman, they stay at the Red Cross store both day and night.

> Now, my girl told me this morning, that she done collared a job,
> She gonna take care of me, while the times was hard.

> And I told her, "Yes, Great God, and I won't have to go,"
spoken: (Why, the reason you say that?)
> "Because I can't go down to Hill, you know I can go to the Red Cross store."

> I worked on the mountain, till my shirt got soaking wet,
> I don't want no foolishness, 'bout my Red Cross check.

> Well, I saw two women, they was arguing on the street,
> Say, "I believe I'll go to that Red Cross store, tell 'em to give me something to eat."

Scott's third stanza was borrowed from Walter Roland's first version, and his fourth stanza had also been used by Lucille Bogan. In his final stanza Scott introduces "two women" who want to get food from the Red Cross store. This theme would be developed in "Red Cross Blues No. 2," which he recorded two days later:

> Lord, I had two women, they were long and tall,
> They went to the Red Cross store, then made a water haul.

chorus: *I told 'em, "No, Great God, and I don't want to go,*
I can't go down to Hill, but I'm going to the Red Cross store."

I saw two women, they was arguing on the street,
They was talking about that Red Cross meat.

I dreamed last night, that I never dreamt before,
I dreamt I saw the head clerk, down in the Red Cross store.

Lord, I had two women, walkin' hand in hand,
They said they didn't want no Red Cross man.

The two women are long and tall, and they are arguing about the "Red Cross meat." In the surface meaning they may both be disparaging the Red Cross meat. However, the phrase might have sexual overtones. In the final stanza the two women are "walking hand in hand" and they say they don't want a "Red Cross man." This might mean that they have a lesbian relationship, or that they have something going with the head clerk from the Red Cross store referred to in the previous stanza. The "Red Cross meat" could then be identified as the head clerk.

One of the most popular versions of "Red Cross Blues" was recorded in 1940 by Jackson, Tennessee-born harmonica player John Lee "Sonny Boy" Williamson (1914–1948). As Speckled Red had done in 1938, Sonny Boy changed the title to the more topical "Welfare Store Blues," and three stanzas were taken from Walter Roland's influential first version. There were also two new stanzas:

Now me and my baby, we talked last night, and we talked for nearly an hour,
She wanted me to go down to the welfare store, and get a sack of that welfare
flour.

chorus: *But I told her, "No! Baby, and I sure don't wanna go,"*
I say, "I'll do anything in the world for you, I don't wanna go down to that welfare
store."

Now you need to go get you some real white man, you know, to sign you a little
note,
They give you a pair of them keen-toed shoes, and one of them old pinch-back
soldier coats.

President Roosevelt said, "Them welfare people, they gonna treat everybody right,"
Said, "They give you a can of them beans, and a can or two of them old tripe."

Well, now me and my baby, we talked yesterday, and we talked in my back yard,
She said, "I'll take care of you, Sonny Boy, just as long as these times stay hard."

And I told her, "Yeah! Baby, and I sure won't have to go,"
I say, "And if you do that for me, I won't have to go down to that welfare store."

In his second stanza Williamson explains how difficult it was for many blacks under sharecropping to receive welfare goods without the patronage of "some real white man." The pair of "keen-toed shoes" and the "old pinch-back soldier coat" that Sonny Boy gets after his bossman has signed "a little note" were not forgotten when his admirer "Forrest City" Joe Pugh recorded a "Red Cross Store" nineteen years later. Some of its verses are derived from recordings by the Alabama artists, but its main source of inspiration is the version by Williamson. In this rendition the shoes are "hobnailed" and the old soldier coat is "box-back(ed)." Again army surplus is dumped via the Red Cross stores.[22]

Here is a list of goods supplied by the Red Cross stores, in order of the frequency with which they occur in the forty-seven different stanzas in the twenty-six versions of "Red Cross Blues" recorded between 1933 and 1986: one to three little cans of beans, a sack of Red Cross/welfare flour, a hunk of old, white meat (tripe?), one to five little cans of molded tripe, a sack or bag/a dime's or a nickel's worth of bolted meal, a nickel's worth of sugar, a dime's worth of lard, a nickel's worth of rice, two cans of kraut, a little old can of them old pork (and beans), one of them old pinch back/box-back soldier coats, a pair of hobnailed/keen-toed shoes, one little can of corn, a nickel's worth of veal and a can of chopped beef. The items may appear as coats and shoes (clothes), flour, meal, corn and rice (grain), sugar (groceries), tripe, veal, lard, pork and beef (meat) and beans and kraut (vegetables).

To try to understand the origins of "Red Cross Blues" we have to listen to the three versions of the song recorded by Louisiana guitarist Huddie (Leadbelly) Ledbetter (1889–1949). Leadbelly is one of the giants of the blues. His versatility and huge repertoire made him one of the most prolific of the recorded blues artists. From the beginning of this century Leadbelly played all over Texas and Louisiana. He led Blind Lemon Jefferson (1897–1929) around and was very much influenced by him. Leadbelly had to spend time in prison on homicide charges. From 1933 on Leadbelly was recorded in depth for the Library of Congress by John and Alan Lomax. This first version of the song was recorded in 1935 and was entitled "Red Cross Sto'":

chorus: *And I told her, "No, baby, you know, I don't wanna go,*
          Yes, and I ain't goin' down to that Red Cross store."

          She said, "Daddy, I just come by here to let you know,
          They want you down to that Red Cross store."

          She said, "Daddy, I'll come here and sit down on your knee,
          Ain't you goin' there to fight for you and me?"

          She said, "Daddy, I just come here, 'cause you know I'm your wife,
          Ain't you goin' fight for me and your life?"

          She come back here again, and she shook my hand,
          Said, "Can't you go down there and fight like a man?"

spoken: *You better get away from here, gal, 'cause you know I ain't goin' to no Red Cross*
                                                      store.
          I ain't never been down there before, and I ain't goin' down there.

          She said, "Now, come here, daddy, cause they're feedin' mighty fine,
          Mixin' everything up with whiskey and wine."

          She said, "Daddy, they're feedin' better than I ever seen,
          Feedin' everybody off of pork and beans."

          She come back here and she said they're feedin' her marbled ham,
          Said, "Get away from here, gal, you know I don't give a damn."

Again the woman uses all the tricks in the book to make her husband go to the Red Cross store, but he refuses. The second, third and fourth stanzas make clear why he has to go to the Red Cross store: to "fight for you and me," to "fight for me and your life" and "to fight like a man." The Library of Congress microfilm of notes on Leadbelly's songs made by John A. Lomax has the following comment on Leadbelly's "Red Cross Sto'": "Some negroes, at least, weren't carried away by a patriotic desire to enlist during the last war: this Negro man shows a wise animal suspicion of the strange agency which was 'mixing ev'rything up in whiskey an' wine' and sending men off to be made into soldiers. He is beautifully indifferent to his wife's desire to make a hero of him and the dialogue is authentic both as to diction and manner."[23]

Lomax shows a callow approach to war and the armed forces, and has made an unfortunate choice in the rather patronizing term "wise animal suspicion." Blacks' fear of entering a Red Cross store is made all the more explicit in a

BLUEBIRD
Electrically Recorded
PHONOGRAPH · RECORDS

Not Licensed for Radio Broadcast

RED CROSS BLUES
(W. Davis)
Walter Davis
Blues Singer with piano by Willie Kelly
B-5143-A

©RCA Manufacturing Co., Inc., Camden, N.J., U.S.A.

PERFECT
ELECTRIC

Not licensed for
Radio broadcast
(13551)
Vocal
with Guitar

RED CROSS BLUES NO. 2

Walter Roland
0291-A

PRODUCT BY AMERICAN RECORD CORPORATION
MADE IN U.S.A.

PERFECT
ELECTRIC

Not Licen
Radio Broadcas
(13550)
Vocal with
Piano Acc.

RED CROSS BLUES

Alabama Sam
0251-A

BLUEBIRD
"HIS MASTER'S VOICE"
REG. U.S. PAT. OFF.   MARCA REGISTRADA

For best results
use Victor Needles
B-8709-B

THE RED CROSS STORE BLUES

Huddie Leadbelly
Blues singer with guitar

RCA MANUFACTURING CO., INC., CAMDEN, N.J., U.S.A.

commercial 1940 recording of the song by Leadbelly for Bluebird Records, "The Red Cross Store Blues":

chorus: *I told her, "No, baby, you know I don't wanna go,*
Yes, and I ain't going down to no Red Cross store."

She come down here, said, "Daddy, I'm gwina talk with you a just a little while,
Ain't you goin' down and fight for your wife and child?"

She come down here and she shook my hand,
She said, "Daddy, I want you to go down there and fight for me like a man."
She said, "The Red Cross people is feedin' mighty fine,
They mixing everything up with whiskey and wine."

She come down here, talkin' to me about the war,
I told her, "Baby, I ain't done nothing to go there for."

She come down here and she fell down on her knees,
I said, "Baby, you better look somewhere for your butter and cheese."

She said, "Daddy, I just come down here to tell you so,
You better go running down to that Red Cross store."

As the first, second and fourth stanzas make clear, the man has to go to the Red Cross store to be enlisted in the army. He has to fight for his wife and child, but the man feels he "ain't done nothing to go there for." In 1940 Alan Lomax wished to discuss with Leadbelly the origins of some of his songs. Portable recording machines had become much improved, and Lomax could use sixteen-inch discs enabling Leadbelly to go beyond the usual three-minute limit.[24] The result was a third version of "Red Cross Sto'," this time preceded by an interview about the song's history.

spoken: *Leadbelly, eh, I'd like you to sing us the song about the Red Cross store.*
And, tell us all about what it means and why you sing it and why it was made up in the first place.
Tell us the story of it, is it a true story or isn't it?

spoken: *It's a true story, Red Cross store, and it was a man he . . .*

spoken: *When did it happen, Huddie?*

spoken: *Well, that's been not so long ago. Well, way, pretty good while too. Well, that's since 1917 on up.*

So a woman she had a husband and she had quit this man. She had a little boy child about seven years old. And so, when she heard about they're gonna draft mens to the army. Well, she knows boys got bonus before, she had been quit him, four years. But she know boys had got bonus in 1917, so she run and hunt up her husband. When she found him, she brought her little child, when she got to him. She told him, "Say, looka here," says, "you better go down to the Red Cross store. Ain't you goin' to the army and draft for the army?" Says, "Cause they're registerin' up down there." Say, "You better go down there and register up, so you can go back to the army." Now, she done quit the man for four years, she just studied up and come down and brought her little child. But that didn't mean nothin' to that man, because every time she come there and tell him something about goin' to the war, he'd sit down and he'd begin to talk to her and he'd tell her:

chorus: I told her, "No, baby, you know I don't wanna go,
         Yes, and I ain't goin' down to no Red Cross store."

         She come down here and she brought her little seven-year-old child,
         "Daddy, ain't you goin' down and fight for me and you a little while?"

         She was a good-looking woman, she had great big legs,
         She walks like she walkin' on a soft boiled egg.

spoken: I ain't goin'!

         She come down here and she bowed down on her knees,
         I said, "You better look somewhere for your butter and cheese."

         Every time she come a-pleadin' to me 'bout the war,
         I tell her, "Baby, you know I ain't done nothin' to go down there for."

spoken: Go ahead now, and talk to me a little bit! That's all right! Well! Do it again, I didn't
                            understand you!
         That's all right! Well, all right then!

         She said, "A toadfrog jumped in the bottom of the well,
         And this poor boy, God, he done jumped in hell."

spoken: Gonna change my mind!

         She says, "Old cow died down in the middle of the branch,
         Jaybird whistled and the buzzard danced."

spoken: Try to change her mind!

According to Leadbelly the story was inspired by a real event. A married couple had a child, and the woman quit her husband. Hearing a rumor that men were to be drafted into the army, she remembered an enlistment bonus paid in 1917 and looked him up again. When she had found her ex-husband, she took along their seven-year-old child and tried to persuade him to go to the army to fight for his wife and child. He was not impressed and advised her to look somewhere else for her "butter and cheese." Obviously the woman was confused and had a misunderstanding about the purpose of the Red Cross stores. The last two stanzas are very interesting. At first sight they seem unrelated and appear to belong to a different song,[25] but the words refer to "jumping into hell," and the excitement of carrion-eating birds at the death of a cow. Is it possible to see here metaphors for the horrors of the battlefields of the Great War? When Leadbelly recorded the song in August 1940, the United States was preparing for the first-ever peacetime draft, though the 1935 version also seems to refer to a draft.

It is possible that someone, perhaps Marshall Owens, composed a "Red Cross Blues" in 1917, drawing inspiration from real events. No version of the song from before 1933 has been found, but Leadbelly connects the song to a remembrance of events around 1917. In 1933, Walter Roland may have revived the old theme for another attack on the Red Cross stores. This time the distribution of food and clothes instead of cash was criticized and, in sometimes veiled terms, the discriminatory attitude of the distributors was analyzed: black clients were addressed as "boy," and the goods supplied were often past their best.

As we have seen, Leadbelly explains that blacks were afraid that going to the Red Cross stores would result in conscription. The phrase "I have to go to (the) hills" may originally have referred to the hills where blacks escaped the high water and the barbed wire relief camps at the time of the 1927 Mississippi flood. Paul Oliver has analyzed songs by Charley Patton and Blind Lemon Jefferson in which escape to the hills is mentioned.[26] By the time of the 1933 recordings by the three Alabama blues artists, "the hill" may have been changed into "Hill's," the Birmingham grocery store. Later recordings by artists from outside Alabama again refer to "the hill" as the phrase has become obscure once more. Fear of the unknown, of discrimination, forced labor or the draft, was still there in the thirties. The song "I Don't Wanna Go to the Red Cross Sto'" was so popular because it voiced common fear among black people. Another theme is pride. The singers want to be able to buy what they want, instead of receiving handouts.

The connection between the Red Cross saga and the Hoover days is borne out by the unissued Brownie McGhee recording from 1942 discussed in chapter 2. Basically McGhee's song is one of the many adaptations of Walter Roland's first version, but it also contains no fewer than three references to President Hoover.

Forrest City Joe, "Bubba" Brown, Thomas Shaw, Roy Dunn and "Boogie" Bill Webb were not the only blues artists who recorded "Red Cross Store Blues" after World War II. Guitarist Mississippi Fred McDowell (1904–1972) (who, in spite of the nickname, which he disliked, came from Tennessee) recorded no fewer than five versions of the song from 1962 to 1969.

McDowell lived on his parents' farm in Rossville, in Fayette County, Tennessee, until 1926. He then hoboed, played music and farmed in Tennessee and Mississippi. In 1940 he settled north of Holly Springs, around Hudsonville, Mississippi.[27] In the fifties he moved to Como, Mississippi, where he lived the rest of his life, and where he was buried.

For textual reasons we shall quote the fourth of the five recordings McDowell made of the song. It was recorded live in England, during a 1969 European tour. McDowell's "Red Cross Store" has an interesting spoken introduction, which is marred by the sheepish laughter of the audience:

spoken: *Well, eh, some of you may have heard talk of it, but we're goin' down to the Red Cross store now.*

You know, eh, I lived on a farm for so many years, farmin'. And you go to the merchant, after July, that's when you're supposed to be through layin' by. Now, he ain't gonna give you nothing else to eat, you understand, see? I'm gonna explain to you real close, so you'll understand what I'm talking about. And I, eh, then you, as he won't furnish you nothin' else to eat, you're goin' down to the Red Cross store, you understand, see? Now, that's what this is, the title of this song.

Eh, I want you to understand it real good. I'm gonna sing it for you:

chorus: *Well, now, I'm goin' down to that Red Cross store.*

Well, them Red Cross people, sure do treat you mean,
Lord, them cans of kraut, baby, them old pork and beans.

Lord, I went to the merchant, asked him for some meat and meal,
Lord, it's, "Go away, boy, you know, you got boll weevils in your field."

Lord, I went to the merchant, asked him for some meat and lard,
"Lordy, go away, boy, you know times is done got hard."

Well, them cans of kraut, them old pork and beans.

Lord, that Red Cross, Red Cross store, meanest store, baby, ever seen.[28]

The farmer got credit as long as he still had work to do in the field. Now the crop is laid by and the credit has been cut off. At harvest time he will pay his debt and probably buy more with any cash he has left, or get more credit against next year's crop. McDowell does not manage to explain this clearly to the nonfarming British audience.

Some other songs were sung about the Red Cross stores which do not follow the Bogan/Roland/Scott pattern. In July 1933, less than a month after the Lucille Bogan/Walter Roland/Sonny Scott recordings, pianist Walter Davis (1912–1963) recorded his "Red Cross Blues":

The Red Cross is helping poor people, who cannot help themselves,
I went down there this morning, they said they wasn't helping no one else.

Uncle Sam's flag is painted, painted in red, white and blue,
'Cause the Red Cross won't help us, what in the world is we goin' to do?

I spent all my money, did not save a lousy dime,
I didn't ever think I would be worried, people, with these hard, old times.

So I will remember this: the longest day I live,
The Red Cross has told me, they did not have nothing to give.

My little children was screaming, cryin', "Papa, we ain't got no home!"
The Red Cross has cut us off, man, and left us all alone.

Four months later Walter Davis recorded a sequel, "Red Cross Blues—Part 2," which was released on a different record.

The Red Cross is helping people, each and every day,
But the rentman has put me out, and I ain't got no place to stay.

I believe to myself, I am just a bad luck man,
The Red Cross is helping everybody, and don't give me a helping hand.

I believe I'll go back south, tell me cotton will be good price next year,
I might as well be gone, because I ain't doin' no good 'round here.

The NRA is warning, people, that things will break someday,
And it will be all right, everybody will have a place to stay.

I'm goin' back to the country, and raise everything I need,
And if I don't make nothin' off-a my cotton, the boss will pay me out the seed.

Walter Davis had run away from the Mississippi farm he was born on when he was about thirteen and had lived in St. Louis and Chicago ever since; his suggestion of a return to the country as the solution is ironic. When the song was recorded, the National Recovery Administration (NRA) had been operational for half a year. The remark about the NRA is meant ironically as well.

Three months later, in March 1934, the second part of the Walter Davis song would be recorded by Josh White.[29] Although the lyrics are very much alike, Davis had sung that "things will break some day," to which White now added, "Depression is waning, people." Roosevelt had given people hope, but many people were still barred from relief in the Red Cross stores.

You have to "sit there all day" and "they ain't gonna help you, till you have told everything you know," sang Arkansas-born blues guitarist Samson Pittman in his "Welfare Blues," recorded in Detroit in 1938:

Welfare's helpin' people, that cannot help theyself,
I said, boys, they ain't gonna help you, less you lived in Detroit one year.

After your case is opened, they will give you plenty of fuel and clothes,
I said, boys, they ain't gonna help you, till you have told everything you know.

You go down to the welfare, they'll make you sit there all day,
I said, they know they ain't gonna help you, they'll make you sit there and wait.

Oh, boy, I believe I'll go there myself,
I say, I'll tell 'em I ain't got nothing, I declare I need they help.

spoken: *When did you compose this song?*

spoken: *This song was composed in nineteen and thirty-six on the twenty-second of*
           December by Samson Pittman in Detroit, Michigan.

spoken: *Is it the truth?*

spoken: *It's the true facts in Detroit about the welfare and the condition of the people.*

When Lomax next asked why Pittman remembered the date (three days before Christmas!) so well, the answer was "because that's the day I got so hungry."[30] As John Cowley has pointed out in his unpublished notes to the album that issued the Pittman recordings, the Library of Congress Archive of American Folk Song was an agency sponsored by the United States government. One of its aims was to document in song people's reactions to rural life and the effects of Roosevelt's New Deal program. A catalogue of the archive's recordings, made between 1933 and 1940, was compiled by the WPA music unit under the direction of Charles Seeger. This was published as a "Checklist of Recorded Songs in the English Language in the Archive of American Folk Song to July 1940," Washington, D. C., Library of Congress, 1942. As Cowley explains, Pittman's "Welfare Blues" was omitted from the checklist to avoid political embarrassment.

For some people like Blind Teddy Darby (b. 1906), going back to the country was impossible. They could not bear it any longer. "Uncle Sam is helping millions, seem like he'd help poor me." But Uncle Sam did nothing and Darby threatened to help himself using a pistol in his 1935 "Meat and Bread Blues (Relief Blues)."

> Now, all my meat is gone, no more flour in my barrel,
> And if I don't get me some groceries, I'm sure gonna lose my gal.

> Now, I'm going down to the relief, I want a order today,

spoken: (I sure do, boy!)

> For if I don't get some groceries, my babe gonna run away.

> Now, if Uncle Sam is helping millions, seem like he'd help poor me,
> Now, I'm going down there tomorrow morning, and ask for sympathy.

> Now, if they deny me, and they won't help me none,
> I'm going to help myself, with my 32-20 or my .41.

> And then it will be too late, too late, to call up the chief of police,
> For I've got to have me some groceries, and I've been denied by the relief.

In June 1941 Mississippi-born blues guitarist Tony Hollins recorded a "Stamp Blues" in Chicago. The food stamp program had started in 1939 to provide the poor with a cheaper way of obtaining food.[31]

> Well, I woke up this morning, half past four,
> Met a big crowd, at the charity store.

chorus: 'Cause they're gittin' them stamps, (3x)

> That the government givin' away.

Cartoon by Henry Brown in the
Chicago Defender, 18 March 1933.

Well, I'm a country man, never go to town,
The women in Chicago, tryin' to jive me around.

spoken: Yeah!

Well, if you're ever in Chicago, and the times get hard,
Take a little walk down on South Park.

Well, the womens up here play me to be a fool,
Think I'm the boy ain't never been to school.

spoken: Yeah!

Well, when I got here, I had good luck,
The woman I love, she keeps me up.

Well, I woke up this morning, half past two,
Streets was crowded and I couldn't get through.

spoken: Yeah! Play it a long time now, boy!

In this song Hollins shows the increasing negative effects of welfare. It pro-
duces dependency and disrupts the man-woman relationship by making women
the recipients of government largesse and thus, in a sense, married to Uncle
Sam. There must have been a stamp dispensing office on South Park where
people, mostly women, lined up early in the morning to get their stamps. A man
might look for a woman receiving food stamps to support him, as Hollins seems
to suggest in his next-to-last stanza.

An earlier complaint about the dependency caused by welfare stores had
been recorded by Louisiana Johnny seven years before in his October 1934
"Charity Blues": "You want to see them peoples, troubled in mind, let their
charity box, get three days behind. Then they're troubled, Lord troubled in
mind, they don't want that charity box, to be three days behind."[32]

Evidently the Red Cross had many discriminatory practices for which they
were to be held responsible. After his election Franklin Roosevelt took the
organization of the distribution of welfare into government hands. "The government done taken it in charge now" the blues singers sang in 1933, hoping that
everybody would be treated correctly. Roosevelt's "three r's"—relief, recovery
and reform—were under way. The letter "r" was just one of the many letters in
the alphabetical soup the president was cooking.[33]

CWA, YOU'RE THE BEST PAL WE EVER KNEW

Roosevelt is a mighty fine man, darling, got to be the president of our land, darling," Georgia guitarist Blind Willie McTell (1901–1959) sang in his 1935 "Hillbilly Willie's Blues."[1] There had been earlier tributes to FDR. Jug band leader Jack Kelly recorded a "President Blues" in August 1933, six months after Roosevelt's inauguration. In the American Record Company files the original title of this song, the first blues recording about Roosevelt, was "President Roosevelt Blues." It is not clear why the more topical title was rejected. When Kelly's song was recorded three "fireside chats" had been given: 12 March 1933, the "Banking Crisis," 7 May, "Progress Made During the New Deal's First Two Months" and 24 July, "Praising the First Hundred Days and Boosting the NRA." "Fight on, boys, fight on, I'll make everything all right," the president encourages in Kelly's paraphrase. "If I don't see you November, I'll see you, boys, Christmas night." In this encouragement the first date probably refers to the last Thursday in November, Thanksgiving Day. And Roosevelt kept his promise: Christmas 1933 saw the people in the shops again. Shelves were finally emptied. In this song life is seen as a series of fights. Roosevelt kept Kelly from death, the "last big fight."

> I was walkin' around in Memphis, until my foots got thin as a dime,
> Don't be for President Roosevelt, I would have done a penitentiary crime.

He woke up one mornin' (spoken: Yeah, man!), he was feelin' mighty bad,
He begin to thinkin' about his poor people, and he begin to feel sad.

"Fight on, boys, fight on, I'll make everything all right,
If I don't see you November, I'll see you, boys, Christmas night."

I believe, I believe, President he's all right,
spoken: *(Now, sing 'em!)*
He kept me from goin', I say, to the last big fight.

The previous day, 1 August 1933, Jack Kelly had recorded "R.F.C. Blues," the song that was to become the flip side of "President Blues" on all five 78 record labels on which it was issued. It refers to the Reconstruction Finance Corporation (RFC), an agency set up by Herbert Hoover in 1932 to aid bank and insurance companies in financial difficulties; Hoover explained that it was "the first of governmental props under the credit structure made necessary by our rotten banking system and pressures from abroad."[2]

That RFC sure is not envied of many men,
spoken: *(Yeah!)*
It caused me to walkin', down through the lowland.

And early one morning, I went out on my job,
spoken: *Yeah, man!*
Began to think, the work had done got hard.

I worked so hard, until I got tired,
Then I went to town, to get my wife some lard.

I sat and I wondered, about RFC today,
spoken: *(Yeah!)*
It's drivin' many men, and they'll have to obey.

This song has been a bone of contention among blues experts. Was it really about Hoover's Reconstruction Finance Corporation? What does a government agency set up to assist "banks and insurance companies in financial difficulties" have to do with a black jug band? Surely the lyrics did not present any clue at all?[3]

At face value the lyrics tell us that the "RFC" is the cause of Kelly's hard, tiring job on the "lowland." "It's drivin' many men, and they'll have to obey," Kelly sings. Men who would evidently prefer to stay at home are forced to work. The "lowland" may be the location of work that is utterly disliked. Laborers may have been forced to work in levee camps. An industrial recovery agency like the RFC financed the Commodity Credit Corporation, which was used by Roosevelt to destroy crops in the struggle against overproduction. During the summer of 1933 farm owners and planters collected $100 million in benefit payments.[4] Sharecroppers who had lost their jobs as a result of the fight against overproduction had to seek other, often harder, work, like the building of levees.

Jack Kelly's record company chose another political song for the flip side of "President Blues," but one that contains political criticism rather than just glorification of Roosevelt's charisma. Franklin Roosevelt tended to downplay his predecessor's RFC, although he made effective use of it.[5]

A fortnight after Jack Kelly's recordings, South Carolina-born blues guitarist Joshua White recorded his song "Low Cotton." Fellow guitarist Willie Trice remembered Blind Boy Fuller (1908–1941), the master of Carolina blues guitar, sitting in front of a phonograph, learning it by heart.[6] On one level the song is a literal complaint against "low [growing] cotton." White wonders who planted it and gave him such "a dirty deal" because he has to get down on his "bended" knees to pick it. There is, however, a double meaning to White's "low cotton":

> I've been pickin' low cotton, no more high cotton can I see,
> I'll be glad when this cotton is picked, I'll be happy as I can be.
>
> When you're pickin' low cotton, you gotta get down on your bended knees,
> Wonder who plant this low cotton, that gave me such a dirty deal.
>
> I'm gonna pray to my father, I'm goin' to bow my head and knees,
> Wonder who plant this low cotton, always makes me rock and reel.
>
> If I was the president, I'd destroy this cotton that's worryin' us,
> Plenty corn liquor, make you darkies want to fight and cuss.
>
> Mmm,
> Mmm.
>
> I'm not the president, so there's nothing can I do,
> Cotton is worryin' me, just the same as it's worryin' you.[7]

Josh White, who, as we have seen, was to become a frequent visitor to the White House, is not the president himself, so there is nothing he can do. If he were the president, he would "destroy this cotton that's worryin' us." This is exactly what Roosevelt did. Cotton crops were destroyed because cotton was "low": prices for cotton were dramatically low because of overproduction. Although the line about the corn liquor and the "darkies" is framed in stereo-types, the juxtaposition with the line about advice to the president seems to hint at the possibility that the anger and violence could be directed against the establishment.

Roosevelt had to face the economic crisis in his own way. He had to forget old programs and take drastic new measures, for the situation was so desperate that fears of a revolution were real. There was to be a peaceful revolution instead.

Harry Hopkins, a newcomer selected by Roosevelt, was to start a new program that could guide America through the winter of 1933–34. Hopkins had told Roosevelt that 4 million jobs must be created to avert the crisis. "Four million people—that means roughly four hundred million dollars," Roosevelt estimated.[8] Large funds were provided by the Public Works Administration, which was also started in 1933. The PWA itself needed quite some preparation for an effective implementation. Harold Ickes, the architect of the PWA, finally agreed with Hopkins that the new agency would restrict itself to "projects of minor character" and would "undertake no contract work."[9]

By mid January 1934, 4.2 million people were employed by the new Civil Works Administration (CWA). Five hundred thousand miles of road were built, forty thousand schools built or improved, three thousand playgrounds or athletic fields constructed, fifty thousand teachers employed, three thousand writers and artists assigned special projects, five hundred new airports laid out and another five hundred upgraded, streets were repaired and parks cleared.[10] All these activities were carried out in a winter of record cold, but the people felt uplifted. No longer dependent on relief, they now earned real money that they could spend as they themselves thought best. There are no complaints in blues and gospel songs about the CWA, and this tallies with historian Anthony Badger's observation that "the CWA was remarkably free of corruption."[11] Roosevelt's paternal fireside chats had comforted the people, but the CWA showed that the new President also knew how to act. In April 1934 Houston blues singer Joe Pullum[12] sang a "CWA Blues":

> CWA, look what you done for me:
> You brought my good gal back, and lifted Depression off-a-me.
>
> I was hungry and broke, because I wasn't drawing any pay,
> But in stepped President Roosevelt, Lord, with his mighty CWA.

> I don't need no woman now, nor no place to stay,
> Because I'm makin' my own living, now with the CWA.
>
> You didn't ever think, woman, some day things would come my way,
> And especially, baby, in the form of the CWA.
>
> So you go your way, I don't want you anymore,
> I made a very great change, in nineteen and thirty-four.
>
> CWA, you're the best pal we ever knew,
> You're killing old man Depression, and the breadlines too.

The same year Rev. J. M. Gates contrasted earthly breadlines with the freely available "bread of heaven" in his sermon "No Bread Line in Heaven," and gave firm support to President Roosevelt's efforts:

> Ah, there's no breadlines in heaven, the breadline has been broken, long time ago,
> There's no breadline in heaven, I've been grieved, seein' my peoples and others,
> Standin' in the breadline, beggin' for bread, waitin' for bread, hungry!
> But there's no breadline in heaven.
> When I was walkin' through the streets of Philadelphia, I saw a long line: in the breadline.
> And over in Columbus, Ohio: in the breadline.
> Atlanta, Georgia: in the breadline.
> Throughout this country: in the breadline.
> But there's no breadline in heaven.
> There's no breadline in heaven and God has fixed it so, that you can eat bread here.
> I believe I can get a witness!
>   Amen! Reverend, I believe our president is a God-fearin' man,
> Yes!
>   A true Christian,
> Yes!
>   A real Christian,
> Well, we got plenty bread!
>   He did so many good things since he's been on.
> Yes!
>   Did things no president haven't done.
> Yes, he did, daughter, and there's no breadline in heaven.
>   Amen!

Through our president, daughter, God have made it possible.

No breadline in heaven. No breadline.

   Ah, Brother Pastor?

Yeah?

   Since our president has been on,

Yes!

   We have all been able to eat bread and to drink water, and to drink it free.

Yeah!

   We haven't been able to drink water and neither eat bread free.

Yeah!

   Until this president have taken place, our President Roosevelt.

Yeah! Well, I don't blame you for sayin' that, brother.

'Cause this here breadline has been on a long time.

But there's no breadline in heaven.

Now, I'm tryin' to get you to lift up your head.

There's no breadline in heaven.

   I thank God for Mr. Roosevelt, he sure has been good to me.

Yeah!

   He give me bread when I was hungry, he give me meat to eat.

Yeah!

   And he's still helpin' me, Brother Pastor!

Yeah! And when you say that, you want to say that, just like you said, I thank God for him.

And it is God workin' through him and not human stuff, it is God usin' him.

There's no breadline in heaven.

   Brother Pastor, and I tell you I wanna say this:

   He paid my rent when I was outdoors and I'm still in a house, under Mr. Roosevelt.

Amen! Yes, sir! But it's God's work.

   Yes!

God answerin' prayer, and God answered prayer,

And worked it out through the programs under your president.

   There's no breadline in heaven.

Well!

   Brother Pastor?

Yeah?

   I'm glad that God give us bread in heaven, Roosevelt give us bread on earth.

Yeah! Amen! Now listen, daughter: You know one thing?
You said somethin', ah, sister Betty, you know, I like the way you talk.
No breadline in heaven.

The president is depicted by the congregation as a "god-fearin' man" and a "true Christian." He provided bread to eat and water to drink: in the eyes of the black population, Roosevelt is God's agent. "God answered prayer and worked it out through the programs," Brother Pastor Gates explained.

The average CWA wages amounted to fifteen dollars a week, 2.5 times the regular relief wages.[13] In his July 1934 "C.W.A. Blues" Alabama blues artist Walter Roland was overjoyed with CWA wages of only $9.60 a week:

My woman told me to get up this morning: "Go get yourself a job,
I want you to try to take care of me, while the times is hard."

chorus: *I hollered, "Hey, woman, Great God, is you goin' my way?"*
Says, "I believe I'll go try to get me a job, workin' for that CWA."

She told me, "Let's go fall in line here, talkin' about they got jobs for sale,
If you want a good job, just go to that old county jail."

You know that CWA, they'll pay you nine-sixty a week,
You don't have to worry about that welfare, somethin' to eat.

You know, I told my woman this morning, just about half past three,
I said, "Wake up early, and come go with me."

You know, I wanna take my woman, down to that welfare store,
I'm gonna carry her this time, and I won't have to carry her no more.[14]

Like Joe Pullum, Walter Roland rejects the woman who has been nagging too much when the times were hard. To a degree Roland's song is musically and textually similar to his "Red Cross Blues," but this song has a happy end for the blues singer.

The Civil Works Administration lasted for four and a half months only, from 15 November 1933 to 31 March 1934. It had provided jobs for 4,263,644 people during the bleak winter months, and released them from the stigma attached to the welfare recipient. Roosevelt put an end to the CWA because of the costs involved ($933 million). He felt that local authorities should provide for their unemployed. "Nobody is going to starve in the warm weather" the president disingenuously argued.[15] In spite of the enormous popularity of the agency, as witnessed by the arrival of more than sixty thousand letters a week at the White House, FDR was not to be persuaded. Harry Hopkins was deeply disappointed, but remained totally loyal to the president.

Both the Roland and the Pullum songs about the CWA were recorded immediately after the demise of this agency on 31 March 1934, which may account for their being reflective songs. The post-CWA dates may have prompted English blues writer Bob Groom's speculation that the record producers misunderstood their artists' pronunciation of CWA; he concludes that the two songs are really about the PWA. However, both artists clearly pronounce a "c" and not a "p." Besides, as we have seen, the lyrics perfectly match the conditions under which the CWA took place.[16]

Soon after the demise of the CWA many people became desperate once more. There were strikes in New York and riots in Harlem in 1935. In February 1935 Mississippi guitarist Big Joe Williams (1903–1982), recorded a critical observation of the situation, strangely entitled "Providence Help the Poor People." "Big" Joe was referring to the provident/charity organizations that supplied food and shelter; the record company misspelled it as "providence." The first line of the song was probably inspired by Walter Davis's "Red Cross Blues," and the refrain and melody may have been influenced by Walter Roland's "Red Cross Blues."

> Well, the providents helpin' the poor people, Lord, those could not help themselves,
> They give them all the meals a day, boys, and they help someone else.
>
> I went in the office this mornin', 'bout half past four,
> Heard Mr. Roosevelt say they wasn't gonna help no more.
>
> Told 'em, "No, providents ain't gonna help no more,"
> Well, well, it may be tomorrow, ooh, Lord, I don't really know.
>
> Well, Mr. Roosevelt told me, "Ain't gonna be no hard times no more,"
> He's gonna let the poor people go, any place they want to go.
>
> I told him, "Yes, providents ain't gonna help no more,"
> Well, well, it may be tomorrow, ooh, Lord, I won't be back no more.
>
> I got up this morning, 'bout half past eight,
> Started down Pine Street, boys, to get my meal ticket straight.
>
> They told me, "No, provident ain't gonna help no more,"
> Well, well, it may be tomorrow, ooh, Lord, I might dust my bed and go.

Well, there's some have a shovel, some have a spade,
You know the provident is givin' me and my baby a place to stay.

And I told him, "No," he wasn't gonna help me no more,
Well, well, it may be tomorrow, ooh, Lord, I don't really know.

Well, the rooster told the hen, said, "Hen, go lay,"
She told him, "No, the provident gived me a place to stay."

She told him, "No," she don't have to lay no more,
Well, well, it may be tomorrow, ooh, Lord, I won't be back no more.

I asked my woman this mornin', could I fill her place?
She said, "No, Joe, the provident given me a place to stay."

She told me, "No," Lord, I could not fill her place,
Lord, I believe I'll get up in the mornin', ooh, Lord, I believe I'll leave this place.

Every mornin' the clock be striking eight,
I go down to the provident, boy, and I can't get my business straight.

He told me, "No," he wasn't gonna help no more!

Gone are the shovels and spades of the CWA. Back are the troubles the blues singers had with their women. Women want men who can "get their business straight," but now that the provident is no longer helping Joe he cannot "fill her place," just as the hen refuses the rooster's command to "go lay." The woman, however, has "a place to stay," thanks to the provident, and now views Joe as a moocher.

Another victim of the changing mood was the National Recovery Administration. In his third "fireside chat" of 24 July 1933 Roosevelt had enthusiastically announced his plans. He asked all employers to pay the same reasonable wages and to require the same hours. He next "waxed poetic" as Kenneth Davis put it: "In war, in the gloom of night attack, soldiers wear a bright badge on their shoulders to be sure that comrades do not fire on comrades. On that principle, those who cooperate in this program must know each other at a glance. That is why we have provided a badge of honor for this purpose, a simple design with a legend, 'We do our part': and I ask that all those who join with me shall display that badge prominently."[17] Roosevelt's mighty persuasive powers ensured that a "blue eagle" appeared widely, in spite of a design that evoked comparisons with Nazi symbolism.

Logo of the National Recovery Administration.   **WE DO OUR PART**

Walter Vinson (1901–1975) sang the glories of the NRA in his January 1935 "I Can't Go Wrong":

> *Now, the Government said right from the start,*
> *Do as he say do: "We will do our part."*

chorus: *Lord, the Government's before me, oh, and I can't go wrong,*
               Oh, the reason I'm singing this old lonesome song.

> *Government went to Rockefeller, carried Maxwell Sand(s) [?],*
> *He says, "Any way, Government, to get this world to stand?"*

spoken: *Play it, man, play it! Yeah, the Government's before us!*

> *He went to Ford brothers and told them like a man,*
> *They didn't care to sign, and he closed down their plan(t).*

> *It's on windows and doors in the shape of a bird,*
> *You don't have to wonder or neither say you heard.*

spoken: *Oh, fiddle that thing!*

Vinson was a Mississippi-born guitarist, and one of the Mississippi Sheiks, a successful blues group whose other members were the Chatmon brothers, Bo, Lonnie and Sam.[18] In his song Vinson personifies the "Government"; to most people at the time "the Government" was Roosevelt.

The president had succeeded in persuading most manufacturers, but, as Vinson sang, he had failed with Henry Ford, who stated "I wouldn't put that Roosevelt buzzard on my cars." Ford had refused to participate in the NRA because he thought that he did not need the government to ensure decent pay and working conditions for his laborers, and in Franklin and Eleanor Roosevelt's opinion, Ford did more than any other man to wreck the agency.[19] Many of the employers who had stuck the Blue Eagle on their windows were also silently avoiding its regulations. It was hardly possible to take measures against Ford, as he had already made promises with regard to wages and standard hours, and because he could not be forced to join the NRA by law. On 27 October 1933 Ford "was declared ineligible to receive Government contracts," but this was revoked on 11 November.[20]

The NRA was too complicated. There were 750 different codes by early 1934, and no one could make sense of it anymore, including the president. Hugh Johnson, who had initially organized the NRA with great enthusiasm, was told by Harry Hopkins that his codes "stunk." NRA became synonymous with "National Run Around," and it folded on 27 May 1935.[21]

As late as 1942 an NRA toast was recorded by the Library of Congress in Mississippi. It shows how the unfortunate agency was remembered:

> There was a gang of crabs on a cock one day,
> Said, "We are the members of the NRandA,
> We'll bite you on your ass just to hear you fart,
> We are the NRandA members and we do our part."[22]

Gone were the NRA and the CWA. Still Roosevelt had promised a "New Deal." Was it not time for a "Brand New Deal"? Guitarist Carl Martin (1906–1979) voiced a common sentiment when he sang his "Let's Have a New Deal" in September 1935:

> Now, everybody's cryin', "Let's have a New Deal,"
> Relief stations closin' down, I know just how you feel.

chorus: Everybody's cryin', "Let's have a New Deal,"
> 'Cause I've got to make a livin', if I have to rob and steal.
>
> Now, I'm gettin' mighty tired of sitting around,
> I ain't makin' a dime, just wearin' my shoe sole down.
>
> Now, I woke up this morning, doggone my soul,
> My flour barrel was empty, where I didn't have no coal.

> Now, you go to your workers, put in your complaint,
> Eight times out of ten, you know, they'll say, "I can't."
>
> They don't wanna give you no dough, won't hardly pay your rent,
> And it ain't costin' them one doggone cent.
>
> Now, I ain't made a dime, since they closed down the mill,
> spoken: (Yeah!)
> I'm sittin' right here waitin', on that Brand New Deal.

As was often the case, the song was coupled with another topical blues on the 78, this time about the "Brown Bomber," boxer Joe Louis.

The Social Security Act was signed in 1935. One of its provisions was old-age pension. Both employers and employees paid monthly to be provided with a pension at the age of sixty-five. Tommy Hicks, vocalist for Texas pianist Dusky Dailey and his band, called for help in his 16 June 1939 "Pension Blues":

> Got the pension blues and I really need your help,
> I been here so long, I just 'bout lose myself.
> I was born June the first in eighteen seventy-four,
> It's no need in staying here long when you're so doggone poor.[23]

The singer is so old that he needs help to establish his age. If he can prove that he really became sixty-five on 1 June he may get a pension. Without it a poor man may just as well give up and die.

A "Second New Deal" was indeed under way. And it was politically urgent, for Roosevelt's credibility was at stake. One of its magic phrases was the "WPA." The new agency was anxiously awaited by Annie Brewer, an Alabama school teacher who recorded a "Roosevelt Blues" for the Library of Congress in 1937. If the statement by Alan Lomax that she composed the song herself is correct, she must have written it for a male performer some years before.

> chorus: I got the blues, I got blues,
> I got the RFC blues.
>
> Goodbye beans and goodbye rice,
> I never had such a good time all my life.
>
> Say, Mrs. Roosevelt, aren't you proud,
> Of such a good husband that God allowed?
>
> Roosevelt tellin' us niggers a law,
> Chillun at home just . . .

spoken: *We got it wrong here!*

spoken: *Go ahead, go ahead! Any time . . .*

Roosevelt tellin' us niggers a law,
Chillun at home, just workin' their jaws.

Chewin' that good old bacon and greens,
Best old prospect you ever seen.

I can dip my snuff, and smoke my pipe,
Got money for my children and my lovin' wife.

Warrants all paid and debts all clear,
Come on, boys, let's shout and cheer.

I got shoes on my feet, and clothes on my back,
Gonna step right back, and rip and rack.

I got cheese and butter, eggs, milk and rice,
House all clean and neat and nice.

Good warm wood fires, and coals to burn,
Sometimes it seems them by the ton.

Roads all paved and health restored,
Sumpin' for everybody, even the dogs.

I now can travel from east to west,
In the finest cars that I like best.

I can sail on the ocean in the best steam line,
Reach my destination in due time.

There's so many goods that I could name,
But all good things mean just the same.

Come WPA, just as quick as you can,
And help us to live like a natural man.

Say, Roosevelt, so true and tried,
What's the U.S. doin', if you had died?

Is there never such a man on earth,
Who've revived this nation to its second birth?

The country one half wet, and the other half dry,
(All will be just) all will be one thing bye and bye.

Make your laws, and eat the best,
Unknot your boots, and take your rest.

Oh, we're goin' to do the best we can,
While we're in this God-sent land.

Go on, Roosevelt, you know your stuff,
If you come to the war, you ought not bluff.

Go on, you . . . , Roosevelt, you're in the fight,
You believe in treatin' your people right.

Please, Roosevelt, don't leave us now,
We'll obey the laws, and to God we'll bow.

spoken: *Now.*

No other version of this song is known. The reference to the attempt to assassinate Roosevelt in Miami on 15 February 1933 may be an indication of an earlier date of composition. "RFC" probably represents a confusion with "FDR" in the composer's mind. The reference to Eleanor Roosevelt is one of only two occurrences of her name in blues and gospel music, Otis Jackson's "Tell Me Why You Like Roosevelt" being the other. One stanza refers to the existence of dry counties and states that forbade the sale of alcohol even after Roosevelt's repeal of Prohibition. The song expresses anxiety about the outbreak of war at the early stage of March 1937. The fact that the black singer addresses the president as "Roosevelt," omitting the normally required prefix "Mr.," shows how intimate a friend and father figure FDR had become. "Roosevelt Blues" is a charming song (even mentioning the dogs!) which presents a clear survey of the reasons for the president's electoral victory in 1936.

GOT A JOB ON THE WPA

After the CWA closed on 31 March 1934, opposition to the president's public spending policy mounted, but Roosevelt remained adamant. FDR wanted to put an end to direct relief, but he needed the support of his Democratic Congress, which felt that there was no longer an emergency situation, and had to be convinced anew of the necessity of the New Deal measures. Harry Hopkins put the problem in a nutshell: "Give a man a dole, and you save his body and destroy his spirit. Give him a job and you save both job and spirit."[1]

Roosevelt finally managed to persuade Congress that new initiatives were urgently needed. After many weeks of debate the Emergency Relief Appropriation Act was signed on 27 April 1935, clearing the way for a new agency. Hopkins saw his chance and changed his Works Progress Division into the Works Progress Administration, abbreviated to WPA. (In 1939 the name of his agency was to be changed for a third time, to Work Projects Administration.) The WPA would become the biggest employment project in the history of the United States, with almost $10 billion spent under its aegis.[2]

Six months after its start on 6 May 1935, the WPA was providing jobs for 3 million people. The guidelines that Roosevelt laid down recommended that people "on relief rolls" should be employed on "useful" projects,[3] and so 2,500

W.P.A. BLUES and SOMEBODY
CHANGED THE LOCK ON THAT DOOR.
Vocal—Piano-Guitar-Bass Fiddle Acc.

"W.P.A. Blues" advertisement, 1936.

hospitals were built or improved and 5,900 schools, 1,000 airport landing fields
and almost 13,000 playgrounds were created.[4] Wages were not high; on an
average, men were paid five dollars a day, women only three dollars.[5] There
were two reasons for the low wages: money was scarce, and the WPA did
not compete with private enterprise.[6] In August 1936, however, the Workers'
Alliance of America demanded that "the wages of all WPA workers that are
now $40 a month or more be increased immediately by 20 per cent, and all
below $40 monthly be raised to that figure."[7]

The first blues artist to comment on the new agency was William "Casey
Bill" Weldon, a guitarist who was born in Pine Bluff, Arkansas, on 10 July 1909.[8]
From 1927 to 1938 he made sixty-seven rather sophisticated blues recordings,
with influences from Hawaiian and white country music, after which he drifted
into obscurity. His February 1936 "W.P.A. Blues" describes a poor man who
has rented a house that is part of a WPA slum clearance project and provides
insight into the complexities inherent in the new policies.

> Everybody's workin' in this town, and it's worried me night and day,
> It's that mean workin' crew, that works for the WPA.
> Well, well, the landlord come this morning, and he knocked on my door,
> He asked me if I was goin' to pay my rent no more.
>
> He said, "You have to move, if you can't pay,"
> And then he turned, and he walked slowly away,

So I have to try, find me some other place to stay,
That house wreckin' crew is coming, from that WPA.

Well, well, I went to the relief station, and I didn't have a cent,
They said, "Stay on where you're stayin', you don't have to pay no rent,"
So when I got back home, they was tackin' a notice on the door:
"This house is condemned, and you can't live here no more,"
So a notion struck me, I'd better be on my way,
They're gonna tear my house down, ooh, that crew from that WPA.

Well, well, I went out next morning, I put a lock on my door,
But though I wouldn't move, but I had no place to go,
The real estate people, they all done got so,
They don't rent to, no relief clients no more,
So I know, have to walk the streets night and day,
Because that wreckin' crew's coming, ooh, from that WPA.

Well, well, a notion struck me, I'd try to stay a day or two,
But I soon found out, that that wouldn't do,
Early next morning, while I was layin' in my bed,
I heard a mighty rumblin', and bricks come tumblin' down on my head,
So I had to start duckin' and dodgin', and be on my way,
They was tearin' my house down on me, ooh, that crew from that WPA.

Casey Bill is caught between the WPA and the welfare. The house is going to be knocked down, and the landlord will not continue to house him if he does not pay the rent that is owed; so he goes on welfare, which means that his rent will be paid for him, and the relief people advise him to stay put, but that is no help if the house is condemned anyway. He puts a new lock on to keep the landlord from putting his possessions in the street, and goes to look for a new place to live, but the real estate agents will only rent to the employed; so he goes back to his old house, which is knocked down around his ears in the interests of slum clearance. Thanks to the cross-purposes of the real estate agents and the WPA, he no longer has a home to rent with his relief money.

This topical song was a great success. In May of that year both "Big Boy" Teddy Edwards[9] and Big Bill Broonzy[10] recorded versions of it, with lyrics identical to Weldon's.

A November 1936 Chicago recording, entitled "That Man on the W.P.A.," involves a common subject in the blues songs about "the alphabetical agencies": the woman who is rejected as soon as the man has found a job. He used to be dependent on her, but now he is "smokin' his good-doin' reefers and talkin' all out his head." The girl who has got to go is Billie McKenzie, and to keep her man from "going down," Billie has "kicked mud all around this town," meaning that she worked on the streets as a prostitute.

> I'll tell you, girls, what my man done to me one day:
> He was so nice and kind, till he started for that WPA.
>
> Before then I gave him my money, even bought his shoes and clothes,
> Got a job on the WPA, and put poor me outdoors.
>
> Oh, be a friend to me, girls, please try and see it my way:
> If you want a good man, don't get one on that WPA.
>
> I've did everything I could, to keep that man from going down,
> I even pawned my clothes, and kicked mud all around this town.
>
> But I knew he was jivin', when he laid down across my bed,
> Smokin' his good-doin' reefers, and talkin' all out his head.

East St. Louis blues guitarist and piano player William Bunch (1902–1941), who voiced the concerns of his race from behind the mask of his semifictional persona, "Peetie Wheatstraw," recorded three songs about WPA projects in 1937 and 1938. All three songs were written by Charley Jordan, who was disabled by an old shooting injury, and would not have been on the WPA himself. The first of the three songs is called "Working on the Project" and dates from March 1937.

> I was working on the project, begging the relief for shoes,
> Because the rock and concrete, ooh, well, well, they's giving my feet the blues.
>
> Working on the project, with holes all in my clothes,
> Trying to make me a dime, ooh, well, well, to keep the rent man from putting me
>   outdoors.
>
> I am working on the project, trying to make both ends meet,
> But the payday is so long, ooh, well, well, until the grocery man won't let me eat.
>
> Working on the project, my gal's spending all my dough,
> Now I have waked up on her, ooh, well, well, and I won't be that weak no more.
>
> Working on the project, with payday three or four weeks away,
> Now, how can you make things meet, ooh, well, well, well, when you can't get no
>   pay?

Evidently payment on this project was monthly. Blacks were paid the same amount as whites under WPA rules, and this was a major breakthrough in black emancipation; women (of whatever color) were not so fortunate, however.

Four months later this song was recorded by blues singer Merline "The Yas Yas Girl" Johnson.[11] Her lyrics, again credited to "Jordan," are almost identical to those used by Peetie Wheatstraw, and they make one wonder if a woman could do such heavy work on the projects. But piano player Blind John Davis recalled that Merline's "old man had a coal business. That gal could take two bags of coal up to the third floor just as good as her old man."[12] Merline Johnson, however, would have earned eight dollars a month less than Peetie Wheatstraw for doing the same job.

A year and a half after his influential "W.P.A. Blues" Casey Bill Weldon recorded a follow-up tune for the same company (Vocalion). It was called "Casey Bill's New W.P.A." Evidently Bill has been living off the money his "baby" earned as a prostitute, and has spent his time gambling.

> Said, My baby told me this morning, just about the break of day,
> Said, "You oughta get up this morning, get you a job on that WPA."
>
> I says, "I'm a gambler, and I gambles night and day,"
> Says, "I don't need no job on that WPA."
>
> She said, "I'm leaving you, now, daddy, yeah, that's all I got to say,"
> She said, "I'm gonna get me a man, that's working on that WPA."
>
> And all the womens hollerin', and they're hollerin' night and day,
> "I'm gonna quit my pimp, get me a man on that WPA."
>
> So hard luck has overtaken me, had to throw my dice and cards away,
> Yeah, I've gotta try to get me a job, on that WPA.

In his 1937 "Project Highway," harmonica player John Lee "Sonny Boy" Williamson, who had come north from Tennessee around 1934, wants to buy a V-8 Ford to ride the new highway "that the project just completed a week ago":

> Well, well, well, I've got to get some money, I wants to buy a V-8 Ford,
> Well, well, I wants to ride this new highway, ooh, that the project just completed a
> week ago.
>
> Well, after I ride this new highway, Lord, now I'm gonna cross the Gulf of Mexico,
> Well, well, well, then I ain't goin' to stop ridin', well, until I park in front of my
> baby's door.

Well, when my baby come out and see me, I know she's gonna jump and shout,
Well, well, well, say that's gonna draw a crowd, ooh, people gonna wanna know
what's all of this racket's about.

Now, when peoples gather around, now, in the front of my baby's door,
Well, well, then I'm gonna tell them, "Don't get excited; Ooh, same Lacey Belle, I
was singing about before."

A total of $4.4 billion was spent on highways, roads and streets under the WPA, 38.9 percent of the total outlay, by far the highest percentage.[13] The result of all this work was six hundred thousand miles of roads, "enough to circle the world twenty-four times," according to WPA historian Donald S. Howard.[14]

Until 1937 most of the WPA songs had been rather optimistic, but when Peetie Wheatstraw made a follow-up recording in November 1937, simply called "New Working on the Project," the situation appears to have changed drastically. Wheatstraw is scared to receive a "304" dismissal form:

Working on the project, what a scared man, you know,
Because every time I look around, ooh, well, well, somebody's getting their 304.

Working on the project, with a big furniture bill to pay,
But time I got my 304, ooh, well, well, the furniture man come and taken my
furniture away.

Working on the project, the rent man is knocking on my door:
"I am sorry Mr. Rent Man, ooh, well, well, I just got my 304."

Working on the project, my partner got his 304 too,
So you better look out, ooh, well, well, because tomorrow it may be you.

Working on the project, a 304 may make you cry,
There's one thing sure, ooh, well, well, you can tell the project goodbye.

Charley Jordan completed his song cycle with the dismissal foreshadowed in the second song, and Wheatstraw duly recorded "304 Blues (Lost My Job on the Project)," in January 1938:

I was working on the project, three or four months ago,
Since I got my 304, ooh, well, well, my baby don't want me no more.

When I was working on the project, I had everything I need,
But since I got my 304, ooh, well, I can't even get any feed.

When I was working on the project, womens was no object to me,
But since I got my 304, ooh, well, well, not a one of them can I see.

When I was working on the project, I drinked my good whiskey, beer and wine,
But since I got my 304, ooh, well, these drinks is hard to find.

Goodbye, everybody, that is all I have to say,
But since I got my 304, ooh, well, well, my good woman, she have gone astray.

Why were WPA workers fired in 1937? On 3 November 1936 Roosevelt had been reelected with 24.8 million votes. His opponent, Republican Alfred Mossman Landon, governor of Kansas, gained only 16.7 million votes. Now that Roosevelt's second term was a certainty, he could try to "balance the budget," and by August 1937, 1.5 million people, half of all WPA employees, had been fired.[15]

The ensuing "new recession" was caused by Roosevelt's drastic spending cuts. The president became alarmed when he noticed parallels with the situation Hoover had been confronted with in the early thirties.[16]

The situation quickly worsened: on 25 March 1938, Wall Street faced another crisis, and unemployment figures rose dramatically. Harry Hopkins managed to convince the president of the necessity of further funds to fight the "second depression," and without much opposition Congress agreed to a $4,862,000,000 package. Of this enormous amount the WPA and three affiliated agencies[17] received $1,250,000,000.

In 1938 Big Bill Broonzy celebrated the revival of the WPA in his "WPA Rag." As Broonzy explained:

In 1934 [sic] I wrote a rag titled WPA Rag. The first verse was an old levee camp holler:

Oh I feel like hollering but the town is too small.

And the other part is: When we was gambling shooting dice we would get a point.[18] When we was rolling dice and when they stopped on six and the other on four, we called that ten for a point and we would roll the dice and say:

Oh six-four I call you.

The next verse is:

I want all you women and I mean all you stags,
To spend your money, while I play this WPA Rag.[19]

The stags means anytime a party was given and there was nothing there but men, they call it a stag-party, and where I would be playing the man who owns the place likes to hear me sing that verse because I tell everybody to spend their money and if they had no money to spend it was time for them to go home.

In that time just about all the men and women was on the WPA. That was the only work you could get at that time and it lasted a long time, too. Louis Armstrong recorded a song called WPA, Casey Bill and Peetie Wheatstraw recorded a WPA Blues. In that time anything you'd say about WPA was all right because that was all you had to live on.

WPA, PWA, CWA, all of these was work projects for men and women. Me and my manager was both on the WPA together. There was no recording at that time. It was easy for us to get a job on the WPA because we had been in the army in 1918 and they called us old veterans. All old veterans had no trouble getting on the WPA.[20]

Big Bill next explains how he was once working on the WPA, laying concrete on 47th Street in Chicago, when "one of the boys" told him that he had just heard Bill's "WPA Rag": Bill's record had just come out. Bill relates that he had recorded the song five months before he had got the job: "The WPA had been going on for about a year before I had got that job. Of course the WPA had been going on for about a year before I got broke enough to get in there."[21] Bill obviously had some trouble remembering the correct time sequence, as his song was recorded in September 1938.[22]

Big Bill's song is the first to mention the WPA shovel: "Jump off that shovel, boy," he jokes. "Leaning on the shovel" had become a proverbial phrase used to attack presumed WPA idleness. Postmaster General Jim Farley sent Roosevelt a clipping about a worker who had fallen while resting on his shovel and fractured a wrist, and jokingly suggested a "nonskid shovel handle."[23] As Big Bill recalled: "We had a boss that we called 'Big George' and when he would see one of the men standing, leaning on his shovel he would holler: 'Get up off that shovel, boy, if you're tired go to the office and check out, and come back tomorrow and try it again.' So we all started to tease each other about leaning on our shovel and I got to like working on the WPA."[24]

In 1940 New Orleans jazz trumpeter Louis "Satchmo/Pops" Armstrong (1900–1971) recorded his "W.P.A." with the Mills Brothers. The song was composed by Jesse Stone.

> Now, wake up, boys, get out on the rock,
> It ain't daybreak, but it's four o'clock.

A WPA crew repairs a flood-damaged street in Louisville, Kentucky. Reproduced from the collections of the Library of Congress.

Oh, no, no, no, Pops, you know that ain't the play!
What you talking about? It's the WPA.

Oh, oh, the WPA (now, I said that!)
The WPA,
Sleep while you work, while you rest, while you play,
Lean on your shovel, to pass the time away.
'Tain't what you do, you can jive for your pay.
Where is that?
The WPA, the WPA, the WPA.
Now, don't be a fool, workin' hard is passé,
You'll stand from five to six hours a day.
Sit down and joke,
While you smoke.
It's O.K.,
The WPA.

chorus: *I'm so tired, I don't know what to do,*
Can't get fired, so I take my rest, until my work is through.
The WPA, the WPA.
Don't mind the boss, if he's cross when you're gay,

He'll get a pink slip next month anyway.
Three little letters that make life O.K.:
WPA!

Two other 1938 blues songs that refer to the WPA shovel are "This Old World's in a Tangle" and "Welfare Blues" by Arkansas-born guitarist Calvin Frazier (1915–1972).[25] In the late thirties Frazier moved to Detroit, where he recorded for the Library of Congress. The recordings themselves were part of a WPA project, the Federal Music Project, which "made a special effort to preserve, record, and publish Negro folk music."[26] Frazier's songs both contain lines comparing WPA men to the Devil for "they don't do nothing but sleep and lay on the shovel." According to the lyrics of these songs, Frazier had not been able to find employment on the WPA himself. The image of those who had been lucky, but were now idly leaning on their shovels, made him so angry that he compared them to the Devil.

Historian Donald S. Howard devoted a special paragraph to the phenomenon in his 1943 *The WPA and Federal Relief Policy*:

WPA: "Shovel-Leaners." On the one hand there have been claims that WPA workers, for the most part, are "shovel-leaners" and "bums." Whatever the facts about the efficiency of WPA workers may be, it is undeniable that in the public mind these workers have frequently been regarded as substandard and as bearing what Colonel Somervell once termed "the WPA look." Among evidences of public opinion on this subject have been an allegedly "popular" song ridiculing the industry of WPA workers, the wave of "WPA stories" and cartoons.[27]

In a footnote the song is identified as the Louis Armstrong tune by means of two quotations. The note further adds that the song was banned by the American Federation of Musicians and the major radio networks. According to *Time*, a talent scout for Columbia thought the song "insulting to workers, degrading to Negroes."[28] The banned Louis Armstrong song also contains yet another reference to the pink slip, no. 304.[29] In practice, this was not the likely outcome: Armstrong is pandering to the image of the feckless Negro, who does not heed the consequences of the "shirking" with which he is stereotyped.

Code "304" had become such an obsession to African Americans that there is even a "Pink Slip Blues." It was written by composer Porter Grainger and recorded by blues singer Ida Cox (1896–1967) in October 1939:

One day every week, I propped myself at my front door,
And the police force couldn't move me, 'fore that mailman blowed.

'Twas a little white paper, Uncle Sam had done addressed to me,
It meant one more week, one week of sweet prosperity.

But bad news got to spreading, and my poor hair started turning gray,
'Cause Uncle Sam started chopping, cutting thousands off the WPA.

Just a little pink slip, in a long white envelope,
'Twas the end of my road, 't was the last ray of my only hope.

After four long years, Uncle Sam done put me on the shelf,
'Cause that little pink slip, means you got to go for yourself.

The image of the poor black woman propped up at her front door waiting for "the little white paper" brings the problem home. "The welfare check becomes the controlling force," Daphne Duval Harrison explains in *Black Pearls*.[30]

"Uncle Sam started chopping, cutting thousands off the WPA," Ida Cox sang on 31 October 1939. Was FDR trying "to balance the budget" again? In July and August of that year 775,000 WPA employees had indeed received the dreaded "pink slip." The conservative coalition in Congress had decided to slash "$150 million from the President's proposed relief appropriation."[31] The New Deal was already dying a slow death.

In June 1940 New Orleans blues pianist and ex-boxer "Champion" Jack Dupree (1910–1992), who later became an expatriate in Europe, lamented the closing down of the relief stations in his "Warehouse Man Blues," although he complained about the way his grandmother was treated by the "white folks" at the relief warehouse:

I want you people to know, that the relief is closing down,
If you ain't got no money, you better try to leave the town.

I've got a friend in New Orleans, working on the WPA,
He done lost all his money, he ain't got no place to stay.

My grandma left this morning, with a basket in her hand,
She's goin' down to the warehouse, to see the warehouse man,
She got down to the warehouse, them white folks say: "It ain't no use,"
For the governor ain't givin' away nothing, but that canned grapefruit juice.

It's a low, lowdown, dirty shame,
It's a lowdown, dirty shame, the way these projects doing.

Now, Uncle Sam paid you men that bonus, you know that was mighty fine,
You tried to fill them street-walking women, up with that moonlight wine,
You spent all your money, you done spent it mighty fast,
Now, this winter breeze 'bout to jam you, with a raggedy yeah-yeah.

Well, I know the relief is closing down,
It is a lowdown, dirty shame, the way the relief do.

The veterans' bonus money has been spent, the relief is closing down and winter is approaching. Champion Jack objects to his grandmother's being given grapefruit juice (good for vitamin C deficiency) rather than food. He seems to feel that the reduction in handouts involves discrimination. The government did its utmost to prevent discrimination, but many conservative local relief administrators continued to slight blacks. When a black man in Baton Rouge complained to a relief official that "the President promised all a fair deal," the response was clear: "He told me Dam [sic] the President and said he did not care any dam more for the President than he did for a dam nigger, and not as much. And said he was running the office down here and not the dam President or no one else."[32]

In April 1934 *The New York Age*'s main headline read "Urge Home Relief Investigation." "For months the Home Relief Bureau at 124th and Lenox Avenue, which is largely used by Negro and Latin-Americans, has been a hotbed of prejudice," the report explained. It noted various examples of discriminatory behavior: "Miss Bryan, a clerk, is alleged to have referred to Camille White, who came in seeking relief, as a 'black ape'. She is also alleged to have remarked, 'Why should I have to sit next to those stinking niggers?' "[33]

Plans to end relief bias were offered the WPA at a New York hearing in November 1935. A suggestion to set up an impartial tribunal to hear all cases alleged to involve discrimination was endorsed by Roy Wilkins of the NAACP. Wilkins pointed out that "all the burden of proof in cases of discrimination is upon the worker—an unhealthy situation because workers often cannot afford to take the chance of losing their jobs by protesting these cases." Another suggestion offered was "that more real authority be given Negro appointees in order that they might function in other than a purely advisory fashion."[34]

In a December 1935 *Pittsburgh Courier*, WPA's deputy director Aubrey Williams "admitted the Negroes had been 'the worst victims of the Depression.'

Constituting one-tenth of the population, the race made up one-sixth of the relief rolls. Chief trouble in relief disbursements came from 'local traditions' invoked in many sections of the country."[35]

Whereas blues songs had not complained about the CWA, the WPA was the subject of some rather outspoken criticism. Another striking example of dissatisfaction with the WPA is the December 1938 "CCC Blues" by Washboard Sam. Sam had his own brand of humor:

chorus: *I'm goin' down, I'm goin' down, to the CCC,*
          I know that the WPA, won't do a thing for me.

          I told her my name, and the place I stay,
          She said she'd give me a piece of paper, come back, some other day.

          I told her I had no people, and the shape I was in,
          She said she would help me, but she didn't say when.

          I told her I needed a job, and no relief,
          On my rent day, she sent me a can of beef.

          She said she'd give me a job, everything was nice and warm,
          Takin' care of the dead, in a funeral home.

Sam's tune is the only blues song to mention the Civilian Conservation Corps. On the advice of the "brain trust," his highly intelligent team of young advisers, Roosevelt had started to set up the CCC camps on 31 March 1933.[36] About 2.5 million young men thus found useful work in national forests and parks. They all wore green uniforms, lived in army camps, received a monthly payment and were offered an opportunity to learn how to read and write.

New Orleans blues pianist Roy "Professor Longhair" Byrd (1918–1980) explained what was expected of him when he was in a Shreveport, Louisiana, CCC camp in 1937: "We did everything; plantin' trees, diggin' spillways, gradin', slopin', buildin' banks. We was cuttin' soil, we was layin' soil, openin' up spillways, gradin' roads, puttin' gravel down. We cut trees if necessary, cleanin' off land."[37] In the camp Byrd was drilled like a soldier, but was allowed to play the piano in the recreation hall to entertain the "soldiers." He received fifty dollars a month, out of which the laundry bill had to be paid.

The surprising end to the song by Washboard Sam might indicate that the Civilian Conservation Corps also took care of the conservation of civilian corpses, but close reading of the lyrics shows that in spite of the song's title, the blues in the song was not the result of the CCC, but the WPA. Sam apparently shares Harry Hopkins's view that a job is better than a handout, and is so dissatisfied with his treatment by the WPA officials that he intends to join the CCC instead.

The slashing of funds had caused the number of WPA workers to drop to a record low by 1941, when Josh White sang his "Bad Housing Blues." Although his house is leaking, Josh cannot get a WPA job, and has no way out but to visit the president. As a frequent visiting artist at the White House Josh was probably the only blues artist to come into any sort of regular contact with FDR, but here he is speaking for black people in general, and his threat to visit "the White House lawn" may be a call for demonstrations:

> I woke up this morning, rainwater in my bed,
> You know my roof was leakin', Lord, leakin' on my head.
>
> Now, it ain't no reason, I should live this way,
> I done lost my job, can't even get on the WPA.
>
> Lord, I wonder, when I'll hear good news,
> Right now I'm gonna tell you, I've got them bad housing blues.
>
> I'm going to the capital, going to the White House lawn,
> Better wipe out these slums, been this way since I was born.

Three 78s of this 1941 Josh White session were issued in an album called "Southern Exposure: An Album of Jim Crow Blues." In the liner notes black author Richard Wright, who worked for the Federal Writers Project, writes that White's songs present "the 'other side' of the blues . . . noncommercial because of its social militancy . . . Where the Negro cannot go, his blue songs have gone, affirming kinship in a nation teeming with indifferences, creating unity and solidarity where distance once reigned."[38]

All the songs in the 1941 album were written by "Cuney-White." Waring Cuney was a black poet of the Harlem Renaissance whose lyrics are rather artificial, and lack real blues feeling. The words were inspired, as Richard Wright noted, by left-wing ideals of unity and solidarity; this political content, however, was imported into the music, rather than constituting "the 'other side' of the blues."

Richard Wright was a member of the Communist Party, and, as British blues writer Bruce Bastin explains, in 1950 Josh White himself was to appear before a subcommittee of the House Un-American Activities Committee on the

Work Projects enrollees filling in a gully on eroded farmland, Yanceyville, North Carolina, 5 May 1940. Photo by Wilfred J. Mead, reproduced from the collections of the Library of Congress.

grounds of his alleged Communist affiliation.[39] The former White House guest, who had even played at the president's 1945 inaugural ball and who remained close friends with Eleanor Roosevelt after the president's death,[40] had evidently created quite a stir with his social protest songs in the paranoid Cold War atmosphere of the postwar years.

The WPA had served its term and was given, as Ted Morgan puts it, "an honorable discharge" on 30 June 1943.[41] It had provided work for almost 9 million people and established a shift from relief distribution to useful work. Following the attack on Pearl Harbor, the United States declared war on Japan. The war industry achieved what the agencies had not been able to accomplish: full employment.

SYLVESTER AND HIS MULE BLUES

As soon as the new president had taken office he ordered his staff to pay special attention to people in distress who phoned the White House. In his *F.D.R.: An Intimate History*, Roosevelt biographer Nathan Miller explains Roosevelt's instructions: "Roosevelt said that if someone was desperate enough to call the President, then a way ought to be found, if at all possible, to help him. Many such calls were received—from farmers threatened with imminent foreclosure of their land and householders about to lose their homes—and some were taken by Mrs. Roosevelt herself. Usually a way would be found to cut red tape at some federal agency and get some help for them."[1]

Not many people would actually have got through to the president himself, but on 10 January 1935 blues guitarist Lizzie "Memphis Minnie" Douglas (1897–1973) recorded a song about such an event, entitled "Sylvester and His Mule Blues."

> Sylvester went out in his lot, he looked at his mule,
> And he decided, he'd send the president some news.
>
> Sylvester walked out across his field, begin to pray and moan,
> He cried, "Oh, Lord, believe I'm gonna lose my home."

spoken: *Play it, Jimmie!*

He thought about the president, he got on the wire,
"If I lose my home, I believe I'll die."

He called the president, on the telephone,
"I wanna talk to you, I'm 'bout to lose my home."

First time he called, they get him somebody else,
"I don't wanna talk to that man, I want to speak to Mr. President Roosevelt."

He said, "Now Sylvester, you can rest in ease,
Catch that big, black jackass, and go on by your fields,"
He said, "Sylvester you can rest in ease,
You can catch that jackass, go and raise all your cotton and seeds."

Blues historians have tried to find a factual source for this story about the poor farmer who is afraid to lose his lot and his mule.[2] We have to listen to an August 1934 sermon by Rev. J. M. Gates called "President Roosevelt is Everybody's Friend" for more details:

I wanna talk about our President Roosevelt,
And when I said that, I'm speakin' free.
I'm a man who is now a half a century of age.
And never have I witnessed,
Never have I read, in history,
Of a man greater than our President Roosevelt.
When I say that, I mean he's a friend to everybody,
Both white and black, both brown, everybody.
Don't make any difference about your religious creed,
He is a man that believes in "equal rights for all,
And special privilege to none."
I wish the president of this earth.

I will speak now of, uh, President George Washington,
I believe his spirit could turn over in his grave,
And say, "Well done, wield your gavel, President Roosevelt,
Ah, for you is a man for the people, and by the people,
And the people believe in you."
And I'm tellin' you: He's a man that can't be touched.

Look at Mississippi, yonder on the river,
A Negro with his mule,

And when they had pressed him sore, he lost his mule.
He did not feel worried, but called up President Roosevelt,
Talked with him himself . . . Help me! Help me!
His name was, help me, somebody tell me!
His, his name was Sylvester Harris.
That's right: Sylvester Harris, a Negro down yonder in Mississippi.
I don't mean he talked around Washington,
Called him up and told him that "They've taken my mule and my farm,"
And says, "I want you to do something about it."
The president himself, not a subject, said to him:
"I'll send somebody down in a few days."
Somebody was down there. Sylvester had his mule.
And his farm.

He's our president!
I used to say "the president," "a president,"
But when I say "Our president,"
I'm talkin' 'bout a man that has been touchin' everybody.
CWA, look at it if you please,
Throughout the length and breadth of the United States.
Have they given you a job, brother? Haven't you had a job?
Didn't they make it possible for you?
Have you worked five days in the week, brother?
Have you been in the office, daughter?
It was through the CWA, and it was our own president.

Gates identifies "Sylvester" as Sylvester Harris, a Negro from Mississippi, who was afraid of losing his farm and mule and rang the president. He did get the president on the line, and Roosevelt promised to "send somebody down in a few days." This was no empty promise, for indeed Sylvester "had his mule and his farm." According to The New York Age Sylvester Harris's telephone call to the White House took place on 19 February 1934.

Lizzie McDuffie, FDR's black maid, remembered the phone call: "Mae had rolled him into his study one evening when the telephone began to ring. Usually Miss Marguerite (Missy) LeHand was there to take care of the calls and, of course, it was only the most important ones that were put on the President's line. Since Mr. Roosevelt was a little early, Miss LeHand had not arrived, and he picked up the phone himself."[3]

A 1936 article in *The Crisis*, the NAACP magazine, entitled "Roosevelt, the Humanitarian," said that the headquarters of the Democratic National Committee used Sylvester Harris as election propaganda:

> The 'phone in the White House rang. One of President Roosevelt's secretaries picked up the receiver and answered, "Hello!" A far away voice came over the wire: "Dis is Sylvester, an' I wanna speak to the President." Mr. Roosevelt, who overheard the distressed voice, took the receiver and said, "This is the President." "Mr. Roosevelt, I is Sylvester and these white folks down here is gwine take my farm. I hear you wouldn't let them do it if I asked you." After ascertaining where Sylvester was, the President assured him that he would not let the white folks foreclose on his farm. The President immediately directed his secretary to command the Home Owners Loan Corporation (HOLC) in Mississippi, where farmer Sylvester lived, to save his property. It was done.[4]

It is surprising how much Sylvester Harris's speech was patronized, even in a progressive black magazine. The Home Owners Loan Corporation (HOLC) was established in 1933. In its first three years the corporation spent more than $3 billion refinancing more than 1 million homes.[5] In Sylvester's case the HOLC apparently took care of the financing of his farm.

Nineteen days after Sylvester's call for help *The New York Age* printed what must be the most accurate account of the event:

> Columbus, Miss.—Sylvester Harris, who operates one of the most successful small farms in this section, made a personal appear [sic] to President Roosevelt by telephone last week, and his plea saved his property from being sold in a foreclosure action. After several unsuccessful attempts to contact the President at the White House, the colored farmer finally got Mr. Roosevelt on the phone and said: "I'm Sylvester Harris, down in Mississippi. A man is getting ready to take my land and I want to know what to do. The papers say to call you, and here I am." The President is reported as having replied, "Sylvester, I'll investigate and you'll hear from me." This telephone conversation occurred on February 19. Since then George Hamilton, local representative of the New Orleans Federal Land Bank, received a telegram from Washington requesting investigation of the mortgage on Harris' farm, and an adjustment was worked out through extension.[6]

From this report we learn that Sylvester Harris operated "one of the most successful farms" in Columbus, Mississippi. As he had mortgage debts his property was about to be sold. He called the president after reading in the

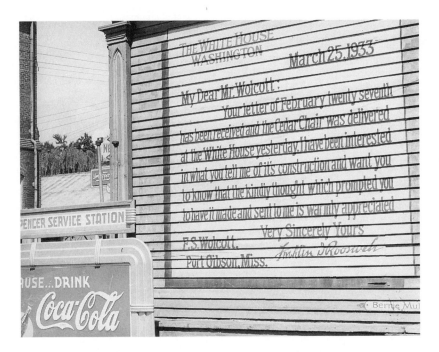

Facsimile of a letter written by President Roosevelt to a resident in Port Gibson, Mississippi, F. S. Wolcott, painted on the side of a building. Wolcott was the owner of the Rabbit Foot Minstrels, a touring minstrel show with an all-black cast. Photo by Marion Post Wolcott, reproduced from the collections of the Library of Congress.

newspapers that it was possible to do so. Roosevelt requested that the mortgage be extended, which no doubt amounted to a command for a bank representative fearful of bad publicity for his employers. In October 1934 Milo Reno, of the Farmers' Holiday Association, was to call for an agricultural strike. One of the four principal demands was "a National moratorium on farm mortgage foreclosures." Sylvester's plight was a national problem.[7] Depression economist Raymond Wolters explained the problems black farm owners encountered with their mortgages: "Thus in many cases the Negro farmer who wanted to save his farm had to go to the very men who held the mortgage, and under these circumstances it is not surprising that the Negro applicant occasionally received less than fair treatment. Rayford Logan reported in 1937 that 'not a single Negro farmer in Arkansas was able to obtain a loan through the Farm Credit Administration,' and he objected to what he called 'the prejudiced machinations of white appraisers . . . who purposely refused to place a large enough appraisal on the land.' He cited several examples of Negro farmers who lost 'splendid farms' because the white appraisers themselves held the mortgages and wanted to foreclose."[8]

The Sylvester Harris story has a sequel not mentioned in the two recordings. Nine months later, Thursday, 29 November 1934, Roosevelt celebrated Thanksgiving in the Little White House in Warm Springs, Georgia. To hear what happened that day we return to White House maid Lizzie McDuffie: "One Thanksgiving a pretty big gift arrived at Warm Springs: a huge turkey, delivered at the Little White House, 'compliments of Sylvester Harris.' Mae and I took the crate for him to see the turkey. We gave him the card and waited to remind him who 'Sylvester Harris' was. But the minute he read the name his face broke in a smile. 'Why! It's from Sylvester Harris! I wonder how his farm is these days?' . . . Come Thanksgiving, Sylvester Harris remembered . . . and so did FDR."[9]

In her study of black politics in the age of FDR Nancy J. Weiss concludes that "[t]he uniqueness of Roosevelt's personal intervention in the Harris case was really beside the point. What mattered was the habit of the White House to solve the problems of ordinary people."[10]

As late as March 1957, twenty-three years after Sylvester's telephone call to the White House, *Ebony* magazine devoted an article to him:

> At the height of his fame, Sylvester Harris was lionized and feted. He got stacks of fan mail. "I got letters," he recalls, "from everywhere. I guess I couldn't get them all in my pickup truck. Letters came by the sackful. They asked for dirt, seed and everything."
>
> The strong-willed farmer discovered, however, that fame is a fleeting thing. When the depression ended Sylvester was shunted to the past, along with old NRA stickers. But Sylvester did not forget. Each year, until the day FDR died, he sent a fat turkey to the Little White House on Thanksgiving Day. And he has vowed to keep the farm as long as he lives. "I'll never let it go," he says, "because President Roosevelt wanted me to have it."[11]

In 1948 Harris sold 100 of his 140 acres to follow his children north. In East St. Louis he worked for the railroad. In 1954 he returned to Columbus, Mississippi, with a pension of $120 a month. He found his farm run-down, but, as he said, "A good farmer can live like a king and never be hungry." He sought specialist advice and began to grow diversified crops (corn, soybeans, peas, hay and cotton). The article features six photos. From the captions we learn that Sylvester's wife died in 1935, that he remarried and had five children, that he saved the sacks of fan mail, that he was a member of the local Mount Pleasant Baptist Church, that he was offered one hundred dollars an acre for his land, that he spent his time fishing and hunting in winter and that he relied on his "visions" in making major decisions.

The ordinary people knew that Roosevelt was there for them. "Gonna call up headquarters, I'm gonna write to Roosevelt," Nelson Wilborn (b. 1907), better known under the soubriquet of "Red Nelson" for his light complexion, sang in October 1937. Mississippi-born "Dirty Red," as he was called on a later recording, was really "signifying" when he sang the second part of his "Relief Blues":

> Nineteen and twenty-eight, brought me to the county door,
> I prayed to the good Lord, never go back there no more.

> If you ain't on the charity, you act just like you need to be,
> You's runnin' 'round and spendin' your last quarter, next morning you don't have a
> > thing to eat.

> Get my groceries from the charity, fixin' to give me my doggone coal,
> Where I get my lovin' early in the morning, nobody knows but the Lord above.

> Gonna call up headquarters, I'm gonna write to Roosevelt,
> Tell him, "My woman done got evil, please don't send me nothing else."

> Say, you's a nasty, stinkin' devil, filthy as you can be,
> Signifying little broad, don't mean a thing to me.
> Tell the truth this morning, please don't run 'round lyin' to me,
> I wouldn't have been like I am, mama, hadn't done put that thing on me.

> It's a nickel worth of beefsteak, dime's worth of lard,
> Salivate your kidney, tryin' to locate your heart.
> You's no good, little girl, don't mean one man no good.
> Don't do nothing but get a free drunk and raise hell in my neighborhood.

Life on a depression farm was tough, even without the threat of fore-closure. Yet, surprisingly few black agricultural protest songs survive. Lemuel Jones, presumably working on the state farm in Richmond, Virginia, under prison conditions, recorded his "Po' Farmer" for the Library of Congress in 1936:

Work all the week and don't make enough,
Pay my board and buy my snuff.

chorus: *It's hard, it's hard, it's hard on we poor farmers, it's hard.*

Every night when I get home,
Peas in the pot and a old jaw bone.

spoken: *Whoa gee!*

Work all the week and don't make enough,
Pay my board and buy my snuff.

spoken: *Get up here, Jim!*

Work all the week to sun to sun,
Fifteen cents when Saturday come.

Every night when I get home,
Peas in the pot and a old jaw bone.

Every morning when I wake up,
Got to feed my horse and all hay cut.

Many farmers were tired of "workin' on the starvation farm," as Bob Campbell put it on his 1934 recording,[12] and moved to the big city in search of less frustrating and more rewarding work. Those who remained behind were dependent on agricultural economics. The 1937 recording "Government Money" by Tennessee blues guitarist Sleepy John Estes (1899–1977) sounds a hopeful chord, however.

Now, all the farmers, they oughta join the governor loan,
Now, the government gives you three years' chances, then you could have something
of your own.

Now, the government'll furnish you a milk cow, a rooster and some portion of hen,
You know, 'long through the spring, then you could have some money to spend.

Now, the women used to count on the bonus, but they are hollerin' on the rental
check now,
You know I didn't go to the army, but I'm usin' this government money anyhow.

Now, the governor, he's forced for to plant a-plenty corn and wheat,
You know, 'long through the winter, you can have something to eat.

A sharecropper at Lake Dick, a Resettlement Administration project near Jefferson, Arkansas, June 1938. Photo by Dorothea Lange, reproduced from the collections of the Library of Congress.

Sleepy John Estes, who had been blind in one eye since he was six, had not been in the army and had thus not been eligible for a bonus. Now the loan from the Farm Credit Administration is most welcome indeed, with its promise of an escape from sharecropping dependency. At last he can spend some real money. The final verse may refer to government policy to discourage cotton farming exclusively.

"Poor John," as Estes called himself in some of his poignant blues, remained confident in New Deal farm policies, and Sylvester Harris had secured his mortgage extension by a direct appeal to FDR. Nevertheless, the number of black tenants was cut by a third, and the number of black sharecroppers by almost a quarter, in the decade from 1930 to 1940.[13]

DON'T TAKE AWAY MY PWA

No one in the Roosevelt administration supported the black cause more fervently than Harold L. Ickes, secretary of the interior. In 1933 Congress had given the green light for a $3.3 billion Public Works Administration (PWA). To help the needy through the 1933–34 winter the CWA was organized. It was continued in an altered form as the WPA in May 1935. Direct relief or immediate employment could not be expected from the PWA.

Roosevelt needed an incorruptible realist to manage a fund as large as that. He chose Ickes, a fifty-nine-year-old progressive who had been president of the Chicago branch of the NAACP for a time. It was Ickes's task thoroughly to prepare a massive program in which "useful public works" would provide employment for as many people as possible. "No discrimination and no waste of money," Ickes was told. FDR could not have chosen a better candidate for the enormous task. While Harry Hopkins spent $5 million of CWA money in his first two hours in office,[1] Ickes spent only $110 million of PWA money in his first six months.[2] Many people complained of Ickes's lack of speed, but the president stood by him in his careful preparation.

In August 1934, Mississippi-born blues guitarist Charlie McCoy (1909–1950) sang in his "Charity Blues" that he would love to have a PWA job, which would bring him money instead of the "beef and meat" relief from "Mr. Charity Man" in "Charity Street":

> I said, charity, charity, is my only friend,
> When I lost my job, the charity took me in.
>
> I said, you ain't got no money, and ain't got no place to stay,
> You'd better try to get you a job, on the PWA.
>
> I said, I'm goin' tomorrow, out on Charity Street,
> And ask Mr. Charity Man, "Can I have some beef and meat?"
>
> The rentman keep askin', "When is you goin' to pay?"
> I said, "Just as soon as I get my money, from the PWA."
>
> I said, the charity give me my groceries, even buy my shoes and clothes,
> I said, but who give me my lovin', I swear nobody knows.

So many thousands of roads, dams, post offices, schools, courthouses, city halls, sewage plants, hospitals, public health facilities, stations, tunnels, ports and libraries were built by Ickes that William Leuchtenburg called him "a builder to rival Cheops."[3] Although Ickes was not satisfied with the progress made by the housing division of the PWA, for the black population the forty-nine housing projects were a godsend. Fourteen of these were meant for African Americans only and seventeen for both blacks and whites.[4] An essential part of Ickes's PWA administration was the development of a quota plan, which meant that a fixed percentage of PWA laborers had to be black. To them PWA stood for "Poppa's Working Again!"[5] Although in general the quota was easily filled, it was quite difficult to find "competent Negro craftsmen"; as Gunnar Myrdal explained, "We have to remember that Negro craftsmen had been rather systematically kept out of the larger construction projects where they could have learned newer techniques."[6]

The Negroes had not forgotten the PWA when they voted for Roosevelt in the 1936 elections. In Harlem 81 percent of the black electorate voted Democratic compared with 51 percent in 1932, in Chicago 49 percent compared with 21 percent in 1932.[7] In September 1936 twenty thousand persons had filled Madison Square Garden in New York to rally for reelection of their president: "Elder Michaux, Happy Am I radio preacher brought up 300 followers from Washington on a special train carrying a 20x24 canvas painting of Christ, Lincoln and Roosevelt entitled 'The Three Emancipators.' Christ was termed the

Election banners for the 1936 (Vice) Presidential election, Hardwick, Vermont. Photo by Carl Mydans, reproduced from the collections of the Library of Congress.

emancipator from sin; Lincoln emancipator from bondage and Roosevelt, the emancipator from social injustices."[8]

One Chicago inhabitant who probably voted for Roosevelt was the obscure blues singer Jimmie Gordon. Gordon's 2 October 1936 recording "Don't Take Away My P.W.A." was recorded a full month before election day, 3 November 1936, evidently for release after the election.

> Lord, Mr. President, listen to what I'm going to say:
> You can take away all of the alphabet, but please leave that PWA.
>
> Now you are in Mr. President, and I hope you's in to stay,
> But whatever changes that you make, please keep that PWA.
>
> I don't need no woman, and no place to stay,
> Because I'm makin' a honest livin', now on that PWA.
>
> PWA, you're the best old friend I ever seen,
> Since the job ain't hard, and the boss ain't mean.
>
> I went to the poll and I voted, I know I voted the right way,
> Now I'm praying to you Mr. President, please keep that PWA.

Cartoon by Jay Jackson, in the *Chicago Defender*, 1935.

Little could Gordon suspect that FDR was waiting until the elections were over to take a budgetary axe to the PWA. No cuts had yet been made in February 1937, when Texas pianist Dave Alexander, better known by the pseudonym "Black Ivory King," recorded "Working for the PWA."[9] Black Ivory King was still earning $9.50 a week from the PWA, but in the White House the president was sharpening his axe. Black Ivory King's song is yet another derivative of the "Red Cross Store Blues" analyzed in chapter 4. This version is based on Walter Roland's "C.W.A. Blues" from April 1934, which was discussed in chapter 5.

In August 1937, led by fear of inflation, Roosevelt virtually stopped PWA operations.[10] As we have seen in the WPA chapter, the president changed his mind by the end of March 1938. The PWA was restarted in June by a Congress that understood that the president wanted to spend in an election year.[11]

There are no PWA blues songs to mourn the temporary halt (August 1937 to June 1938), but PWA workers never knew when the axe would fall again. Fear of a "403," the dismissal note (apparently changed from a 304—or perhaps intended to keep up the PWA/WPA anagramming), is the subject of "Four-O-Three Blues," a November 1939 Lonnie Johnson recording about the PWA:

Relief is all right for some people, PWA's work is all right for me,
'Cause I got a big leg mama, so mellow as mellow can be.
Relief is all right for some people, but money is the thing for me.

Man, the work ain't hard, half of the time you're somewhere asleep,
Wintertime is comin', you better hold on to your job like me,
You can jive me all you wanna, but you can't jive that number 403.

Man, the boss is watchin' you, your head is hard as hard can be,
You better stop your loafin', and shovel some dirt with me,
Boy, you better watch out, 'cause you're heading for that number 403.

I think I better tell you 'bout that number, 'cause you don't seem to understand,
It's an unlucky number, when that boss place it in your hand,
It means you ain't got no more job, and your woman soon will have another man.

I got a big leg mama, she's so fine and mellow to me,
She's got legs just like millpostses, I can't let my baby get away from me,
So, you can do whatever you please, but that man will never hand me that number
403.

By 1939 the PWA was beginning to die a slow death. Harold Ickes urged the president to cut PWA's expenditures in the interests of overall budget balancing.[12] On 1 July 1939 the PWA ceased to be an independent agency. Together with the WPA, the housing division and some other agencies, the PWA now formed a part of the Federal Works Agency.[13]

In June 1941 the PWA was terminated altogether. All in all it had spent $6 billion, and, thanks to the scrupulous management of its director, Harold Ickes, the agency had been quite successful. Discrimination was fought where possible; blues lyrics reveal no complaints about such a problem in the PWA. The agency provided money instead of relief. With the money they earned, the blues singers claimed they could support their women. No wonder that the PWA was a popular agency.[14]

THE SALES TAX IS ON IT

In the twenties, many employers and politicians thought taxes should be paid by the working class and not by the "productive" class of the large employers.[1] To achieve a shift from taxation paid by the rich to taxation of the less well-off many Democrats favored a repeal of Prohibition and a taxation of beer, the working man's drink. The Republicans, with Andrew Mellon as their spokesman, advocated a national sales tax.[2]

In sharp contrast to the opinion of many of his fellow Republicans President Hoover thought the rich should bear the burden of taxation: "It should be seen as their social duty."[3] Hoover later attacked the New Dealers who "further increased and rearranged the taxes supposedly to take the burden from the poor and place it upon the rich." This did not happen: Hoover showed in what he called an "illuminating" table that the lower-income groups paid most of the taxation levied by Roosevelt in his first term.[4]

As Gunnar Myrdal explains in *An American Dilemma*, many white people felt that "a general tax compels white men of the State to educate the children of the Negro" and that most white people in the South are "inclined to stress that Negroes pay practically no taxes." Myrdal argues that poor people are "exempt only in the sense that they have no direct contact with the tax collector."[5]

An "indirect" taxation like a sales tax is a "regressive" tax measure, since it is proportionally higher for the poorer people.[6]

The Republicans were joined by conservative Democrats who wanted to balance the budget by means of a sales tax. In 1932 Congressman Fiorello La Guardia successfully organized opposition against the plan. Although food and cheaper clothing would not be taxed, La Guardia condemned the plans as "grinding the face of the poor" and "taking milk from babies and bread from mothers."

Four years later, however, when he was mayor of New York, La Guardia enacted a local sales tax on some food and all clothing. When he was chided on his inconsistency by former President Hoover during a dinner conversation, La Guardia responded: "You're no politician."[7] The result of the 1932 campaign was that, instead of the proposed sales tax, a revenue act was passed, which raised surtaxes to the high World War I level.[8]

During Roosevelt's first hundred days in office Democratic proposals for a 2.5 percent sales tax were blocked by Roosevelt's personal opposition to a federal sales tax.[9] The 1934 Revenue Act repealed some excises on luxury and consumption items, but those on gasoline, cigarettes, and first-class postage were either retained at the same rate or increased.[10] In 1935 Roosevelt proposed tax measures in line with the so-called "soak the rich" tax scheme, which was applauded by people like Huey Long and Upton Sinclair. However, the plan met with such staunch opposition from the rich that the actual results of FDR's programs were often sharply regressive.[11]

In March 1934 the Mississippi Sheiks—guitarists Walter Vinson and Bo Chatmon and violinist Lonnie Chatmon—recorded an amusing song called "Sales Tax," which was preceded by a sketch in which "the boys" (who were then thirty-three, forty-one and forty-five respectively) enter a store where they are waited on by a white shopkeeper (played by A&R man Dan Hornsby).

spoken: *Say, Walter, we need some cigarettes. Let's go in here and get a pack! O.K.!*
    Hello, boys, what can I do for you?
  I'll have a package of cigarettes.
    All right. Here you are. Be three cents more though!
  What's that for?
    Sales tax. Haven't you ever heard of sales tax?
  Sure haven't!

spoken: *What's gonna happen next, man? You know they got a law here they call the sales tax.*

     Sales tax? What is that for?

That's three cents tax on everything that's sold. They say that's the government's rule.

     The government's rule? Well, there's a lots of things sold that the government knows anything about 'em.

Well, I'll just sing you a little song about these sales tax:

These times now ain't suiting me,
Corn is costin' a dollar and three.

chorus: *Oh, the sales tax is on it, (3x) everywhere you go.*

Old Aunt Martha lived behind the jail,
A sign on the wall sayin': "Liquor for sale."

I never seen the like since I've been born,
The women got the sales tax on the stuff at home.

spoken: *You know these sales tax is a pain!*

You used to could buy it for a dollar a round,
Now sales tax is on it, all over town.

"I'm as lovin' as a woman can be,
The stuff I've got'll cost you a dollar and three."

Now, you may take me to be a fool,
Everything is sold by the government's rule.

The point of the song, of course, is that although everything sold should be taxed by "the government's rule," bootleg liquor and sex, being illegal commodities, escape it.

In August 1938 the same ironic observation was made by another popular blues group, the Harlem Hamfats. The women sell the same old stuff: "Sales Tax on It, But It's the Same Old Thing."

Listen here, boys, don't start no fuss,
'Bout these women, sellin' their stuff.

chorus: *'Cause it's the same thing, it's the same thing,*
They got sales tax on it, but it's the same thing.

Some sell it high, some sell it low,
It's done gone bad, and they can't sell it no more.

Now, I'm goin' up the river, to sell your sacks,
It'll be here, when you get back.

I done been up the river, sold my sacks,
I can buy, but I can't pay no tax.

Big mama told me, little mama told me too:
"Come on home, let that do."

Went out last night, sure I could be fooled,
Tried it once, broke my tool.[12]

The 1935 tax measures did little to redistribute wealth. The president's perceived options were limited by what he saw as the political power of the wealthy. Still, 1935 marked the beginning of what some historians have called the Second New Deal, the era in which FDR focused his attention more on the working classes.[13]

To "insure a Roosevelt victory in November" in 1936 a full-page advertisement was placed in the *Chicago Defender*: "Mayor Kelly urges us to support Bundesen for Governor." The ad shows photos of Mayor Edward J. Kelly, Herman N. Bundesen, Franklin D. Roosevelt and Joe Louis and claims that "Bundesen doesn't like the unfair 3c sales tax any more than you do. He is pledged to cut it down and in the meantime to see that the money collected is rally [sic] used for relief of the poor and unemployed."[14]

Not all blues singers were convinced of the election promises. In September 1936 Old Ced Odom wryly commented: "You know each politician says his candidate is best, he's more honest than any of the rest, but we always find when election has passed, the taxpayer gets it in the yas yas yas."[15]

Well aware that a sales tax in a recession does not exactly stimulate consumption and personally disliking such a tax, Roosevelt nonetheless helped to spread the regressive sales tax by relying on local authorities in the struggle against unemployment.[16] Although it was not a federal tax, many states adopted this measure. As a result $1.03 became a proverbial amount, ridiculing a 3 percent sales tax. The Mississippi Sheiks sang about it in 1934, but when Willie "Piano Red" Perryman (1911–1985) recorded his "The Sales Tax Boogie" as late as 1952, he referred to the same percentage. Piano Red lived in Atlanta in the first state to adopt a sales tax in 1929. He calls it a "new tax" that they levy "down in Georgia." This song may be an illustration of the local variations in the application of the sales tax.

> Down in Georgia, they got a new tax,
> Three cents on the dollar, you'll never get it back.

chorus: It's the sales tax boogie, yes, the sales tax boogie,
> Three cents on the dollar, you ain't gonna never get back.

> They got tax on whiskey, tax on gin,
> Tax on watermelon, you know that's a sin.

spoken: Now, talk with me!

> Back in nineteen forty-two, they took out withholding tax on you,
> Said, "Now after the war, you'll get it back," but now they done named it "income
>   tax."

> Now you may be rich and you may be poor,
> Got to pay three cents wherever you go.

Judging from the above recordings the sales tax was hardly popular with blues singers. At least the white assertion that African Americans did not pay taxes could be refuted by the sales tax. The blues singers also had great satisfaction in the observation that "the government's rule" did not apply to everything. Whiskey and women were still to be enjoyed for a single dollar bill.

WHEN THE SOLDIERS GET THEIR BONUS

In 1924 Congress had passed the Adjusted Compensation Act over President Coolidge's veto. It ensured that 3 million World War I veterans were to receive a bonus "to equalize the differences in pay enjoyed by the civilian and the service man." Each day at home yielded $1 and a day overseas $1.25. The average sum due was $1,012 plus interest, to be cashed two decades later, in 1945. The maximum amount payable was $1,595.[1]

When the depression was taking its toll the veterans understandably demanded immediate payment of their bonus money, but the Hoover administration was afraid of adverse effects on inflation and the budget.[2]

In May 1932 a group of "bonus marchers" entered the nation's capital. In 1918 they had been the segregated American Expeditionary Force in France; now they were the racially integrated Bonus Expeditionary Force (BEF) in Washington. Ultimately twenty thousand people came together to present the real face of the depression to the administration. They lived in cardboard and tin-sheeting encampments along the Anacostia River in the biggest "Hooverville" of the United States. The president himself saw to it that the veterans were supplied with medical equipment and army supplies. In line with Hoover's Quaker principles no publicity was given to this humanitarian act.

Texas Representative Wright Patman argued that the nation needed the additional purchasing power that the bonus bill would afford. On 15 June 1932 the House of Representatives passed the bill, requiring immediate distribution of $2.3 billion to the veterans of World War I. Two days later the Senate defeated the bill.[3] Consequently President Hoover asked the chief of staff, General Douglas MacArthur, to clear the camp. With the assistance of Major Eisenhower and Major Patton, MacArthur not only burned down the Anacostia camp, but drove the BEF from the city, in direct violation of presidential orders.[4] Hoover did not punish the general's insubordination, however, and took the blame on himself. The newspaper photos of the United States Army attacking its own veterans caused an outrage.

In his *Memoirs*, Hoover defended himself by calling the bonus march "a glaring example of Soviet interference,"[5] and said that both Mr. and Mrs. Roosevelt later misrepresented the bonus march for political motives by portraying him "as a murderer and an enemy of the veterans."[6]

In a conversation with Rexford Tugwell, presidential candidate Franklin D. Roosevelt confessed that he considered MacArthur one of the two most dangerous men in the United States.[7] When he received the 1932 Democratic nomination Roosevelt received an unexpected telephone call from the second of these dangerous men: Huey "The Kingfish" Long, governor of Louisiana. Long offered a suggestion to "clinch" the presidential nomination: "I think that you should issue a statement immediately, saying that you are in favor of a soldier's bonus to be paid as soon as you become President." Roosevelt rejected the suggestion by saying that he preferred a balanced budget to a bonus payment. As "The Kingfish" hung up, he uttered the words: "Well, you are a gone goose"![8]

On 9 May 1933 the veterans returned to Washington. FDR, the new president despite Huey Long's pessimism, directed his private secretary, Louis Howe, to see to proper shelter for the three thousand men of the second BEF. Eleanor Roosevelt made an unexpected appearance at the bonus camp. While Howe took a nap in the government car, the first lady stepped into the mud to lend an ear and even joined the veterans in the singing of "There's a Long, Long Trail."[9] One of the veterans summed it all up: "Hoover sent the army, Roosevelt sent his wife."[10]

In April 1934 the first blues recording to mention the bonus, "Black Gal What Makes Your Head So Hard?," by Texas singer Joe Pullum, was a huge hit. Many cover versions were made of this song, which continued to be sung by zydeco accordionist Clifton Chenier and his fellow Louisianian Silas Hogan as late as the 1980s.

> Black gal, black gal, what makes your head so hard?
> Lord, I would come to see you, but your bad man has got me barred.
>
> She's gone, she's gone, she's forever on my mind,
> She was a real good black woman and she was so nice and kind.
>
> She caught that Katy, she caught that Katy, Lord, and I swung on behind,
> Going to find that black woman or lose my black life trying.
>
> When I got my bonus, had my big money, she followed me all over town,
> Now that she spent all my money, she don't even want me 'round.
>
> I cried out, "Lord," I cried out, "Lord, Lord, Lord, Lord, how can it be,
> That my black woman can leave me and go back to her used to be?"
>
> But I'm going to hunt her, I'm going to hunt her with my smokin' forty-four,
> And when I find that black gal, Lord, her nappy, knotty head won't be hard no
>   more.

Pullum's song was such a big hit that he recorded no fewer than six versions of it, only one of which also referred to the bonus issue. It is called "Black Gal No. 4" and contains the line "You spent my bonus."[11] Part of the song's success may be explained by the identification it provided for the bonus veterans. In the song Pullum complains that his "black gal" has spent all his bonus money. The bonus bill had not passed Congress when this song was recorded, but most of the bonus veterans who were still alive in those years had borrowed on their expected bonus payment. As BEF Commander W. W. Waters explains, they had to pay interest on that loan "set at 2% more than the discount rate, or 5% to 6%."[12] Pullum must have been referring to the bonus money received from such a loan. This explanation becomes even more likely when we hear him sing "I'm going to get the rest of my bonus money" in his 1936 "Bonus Blues," which will be analyzed later in this chapter.

Wright Patman never gave up on the bonus issue. On 28 April 1935, a new bonus bill was passed by both the House of Representatives and the Senate. Vice President John Nance Garner advised Roosevelt to first veto it and then silently acquiesce in a congressional override of the veto. The problem would thus be solved and forgotten by the election year of 1936.[13] On 22 May 1935 FDR vetoed the bill in a personal appearance before Congress, and, as the

Senate did not override the veto by the necessary two-thirds majority, the president's veto was sustained, thus upsetting Garner's political calculations.

On 20 January 1936 the Patman bill was slightly amended to allow that the bonus no longer be paid in fiat (uncovered) money but in interest-bearing bonds (which could be cashed whenever the bearer preferred). Again FDR vetoed the bill, this time in a handwritten note, dated 24 January 1936.[14] Congress now overrode the chief executive in both houses by the required majority. Harold Ickes had his own thoughts about the congressmen's motives: "Man after man, like so many scared rabbits, ran to cover out of fear of the soldier vote."[15]

The blues and gospel artists were not slow to respond. The first artist to comment on the thrilling news was Red Nelson Wilborn, who had been born on a Mississippi farm in 1907 and had come to Chicago in the early thirties. Wilborn was accompanied by boogie-woogie pianist "Cripple" Clarence Lofton (1887–1957) when he recorded his topical "When the Soldiers Get Their Bonus (Even if It Don't Last Long)" on 6 February 1936.

> Yes, good morning, mama, you look mighty swell,
> Now, you say you've got something to sell.

chorus: We'll have a nice time (3x), when the soldiers get their bonus, even if it don't last long.

> I've got some liquor, got some wine,
> We can get drunk, have a whoppin' good time.

spoken: Yes, play it!

> I had two dollars, I don't know where it went,
> Show me what you got, there for fifty cents.

> My gal got a heart, big as a whale,
> Shake up her body, she just won't move her tail.

> I plays a little coon-can, shoots a little dice,
> Sometimes fool with a old man's wife.

spoken: Yes, beat it on out!

> Grandpa told grandma last year,
> You got too old for to shift your gear.

> My black gal's head won't be so hard,
> Even her good man won't have me barred.

The news has come out that the soldiers will get their bonus money after all. Red knows how he will spend it: on women, liquor and gambling. As will be shown, the song's subtitle was quite prophetic; money spent in this way would not last long. The final verse is a clear reference to the opening stanza of Joe Pullum's "Black Gal What Makes Your Head So Hard?" Red Nelson was too young to be a World War I veteran himself, but Pullum's real date of birth is unknown.[16] If he was a bonus veteran, and his lyrics do not rule this possibility out, he may have been born as early as the turn of the century.

A few days later Chicago singer Lil Johnson sang "That Bonus Done Gone Thru," accompanied by pianist Black Bob Hudson, who also assumes the role of the bonus veteran:

> Have you heard the latest news?
> These veterans ain't got no more blues.
> They are planning just what to do,
> Since that bonus done gone thru.
>
> Now, where's that man you used to rave about?
> Time now to see what he's made out.
> You'd better not let him slip through your hand,
> 'Cause some other woman surely take your man.

chorus: Come on girls, (yes)
> Ain't you goin' downtown? (yes)
> What you gonna buy?
> A new evening gown.
>
> Oh, a new pair of shoes,
> Oh, gonna truck away those blues,
> 'Cause that bonus done gone thru.

spoken: Beat it out, boys! Play it, Bob!
> Yes!
> Ain't you gettin' your bonus?
> Sure, baby!
> You goes when the wagon comes, tip up and see me sometimes.
> Sure, baby, when I get my bonus!
>
> Now, when you steps out on the street,
> All lookin' so nice and neat,

Everybody will stare at you so,
Now, looka here, folks, she's out o' the barrel once more.

Now, wait until I get all togged down,
Mens will come from miles around.
Go away, boys, I ain't got no time to lose,
I've got a good veteran who has cured my blues.

Oh, listen to my talk,
Oh, just watch this Mae West walk.
'Cause that bonus done gone thru,
'Cause that bonus done gone thru.[17]

When Lil calls out "Just watch this Mae West walk," and refers to the famous film star with the line "Tip up and see me sometimes," we may get a glimpse of the act of this extensively recorded, but still obscure, Chicago singer. Both the tune and the harmonies are reminiscent of Cab Calloway's "Minnie the Moocher," suggesting a brothel setting for this song. Would the bonus men, with all their bonus money, remain faithful to their partners?

Peetie Wheatstraw, for one, has no intention at all of giving his bonus money to his woman. "You think you can get my money, that is going to be your D.B.A.," he sings triumphantly (D.B.A. is a common slang abbreviation for "dirty black ass"). Wheatstraw's "When I Get My Bonus (Things Will Be Coming My Way)" is sung appropriately to the tune of "Sittin' on Top of the World."

When I was broke, didn't have a dime,
You hinkty[18] *women, wouldn't pay me no mind.*

chorus: *But when I get my bonus, things will be coming my way.*

Then I will be up on my feet again,
I'm gonna drink my whiskey, and goin' to drink my gin.

You told everybody, I didn't do nothing but lie,
I wouldn't give you women, even time to die.

spoken: *Play it a long time, boy! Can't play it long time, play it two times!*

You hinkty women, get yourself a glass,
You can have a little drink, of your yas-yas-yas.

I am telling you women, about my army pay,
You think you can get my money, that is going to be your D.B.A.

The third bonus blues from February 1936, the month in which the bonus "done gone thru," was recorded by the originator of the theme, Joe Pullum, and was simply called "Bonus Blues":

> Nineteen thirty-five is gone, nineteen thirty-five is gone, in come nineteen and
>> thirty-six,
> I'm going to get the rest of my bonus money, Lord, and get my business fixed.
>
> Men be careful, men be careful, who you give your money to,
> Because as soon as you get broke, you know the whole round world is through with
>> you.
>
> Everywhere I turn, everywhere I turn, there's somebody there that wants to talk with
>> me,
> But it's all concerning, nothing but my bonus money.
>
> They are advising me, they are advising me, just like they did before,
> But I'm going to put my money in the bank, and be a fool no more.

In comes 1936 and Joe Pullum is going to get "the rest of his bonus money." He had probably already taken a loan on part of the forthcoming sum. Many people—women, salesmen, investment advisers—want to talk to Joe about his bonus money, but he has learned from the way he had spent his first bonus money, and will now put it in the bank. Both the melody and the scheme of this song show that "Bonus Blues" is yet another derivative of Pullum's big hit, "Black Gal."

How had the blues singers learned the news about the payment of the bonus money? The radio was a very important source of communication and so were the black newspapers. In his 11 March 1936 "When I Get My Money (I Mean That Bonus)" Amos Easton says that he read all about it in his newspaper (in his case perhaps the *Chicago Defender*). In one of its February or March issues Easton would have read about the bonus being passed over the presidential veto:

> Soon one morning, I was lyin' in the bed,
> Picked up the paper, this is what it said:
> "Bonus have been vetoed, but they passed it anyhow."
> I said, "Thank God Almighty, I wished I had it now."
>
> chorus: When I get my bonus, I ain't gonna throw it away,
>   I'm gonna save some to live on, workin' hard won't pay.

Maybe I'll go to the tavern, and drink a little beer,
I'm gonna buy Myrtle a souvenir.
Ain't gonna pitch no parties, and pay the whole bill,
Thought I'd buy me a V-8 Ford, don't believe I will.

spoken: Now, boys, you ought to take it from me,
This is the last round-up, on that bonus business.
You ain't gonna get no more bonus, unless you fight some more war.
You better hold to every dollar you can. That's what I'm gonna do!

Everybody is plannin' to have a nice time,
I ain't thinkin' about nothing, but savin' mine.
When I get broke, can't nobody say,
"Slim got his money, and threw it all away."

I'm goin' to New York City, place I've never been,
And make Harlem ring, from end to end.
Harlem is heaven, so they say.
If I get lucky, that's where I'm gonna stay.

Easton (b. 1905), a barber from Georgia who moved to Chicago and recorded prolifically as "Bumble Bee Slim" from 1931 to 1937 as well as after the war, was also too young to have been a bonus veteran himself. Easton is not going to throw his bonus money away. He will buy himself a beer in the tavern and a souvenir for his pianist, Myrtle Jenkins, but he will not give expensive parties or buy himself a V-8 Ford. The S&L Motor Company ran a page-size *Chicago Defender* advertisement with photos of the Ford V-8 and the Lincoln Zephyr: "Ex-soldiers! Special bonus blanks properly filled by experts. Notary service free. Get your new Ford V-Eight."[19] In the last stanza Bumble Bee Slim intends to travel to New York City, "place I've never been." This statement is belied by the fact that he had recorded there in 1932 for Vocalion.

That same month Easton's fellow Chicago blues singer Carl Martin (1906–1979) was less cautious in his "I'm Gonna Have My Fun (When I Get My Bonus)." He will get himself another woman and will buy no more "moonshine" but instead will drink the more expensive "bottled in bond," legitimately produced whiskey stored in bonded warehouses.

When I get my bonus, tell you what I'm gonna do:
Get me another woman, and quit fooling 'round with you.

Barber shop in Vicksburg, Mississippi, March 1936. Photo by Walker Evans, reproduced from the collections of the Library of Congress.

You can't spend my money, for you don't treat me right,
Go out with your boyfriend, come in high as a kite.

chorus: *And when I get my bonus, I'm sure gonna have my fun,*
I'm just sitting here waiting, waiting until my bonus comes.

Just like I found you, baby, I can find someone else,
That's why, baby, I'm gonna put you on the shelf.
You been spending my money, and doin' the messaround,
So if you're plannin' on my bonus, that's the coldest stuff in town.

spoken: *Play that thing, boy!*

Now, listen all you veteran soldiers, who live in this town,
Let's take off our hats: "Thanks to Uncle Sam."
Lots of you are crippled, gassed, blind and cannot see,
But we came back home, with the victory.

Ain't gonna drink no moonshine, nothing but bottled in bond,
Kick up my heels, pitch a boogie-woogie, boys, from sun till sun.
Ain't had no good time, since nineteen twenty-nine,
Times have been so tight, couldn't save a lousy dime.

Carl Martin, NBBO Blues Festival, Utrecht, 17 February 1979. Photo by René van Rijn, from the collection of the author.

This is yet another bonus blues by a singer who was too young to be a World War I veteran himself, providing further evidence that the blues singer voices common sentiment that is not necessarily autobiographical.

Red Nelson recorded a second bonus blues in April. "What a Time I'm Havin' (Off the Soldiers' Bonus)" has him in the role of a Chicago pimp. His 'Lise needs only "four or five good tricks" to earn her money, and he has eight or nine more vets "hemmed up" in his brothel. If he does not get their bonus money he "ain't gonna let ne'er one out," which proves that one does not have to be a veteran to thrive on bonus money.[20]

Women were inclined to follow the unexpectedly prosperous bonus men wherever they could, if one were to believe the blues singers. In Earl Thomas's July 1936 song, "Bonus Men," they have stolen his woman. The suggestion that is probably made is that Thomas's woman will have to earn her living as a prostitute on "Black Avenue" when the bonus money of the veterans to whom she had also offered her body has gone. One day, when the bonus money is gone, she will try to come back home, but Thomas has seen to it that she will "find two padlocks on her door":

> It's getting here lately, I can't keep a woman friend,
> Boys, but I know the trouble, on account of these bonus men.

My baby left my home, it's been two long weeks ago,
She been following them bonus men, each and everywhere they go.

Boys, I wonder what that girl's gonna do, when them bonus men's money play out,
She'll be standing round there on Black Avenue, looking like a barrel of kraut.

One of these old lonesome days, she'll think about poor me,
But I'll have me another woman, making it good to me.

Boys, but I'll swear she'll try to come back home, find two padlocks on her door,
She will grieve and worry, never have another bonus man no more.

The Edgewater Crows[21] had to sing a "No Bonus Blues" in July. "Bonus money like fire, and it sure will burn your hand":

I didn't get me no bonus, and stayed broke all the time,
And some of these bonus cats done changed my baby's mind.

Bonus money like fire, and it sure will burn your hand,
I didn't get me no bonus, but I'm gonna spend some other man's.

Hey, hey, hey, woman, please come and go my way,
I didn't get me no bonus, but I work for the WPA.

Didn't get me no bonus, and it sure don't worry my mind,
I can spend a bonus dollar, baby, most any time.

Some churchmen seem to have frowned upon the bonus men. To support his admonition, the obscure Rev. R. H. Taylor, who recorded his "The Bonus Have Found the Stingy Mens Out" in Hattiesburg, Mississippi, one week after the Edgewater Crows, quoted (with some small errors) from Isaiah 55:2: "Wherefore do ye spend money for that which is not bread, and your labour for that which satisfieth not?"

Ah, we gonna talk from the fifty-fifth Isaiah and the second verse. Our text is today:
"Wherefore ye spend money for that which is not bread? And labour for that which
satisfieth none?"
    Amen!
Ah, the subject is: "This bonus has found these stingy mens out."
    Oh, Jesus!
Ah, when we think about those mens, who went across the deep water,
    Tell it!

And cast their lives for the freedom of this country, and the Lord has blessed them
and they have returned safely,

   Amen!

And received hundreds of dollars.

   Right!

And since that time they've forgotten their God,

   That's right!

Who carried them safely and brought them back to their homes again.

   Amen!

Since they have received this money, some of their wives haven't seen them in three
days and nights.

   Amen! Brother Pastor, I haven't seen my husband since he got his bonus.

I'll tell you where he is: he is out, ridin' up and down the streets in the automobiles,

   That's right!

Talkin' 'bout his bird liver and his pig liver, all the other kinds of dainty meat,

Ah, but he will have to give an account of the scriptures here.

Ah, those bonus men, remind me of hogs.

   Wait a minute Brother Pastor, did you just call me a hog?

Yes, you're a hog. All of these bonus mens are hogs!

   Amen!

   Don't call my husband a hog!

Oh, yes he's hog! Or remind me of a hog. Under the acorn tree with his head down.

Gruntin' and eatin', never look up to see where it's coming from.

   I wouldn't say that.

Possibly a limb would fall and break his neck. That's the way these bonus mens are.

   Amen!

They are with the head down, enjoying their blessings,

Don't never look up to thank God for nothing he has done to 'em.

   Amen!

They've even forgot the attitude of his wife towards him, or the childrens are gone
astray.

The jailhouses are full of them,

   Come on!

Penitentiaries are full.

   That's right!

God has goned out of their hearts.

   That's right!

> Hearts full of malicy, envy, pride, angry, unkindness, unthankful.
>   Amen!
> Oh Lord!
>   Amen!
> But God will call them in question,
>   That's right!
> They will have to give an account.
>   Preach it!
> Of the surety of hell.
>   Yes!
> Talkin' 'bout the bonus have made good times,
>   Preach it!
> Yeah, for the bootleggers, the beer gardens,
>   That's right!
> The whiskey dives,
>   That's right!
> Undertakers,
>   That's right!
> All other unfittin' things under heaven.
>   Amen!

One year later the bonus money had mostly been spent. The final bonus blues songs, which date from 1937, express regret for the disappearance of bonus money. Big Bill Broonzy, who as a World War I veteran must have received a bonus himself, spent his too fast, as is evident from his "My Big Money."

> I'm on a bum, can't get back home,
> Can't sleep for dreamin', I'm all alone.
>
> chorus: Oh, but when I had my big money,
> I had everything going my way.
>
> I bought a paper, I had it read,
> I had my breakfast right in my bed.
>
> My baby told me to take it slow,
> Uncle Sam may want me to fight some more.
>
> Ah, now, don't be foolish, this is what I know,
> If I'm living, I'll be too old to go.

My big money, didn't last me long,
Had too many friends to spend it on.[22]

"Bye, bye, bonus, till we meet again," Charley Jordan sings in his "Look What a Shape I'm In (Bonus Blues)," "I know I have lost my only and best friend":

When I had my bonus, I had plenty of friends,
Since I've spent my bonus, it came to an end.

chorus: *But it's gone, I ain't got no money to spend,*
Since I spent all my bonus money, look what a shape I'm in.

Says, I bought an automobile, for that gal of mine,
But I couldn't make the payment, upon due time.

So I lost my automobile, lost my good gal too,
Also my bonus, now what shall I do?

Say, the women come runnin', holdin' out their hands,
You can hear them cryin', "Here's my bonus man."

Says, I bought plenty clothes, had never been worn,
Since I spent my bonus, they're all in pawn.

So, bye, bye, bonus, till we meet again,
I know I have lost my, only and best friend.

Charley Jordan (c. 1890–1954) served in the United States army around 1918–19. Consequently, he may have received a bonus himself, so that he actually sang from experience.

Robert Lee McCoy (mother's name) or McCollum (father's name) recorded the final prewar bonus blues, entitled "I Have Spent My Bonus." McCoy, who recorded after World War II as Robert Nighthawk, was born in Helena, Arkansas, in 1909, the place where he would also die in 1967. Again both his woman and his friends have left the veteran who has spent his bonus money.[23]

Meanwhile President Roosevelt's desire to balance the budget had been thwarted by the inflationary effects of paying the bonus. A "lump sum" in the amount of $1.7 billion had been paid out to the veterans, and in 1937 an additional $564 million was paid for the "remainder of the soldiers' bonus."[24] Roosevelt had vetoed the Patman bill, to the amazement of his progressive followers,[25] and the veterans did not have Franklin Roosevelt to thank for their windfall. As Herbert Hoover showed in one of the tables in his *Memoirs*, the number of veterans aided in 1932–33 when Hoover was still in the White House was about 1 million. In 1936, when FDR's veto was overruled, the number dropped dramatically to around six hundred thousand.[26] Still, economic recovery had mainly been caused by government spending, and the bonus payment had been a substantial part of it. Even so, the budget was foremost in Roosevelt's mind, and in the months following the final bonus payment of 1937, government spending, mainly as relief support, "would be reduced significantly."[27]

For the blues singers, the bonus payment was an important theme. Among the three major blues and gospel record companies, RCA, Decca and ARC, some tough competition arose in the struggle for the most topical song about the bonus issue. Most blues singers who recorded on this topic were born around 1905 and were too young to be veterans themselves, the only exceptions being Charley Jordan, Big Bill Broonzy and possibly Joe Pullum. The sixteen bonus blues discussed in this chapter so far can be divided into four distinct phases: the trendsetting "Black Gal" recordings by Joe Pullum from 1934 and 1935, when the bonus bill was still being fought in Congress and the veterans could receive advance loans; the seven songs from the months of February to April 1936, when expectation of the bonus money led to the wildest dreams; the month of July 1936 when the excesses of uncontrolled spending were criticized; and the recordings from 1937 that mourn the loss of money spent too soon.

In 1937 the veterans were waking up. "Bonus money like fire, and it sure will burn your hand," the Edgewater Crows had sung. Understandably this observation is especially true for poor people who have suddenly received a substantial amount of money. The bonus money had taught many veterans who their real friends were, and for all of them it had at least meant some temporary relief in the bleak thirties. Most veterans may not have realized that the president had not been on their side in the issue. The image that would forever stay with the veterans was that of Eleanor Roosevelt visiting the veterans. "I never want to see another war," Mrs. Roosevelt had concluded. "I would like to see fair consideration for everyone, and I shall always be grateful to those who served their country."[28]

As Franklin Roosevelt never intervened when his wife acted as an advocate of the Negro cause, so he was content to let her act as his public relations officer towards the veterans, both black and white.

THE "SCOTTSBORO BOYS"

Without answering the question directly Harlem Renaissance poet Countee Cullen wondered why American poets had not sung about the "Scottsboro boys." Cullen's "Scottsboro, Too, Is Worth Its Song" (1935), subtitled "A poem to American poets" ended with the lines: "Surely, I said, now will the poets sing. But they have raised no cry. I wonder why."

In the thirties "Scottsboro" was a cause célèbre in American law enforcement.[1] On 25 March 1931 nine African Americans, who were among the two hundred thousand people practically living on the trains, were hoboing on the Chattanooga-to-Memphis freight train, when some of them got into a fight with a few white hoboes, who were thrown off the train. Sheriff M. L. Wann, of Jackson County, Alabama, gave his men orders to "capture every Negro on the train and bring them to Scottsboro."[2] To the surprise of the armed men sent out by the sheriff, there were also two young white women on board. These women, Victoria Price and Ruby Bates, accused the boys of rape. The nine "Scottsboro boys" were all from Georgia or Chattanooga, Tennessee, and ranged in age from thirteen to twenty.[3]

Local public outrage was so great that the boys were in grave danger of being lynched. Fortunately this was prevented, and they were taken to an Alabama court. The all-white jury found the boys guilty beyond all reasonable

Onlookers watching a Saturday afternoon ball game, as one of the group plays the guitar, at Gee's Bend, Alabama, May 1939. Photo by Marion Post Wolcott, reproduced from the collections of the Library of Congress.

doubt, and Judge Hawkins pronounced the death sentence, his first, for eight of them. Roy Wright, who was only thirteen years of age, was sentenced to life imprisonment.

Both the National Association for the Advancement of Colored People (NAACP) and the Communist-oriented International Labor Defense (ILD) took an interest in the case, but the NAACP was reluctant to get involved[4] and withdrew from the case on 4 January 1932. That the ILD now took on the case exclusively provided racists with additional ammunition. When, in December 1932, the ILD managed to persuade Samuel Leibowitz, one of the most success-ful criminal lawyers in the country, to defend the Scottsboro boys in a second trial, his Jewishness provided the racists with yet more ammunition. The second trial was ordered by the United States Supreme Court "on the ground that appointment of counsel [was] violative of their constitutional rights."[5]

Leibowitz took command of the case on 13 March 1933. He pleaded that there were illiterate white men on the jury who could easily be replaced by educated Negroes. White witnesses had to admit that there had never been a black jury member in their county. *The New York Age* reported that "one of the witnesses, J. S. Benson, newspaper publisher, said that it would be impossible to convince him that any but a white man possessed that judgment and training in law and justice which he regarded as being essential for a fair and impartial verdict. 'They'll all steal' he answered as Leibowitz sought to find out why he rejected the idea of a Negro upon a jury in his county."[6]

Ruby Bates had disappeared, so Victoria Price was now the star witness.[7] Leibowitz called on Dr. R. R. Bridges, the physician who had examined the women on the day of the arrest of the Scottsboro boys. The doctor declared that he had had great difficulty in finding enough semen for a smear during his examination of Victoria, and that the little he had found was "completely non-motile,"[8] a surprising conclusion, given that she claimed to have been raped six times on the train. A shocked Judge Horton exclaimed, "My God, Doctor, is this whole thing a horrible mistake?"[9] Leibowitz also proved that Victoria Price had had sexual contact with a certain Jack Tiller "less than thirty-six hours before the alleged assault."[10] Victoria Price turned out to be a well-known prostitute in Huntsville, Alabama, who worked under the name "Big Leg Price."[11]

The Scottsboro boys sang gospel songs in jail as the jury deliberated. According to a later report in *Life* one of the boys, Olen Montgomery, "spent most of his time singing and twanging a one-string tenor guitar. He has composed a 'Lonesome Jailhouse Blues', which begins: 'All last night I walked my cell and cried, cause this old jailhouse done got so lonesome I can't be satisfied.' "[12] In spite of the caption the photograph shows Montgomery playing a four-string tenor guitar. It was Montgomery's dream to become a "blues king" one day, so he badly needed a regular six-string guitar.[13]

Despite all the evidence to the contrary, the all-white jury condemned the boys to the electric chair. Twenty thousand angry African Americans now decided to march to Washington. From 2 to 17 May 1933 the ILD secretary wired President Roosevelt's private secretary, Louis Howe, four times, asking if the president would be willing to meet with Ruby Bates, who had repudiated her testimony, and with four Scottsboro mothers (Wright, Patterson, Williams and Norris).[14] Roosevelt ignored the telegrams.

A third trial for Haywood Patterson was granted by Judge Horton, who had concluded that "the conviction was against the weight of evidence."[15] It was held beginning 20 November 1933 under a third judge, the tough W. W. Callahan. The *Afro-American* reported that "the jury finally picked, consists of nine farmers, one merchant, one truck driver and one janitor."[16] Again Patterson was sentenced to the electric chair by a white jury. Leibowitz next went before the Alabama Supreme Court, but "they denied the motion for new trials and set the execution date for 31 August 1934."[17]

In 1934 President Roosevelt asked his secretary for a complete memorandum on the case: "Randolph Preston, a special assistant to the attorney general, read the trial transcripts and reported to the President that he did not 'ever remember to have read a record which is such a mass of contradictions and improbabilities as is the evidence of these two witnesses (Orville Gilley[18] and Victoria Price) upon whose testimony the whole case of the state is found.' If the boys were faced with the death sentence, Preston advised that the President intervene."[19]

FDR's maid Lizzie McDuffie remembered: "Mr. Roosevelt had shown keen interest in the Scottsboro case. Hundreds of letters had been written to him about the Alabama boys who had been convicted of rape. When he held a governor's conference at Warm Springs in 1934, Mr. Roosevelt asked the in-coming governor of Alabama, David Bibb Graves, to remain behind for a while. Mac[20] heard the President say, 'Governor Graves, I know I haven't a thing to do with this matter officially because it's purely a state affair. I don't know how you feel about the Scottsboro case. But won't you do all you can to clear it up?' Governor Graves promised that he would."[21]

On 15 February 1935, Leibowitz went to the United States Supreme Court for the first time in his life. The highest judges in the country said that the ex-clusion of black jury members was contrary to the Fourteenth Amendment, and remanded the Haywood Patterson case back to the Alabama high court.[22] Not until 1937 would a "compromise" be reached. Olen Montgomery, Roy Wright, Willie Roberson (who suffered so badly from syphilis that he could not have raped anyone) and Eugene Williams were finally released. On 26 October 1937 the U.S. Supreme Court "declined to review the seventy-five-year conviction of Haywood Patterson"[23] and in June 1938 the Alabama Supreme Court "affirmed the death sentence of Clarence Norris and the prison sentences of Andrew Wright and Charley Weems."[24]

On 11 November 1938 Walter White, the NAACP secretary, visited Eleanor Roosevelt in the White House at the request of Allan Chalmers, head of the Scottsboro Defense Committee (SDC). Mrs. Roosevelt talked to her husband, and as a result FDR invited Bibb Graves, governor of Alabama, to the Little White House.[25] Graves declined his president's invitation. On 7 December Roosevelt wrote Graves a letter with an emotional appeal "to commute the sentences of the remainder of the Scottsboro boys."[26] To Chalmers, Graves confessed: "I can't go through with it. I am finished politically if I do."[27] It took Graves till 27 December to reply to the president. In his letter he denied ever having made a promise to change the sentences.[28] The five Scottsboro boys remained in jail.

That same December Huddie "Leadbelly" Ledbetter recorded a song called "Scottsboro Boys" for the Library of Congress. He had previously sung it for Richard Wright, who quoted part of it in an article for the *Daily Worker*.[29] On 13 August 1937 the Federal Writers' Project had invited Scottsboro mothers Mrs. Wright and Mrs. Montgomery for a moonlight sail aboard the steamboat *Mayflower*. There Ledbetter premiered his Scottsboro composition.[30] In his first recording of "Scottsboro Boys" on 26 December 1938 the most interesting parts are not in the lyrics of the song itself, but in the spoken comment.

spoken: *Now this is a song, "Scottsboro Boys." When I made this song about Scottsboro boys, 'cause I been all over Alabama, Birmingham, Montgomery. And in Alabama, must be Jim Crow or something like that, because they turn loose some men and try to keep the others. I don't see why they don't turn all of 'em loose. And this is the song, is "Scottsboro Boys."*

chorus: *Go to Alabama and you better watch out,*
       The landlord will get you, gonna jump and shout.
       Scottsboro, Scottsboro, Scottsboro boys,
       They can tell you what it's all about.

       I'm gonna talk to Joe Louis, ask him to listen to me,
       Don't he never try to make no bout, in Alabamaree.

       I'm gonna tell all the colored people, livin' on Sugar Hill,
       Don't you never go to Alabama, to try to live.

spoken: *Oh, shake it!*

       I'm gonna tell all the colored people, livin' in Harlem swing,
       Don't you never go to Alabama, to try to sing.

spoken: *Tell about the Scottsboro boys. Where were they going to? . . .*
       Tell about the Scottsboro boys, what happened to them. . . .

spoken: *This song is 'bout the Scottsboro boys. The boys left on a trip, you know, they was ridin' a freight train. And they met two white women in there, you know, the white*

women was boostin', too, what we call it. And they was beatin' they way along and
they met up with these boys. There was about nine boys and they rode along with
'em and they went out. One of the women says it wasn't so and the other one says
it was. Now they goin' hold all of them for just one sentence, which I don't think
none of it was true. But they turned loose four and now they got a few more. I
think they ought to turn 'em all a-loose. That's what they call happened. So they
puts the boys in jail. Give some of 'em life and some got loose, but I don't think it's
true. But, anyhow, the last word is this:

I'm gonna tell all the colored people, livin' in Harlem swing,
Don't you never be in Alabama, to try to sing.

spoken: Now, I'll tell you about it in Alabama, must be Jim Crow. If a white woman says
something, it must-a be so, and she can say something about a colored person, if
it's a thousand colored men, they kill all of 'em just for that one woman. If she ain't
telling the truth, it don't make any difference. Why? 'Cause it's Jim Crow and I know
it's so, 'cause the Scottsboro boys can tell you about it.

Leadbelly had always been an avid reader of newspapers who was able to
select from the long accounts of such events the kinds of details that caught
people's imaginations.[31] The rabid racism in the Scottsboro case did not escape
him. To Leadbelly, whose account of the Scottsboro Case is accurate, Alabama
justice is so unfair that he advises boxer Joe Louis, an Alabama native, "to make
no bout in Alabamaree," probably meaning that no Alabama referee would give
the fight to a black boxer.

Two years later Leadbelly recorded a second version of "The Scottsboro
Boys" for the Library of Congress. In August 1940 he was invited to Washington by Alan Lomax. Recording machines had improved, and new sixteen-inch
discs were used, which provided Leadbelly with an opportunity to go beyond
the three-minute limit.[32] In answer to questions from Elizabeth Lomax, Alan's
wife, Leadbelly discussed the background of the song.

Yes, ma'am. Yes, I'll tell you all about the Scottsboro boys. 'Cause we had a sail
once. And the Scottsboro boys' folks got out from down in that hard world, that
Alabama's a hard world down there. And the Scottsboro boys had a long time: six
years that time, them four boys what got out. And I met 'em. And the boys had
such a hard time. And I've been through down in that eh, that hard world. But I
didn't stay long. And when I saw the Scottsboro boys I shook their hands, an' I 'gin
to thinkin' about. And here what I said about the Scottsboro boys. 'Cause I know

they had a hard time. And here the advice I give Joe Louis and this is advice I give to all the Harlem colored people and what I mean all the good colored people.

Huddie, what did the Scottsboro boys do, anyway, to get in all this trouble?

Well they was down there and they was supposed to been ridin' in a, on a freight train. And they was ridin' in the box car and they run up on some white women. They was, had on pants, an' they was ridin' too. All of them supposed to been beatin' their way. Up to-comin' this-a-way. And so, down in Alabama, there I guess the train stopped in the yard down there somewhere. Well, and some of 'em found all the boys and girls in the same box car. Some was in different cars. And so I guess it's some of the people down there, they just say, well, they see them boys in there with them white women, that was the trouble about it. Then they went out and made some loud, some loud cry about the boys bein' there with the women, you see. That was all there was to it, they just saw the women, they didn't see nothing else wrong. But anyhow, they put the boys in jail, and they was in there six long years. Well, the state, all the whole United States got together. And they got out four of 'em an' they come to New York. And the lawyer which got 'em out, I know him pretty good. I've met him. And eh, now, he showed me the Scottsboro boys and I shaked hands with 'em. So I made this little song about down there. So, I, I advise everybody to be a little careful when they go along through there, they better stay woke, keep their eyes open.

In this song Leadbelly explains that he met the Scottsboro boys at a "sail" in New York (probably the meeting on the *Mayflower* in 1937) after they had been in prison for six years. On 20 August 1937 the four recently released boys had even appeared at Harlem's Apollo Theatre: "Appearing IN PERSON as a special added attraction with the novel ALL-GIRL REVIEW . . . a cast of FIFTY FASCINATING FEMALES."[33] Leadbelly claimed to know Samuel Leibowitz "pretty good" and to have "shaked hands with" the Scottsboro boys, at the time of the *Mayflower* trip. Leadbelly himself had also been "down in that, eh, that hard world," having served time for assault in Harrison County Prison in Texas in 1915,[34] for murder in Shaw State Prison Farm in Texas from 1918 to 1925[35] and for attempted homicide in Louisiana State Penitentiary in Angola, Louisiana, from 1930 to 1934.[36] After leaving prison he had been in Alabama as John Lomax's chauffeur. Leadbelly knew what the Scottsboro boys had gone through.

After many more years of painstaking negotiations, Charley Weems was finally released in November 1943. In January 1944 the doors flew open for

Clarence Norris. Ozie Powell followed in late 1946. Haywood Patterson escaped from his work gang in the summer of 1948 and remained in hiding for two years, after which he was not returned to the penitentiary. In May 1950 the last Scottsboro boy, Andrew Wright, walked through the gates of Kilby Prison.[37] He had been a prisoner for nineteen years. The nine Scottsboro boys had collectively served 102 years for a crime they did not commit.

As late as 1984 jazz drummer Max Roach recorded the two-part instrumental composition "Scott Free"[38] (to get off "scot-free" means to get away without punishment). Roach explained the concept behind the two-part structure to the writer of the notes for the CD: "They went through two trials—one they were convicted and that was it, then they had to go back and go to the retrial of it. And that's why the first side of the album is one thing, the second side is like starting all over, with the medium-tempo going into the fast-tempo and then the free section again. And the results ended up being the same in both trials, unfortunately; but finally, after a long period of time, they were all exonerated." Although historically not fully correct, Roach's explanation shows that black musicians have not forgotten the Scottsboro boys.

UNCLE SAM IS CALLING

Samuel Wilson, from Troy, New York, supplied meat for the army during the British-American war of 1812. When humorists suggested that the abbreviation "U.S.," stamped on his meat, and on government property in general, stood for "Uncle Sam" (Wilson), the personification of America was born. Many blues singers addressed themselves to their "Uncle Sam." In the early years of blues recording Sara Martin had a fine success with the song "Uncle Sam Blues,"[1] which she had written with her pianist Clarence Williams. It was recorded in 1923 and was so successful that three cover versions were recorded that same year.[2] The song was a complaint against Uncle Sam, who had taken off Martin's husband, her "good man" (her lover) and her "used to be." "He took my buddy out of his box back, put him in his khaki suit," she moaned. As the war was over she could not understand why Uncle Sam did not send back her man.

In the late thirties war was approaching again and the blues singers felt the threat. Big Bill Broonzy, who had served in France, was afraid Uncle Sam would need him again. "I do hope war don't start," Broonzy sang in his March 1938 "Unemployment Stomp":

> I'm a law-abiding citizen, my debts I sure will pay,
> I do hope war don't start, and Uncle Sam have to send me away.

I haven't never been in jail, and I haven't never paid no fine,
I wants a job to make my living, 'cause stealing ain't on my mind.

spoken: *Oh, yeah! Pick it, Mr. Josh!*

I've known times, when I raised my own meat and meal,
My meat was in my smokehouse and my meal was in my field.

Oh, when Mr. Roosevelt, sent out them unemployment cards,
I just knowed sure that work was going to start.

spoken: *Toot it, Mr. Man!*

Broke up my home, 'cause I didn't have no work to do,
My wife had to leave me, 'cause she was starving too.

spoken: *Let's go, boys! Yes, yes!*

However, the main subject of Bill's song is unemployment. Ironically, Adolf Hitler was more responsible for ending the Great Depression in the United States than Franklin Roosevelt was. The military buildup of 1940 and 1941 was to provide much more work than the New Deal had ever done.

On 3 September 1939, the day when the United Kingdom declared war on Germany, Roosevelt broadcast a brief fireside chat. In it he declared—in contrast to Wilson in 1914—that although "this nation will remain a neutral nation," he could not ask that "every American remain neutral in thought as well."[3] The next day twenty-eight Americans were killed when the British passenger ship *Athenia* was torpedoed. FDR could now carefully prepare the nation for a moderate military increase. Five days after the 8 September press conference at which the president explained that reserves had to be called up,[4] guitarist Bill Gaither gave a musical response to Uncle Sam's call. Gaither was born in Kentucky in 1910, and made a living repairing jukeboxes and radios in a small Louisville shop where he also sold records. In September 1939 Bill Gaither sings the "Army Bound Blues" and hopes his baby will write him when he has crossed "the deep blue sea." As in many army blues the pianist imitates a bugle call (in this case reveille) to create the proper atmosphere:

Uncle Sam is calling, I will answer to his call,
I'm army bound, and I may not get back at all.

Early this morning, here's what I heard his bugle say:
"Bid your baby goodbye, and be out on your way."

Give me something, baby, just to remember you,
I may be gone a month, or maybe a year or two.

But I will think about you, baby, when I'm crossing the deep blue sea,
And promise me, dear, that you will write to me.

Well, the train is coming, and it's not so far away,
I hate to leave you, baby, but I hope to see you again some day.

When he sang this blues Gaither was twenty-nine years of age, and accordingly his fears were well founded. The draft was still on his mind when he recorded his imaginative, antifeminist "Changing Blues" the next day. The song is credited to Gaither's (male) pianist Honey Hill. If women so much want to take the place of men, let them, Gaither says, but he predicts that they will soon change their minds when Uncle Sam calls them up to fight.

I'm gonna explain to this whole world, what's the matter with this world today:
Women tell these men what to do, then we let 'em run around and have their
doggone way.

If womens gonna take the place of men, then why not change this whole thing
around?
Dress the women in box-back and drapes, dress men in long evening gowns.

Now, if Uncle Sam calls for soldiers, and sends them right out on the front line,
Before the war was over, a many poor girl would change her mind.

It's a wonder some woman, don't try to take the president's place,
Take the man off of the dollar and stick on a woman's face.

Just imagine how this world will be, in just a few more years:
This whole world will be upside down, and my face streaming down in tears.

Gaither's songs from this period clearly show how the war influenced personal lives. In January 1941, when the world was "upside down" and the draft had become a reality, he sang "Uncle Sam Called the Roll":

Uncle Sam called the roll, just a few days ago,
It's too late to worry, baby, your daddy's booked to go.

chorus: *Yes, but I love you and always will, but it's just too late now.*

Don't mind goin' to war, I'm not afraid to fight,
But I'll miss your lovin' arms, baby, late hours in the night.

> *I love you, baby, with all my heart,*
> *Now the time has come, baby, the best of friends must part.*
>
> *You say I was no good, and too hard to please,*
> *But there you are prayin', down on your knees.*
>
> *I wanted to marry you, way back in thirty-four,*
> *You just made up your mind, three days ago.*
>
> *You know I begged you, I begged you and how,*
> *But if you didn't need me then, baby, you sure don't need me now.*

The final two stanzas refer to a woman to whom Bill had proposed in 1934, but who apparently made up her mind to marry him only on 11 September 1939. According to Pen Bogert, Gaither had met (and lost) a woman called Rose Lee in Indianapolis in 1934. He next moved to Louisville, but when he returned to "Naptown" he was reunited with Rose Lee. He had never been able to forget her, as is evident from the songs he recorded in the late thirties.

Gaither sang that he was not afraid to fight, but he could not foresee what a devastating effect the war would have on him. During his research into the blues in Louisville, Pen Bogert discovered what had happened to Gaither: "His last recordings were made eight days before the attack on Pearl Harbor, and he was drafted into the army in July 1942. He was assigned to the historic all-black 24th Infantry Regiment and saw action in Bougainville and Saipan. He returned to the U.S. in July 1945, but his combat experience left him a changed man. He never recorded or performed again because, as a close friend said, 'something happened to his nerves while he was in the army.' He never seemed able to get back on his feet."[5]

Bill Gaither died in Indianapolis in 1970, alone and forgotten. He had recorded 119 sides before the war ruined his career.

The approaching draft became a much-debated issue in the course of 1940. "Every time I pick up a paper, I could read something about the war," Sonny Boy Williamson sang in his May 1940 "War Time Blues."

> *Did you hear about the news up north, and it was everybody's Santa Claus?*
> *Now, and every time I pick up a paper, I could read something about the war.*
>
> *Now, it ain't no use of you worryin', buddy, that ain't goin' to help you none,*
> *Now, if you can't fly no airplane, maybe you'll be able to carry a gun.*

> Now, I'm gonna be up in my airplane, I'm gonna be sailin' all around,
> Now, but I believe I spied something below, and I'm goin' head in toward the
> ground.
>
> Now, look at that big gun yonder, that big gun hid out in the wood,
> Well, I believe I'll drop a bomb, because my machine gun won't do no good.

spoken: Yeah, yeah, yeah!

Sonny Boy imagines himself the pilot of a warplane, searching for "that big gun hid out in the wood" so he can drop his bomb on the enemy. Would the United States Air Force welcome Sonny Boy the pilot this time?

It seemed unlikely, for discrimination in the prewar effort before Pearl Harbor was so pervasive that A. Philip Randolph, head of the Brotherhood of Sleeping Car Porters, Walter White from the NAACP and T. Arnold Hill from the National Urban League met with the president on 27 September 1940. We know fairly well what went on at this meeting, as Richard Nixon was not the first president to make secret recordings in the Oval Office.[6] Roosevelt said that the Negro soldiers were being put "proportionally, into the combat services." White asked if this also held good for the officers. What about segregation, and could blacks also enlist in the navy? The outcome of the meeting was a statement by the War Department, issued with Roosevelt's approval. It held that Negro civilians should be "accorded equal opportunity for employment" at army posts and arsenals. It also secured aviation training and training as reserve officers for blacks.[7] FDR refused to end segregation in the army, however, and the black population was outraged.

A march on Washington movement was organized to denounce the shameful situation. On 18 June, A. Philip Randolph again visited the White House, where he disclosed that no fewer than one hundred thousand blacks were expected to march on 1 July. After several rejections by Randolph of a suggested compromise, the march was finally called off on 25 June 1941 when the president issued Executive Order 8802. It was now United States policy "that there shall be no discrimination in the employment of workers in defense industries or government because of race, creed, color, or national origin."[8]

Obviously ineligible for the draft, blues guitarist Blind Boy Fuller sang a cynical "When You Are Gone" in June 1940:

> This war is raging, what are you men going to do?
> If Uncle Sam call you in the war, and it's no use to feeling blue.

Yeah, when Uncle Sam calls you, be by one and two and three,
Yeah, you, no use of worryin', leave all these women back here worryin' me.

Yeah, when you're gone, no use to weep and moan,
Yeah, (no) use of worryin', 'cause this good work'll be carried on.

Yeah, when you're fighting, blood running in your face,
Yeah, no use of worryin', you know this world is a funny old place.[9]

The Nazi armed forces had conquered Poland, Denmark, Norway, Holland, Belgium and France in the period from September 1939 to June 1940. To prepare his country for defense, Roosevelt asked Congress for enormous amounts of money. On 8 October 1940 the awesome total sum of $17,692 billion had been granted (within a year the amount required would be more than twice as much).[10] In the election year of 1940, the president was faced with the necessity of greatly increasing recruitment into the army. When Britain was threatened with an invasion in the summer, public opinion shifted in favor of the draft, and on 16 October men from twenty-one to thirty-five registered for the first peacetime draft the nation had ever known.[11] A national Selective Service lottery was organized on 29 October. The president himself was present when a blindfolded Secretary of State Henry Stimson drew the first number (158) from a huge glass bowl.[12]

Only one day after the official start of the lottery Jimmy Rushing revived the First World War Maceo Pinkard composition "Draftin' Blues" that was discussed in chapter 1. Big Bill Broonzy, who had fought in World War I, also provided the nation with a patriotic song on the occasion. In his "That Number of Mine (Number 158)" Broonzy projects himself into the position of the first draftee, and the "goldfish bowl" from which his unlucky number, 158, was drawn becomes the controlling force of his life:

I was just sittin' here wonderin', was my number in that old goldfish bowl?
And when I heard my number called, ooh Lord, I couldn't feel happy to save my
                                                                        soul.

Everywhere I go, I see that same old one-fifty-eight,
I know I'm billed out, baby, ooh Lord, Uncle Sam say, "Bill don't be late."

I got my questionnaire, and I found that old number of mine,
Now, guess I well to start movin', ooh baby, there ain't no need of crying.

All you young men, I mean come on and follow me,
Now the American soldiers winned before, ooh Lord, now boys, why can't we?[13]

Although World War I veteran Broonzy (b. 1893) was by this time exempt from military service, the song shows that he considered the war to be an opportunity for young men of all colors to display their patriotism and forget about racial differences.

In November the Five Breezes, a quintet featuring bassist Willie Dixon (1915–1992), addressed themselves to those of their "buddies" who had reached the age of twenty-one. Vocalist and composer Eugene Gilmore sang "My Buddy Blues":

spoken: *Yes, yes, yes!*

      I have signed my name, it won't be long before I go,
      I woke up this morning, the mailman had my numbers at my door.

chorus: *If you're twenty-one, buddy, I advise you not to hide,*
      Because when that wagon roll 'round, I declare you've got to ride.

      Uncle Sam is calling for you, and you know you got to go,
      He's callin' for all you jitterbugs, like he never called before.
      The charity's been taking care of you, for a very, long, long time,
      Now Uncle Sam is callin' you, and you know what's on his mind.

      If you should happen to see a smoke, mama, and it ain't no wind around,
      Just tell all your friends, "That's the Five Breezes leavin' town."

Willie Dixon did not hide, but neither would he ride. In December 1941, after Pearl Harbor, Chicago police dragged him off the stage of the Pink Poodle, where the Five Breezes were playing. Dixon had ignored the draft and claimed he was a "conscientious objector." At his trial Dixon asked, "Why should I go to work to fight to save somebody that's killing me and my people?" In his autobiography Dixon remembered the circumstances:

I said I wasn't a citizen, I was a subject. I was telling them about the 14th and 15th Amendment. A lot of people in Chicago felt like this, you know. Under the conditions that existed at that particular time, what the hell did you have to fight for? They were mistreating every damn body all over the world, especially our people.

I just stayed in jail, about ten months off-and-on. They put me on bread and water for a while there but I just wouldn't let go. After I got in jail, I started explaining to people why I wasn't going. Some of 'em were mad with me and some were glad. I was creating arguments and making a disturbance so they were glad to get me out of there because I was working up too damn many people.

OKeh

06092
(C 3371)

UNCLE SAM, CALL OF THE ROLL
Blues Singer with Piano,
Guitar and Bass Acc.
-Crudup-
LITTLE BILL GAITHER

OKeh

Licensed by Mfr. under U.S. Patent Nos. 1625705 and/or 1702154 and
other patents pending; only for non-commercial use on phonographs in homes.
See detailed trade mark and patent notices on envelope. Made in U.S.A.

Use Columbia
or Okeh Needles

6709
(C 4057)

TRAINING CAMP BLUES
Blues Singer with Piano and Bass
Acc.   -Sykes-
ROOSEVELT SYKES
(The Honey Dripper)

BLUEBIRD

For best results
use Victor Needles

B-8580-B

WAR TIME BLUES

(Sonny Boy Williamson)

Sonny Boy Williamson
Blues singer with instrumental acc.

DECCA

MANUFACTURED BY DECCA RECORDS, INC., NEW YORK, U.S.A.

(70346)

Fox Trot
Vocal Chorus by
Trevor Bacon
and Ensemble

WE'RE GONNA HAVE TO SLAP
THE DIRTY LITTLE JAP
(And Uncle Sam's The Guy Who Can Do It)
(Bob Miller)

LUCKY MILLINDER
And His Orchestra

4261 B

They just started telling 'em, "Well, you were born in the United States." Hell, that doesn't make you anything. All my folks were born here but they never had papers or anything. I told the judge one time, "An egg can be hatched in a stove but that doesn't make it a biscuit just because it came out of the stove."[14]

Dixon had to appear in court a great many times. As an avid newspaper reader he was well aware of the politics of the day. "They claimed I must have been educated somewhere else and all like this but the only education I had was from the actual experience up and down the highway." Eventually Dixon was released with a 5-F classification. "I don't know what that meant and nobody else did, either."[15]

Pianist Nat "King" Cole (1919–1965) was classified 4-F. The press reported that the reason was "hypertension" although Cole's wife, Maria, claims her husband's flat feet were the real cause.[16] Whatever the reason, Cole's flat feet are mentioned in his December 1940 "Gone with the Draft," which clearly puns on the 1939 movie classic Gone with the Wind. The song was written for him by his bass player Wesley Prince, who was drafted himself in August 1942, and contained the lines: "When Franklin D. did sign the draft, the cats all had a chill. The boys turned pale and ceased to laugh, 'cause this is a serious bill."[17]

There are several songs that mention the army camps where the soldiers were trained. One of these was pianist Roosevelt Sykes's November 1941 "Training Camp Blues." Sykes, like Fuller, expects to step into the absent soldiers' shoes and "carry their lovin' on."

> When you look in your mailbox, and find your questionnaire,
> If you pass examination, won't nothing help you but prayer.
>
> There's no need to worry, hate to leave your happy home,
> Because there'll be someone left behind, to carry all of your lovin' on.
>
> You may be mean as a lion, you may be humble as a lamb,
> Just take your mind off-a your wife, and put it on Uncle Sam.
>
> I want all of you draftees to put your mind on your training camp,
> So when you meet Hitler, your powder won't be damp.
>
> So just pack your suitcase, get ready to leave your mate,
> You know you got to go, and help save them United States.[18]

Employment was soaring during the wartime preparation. As we have seen in Sonny Boy Williamson's "War Time Blues" blacks were ready to fly fighter

Roosevelt Sykes, NBBO Blues Festival Amstelveen, 18 May 1974. Photo by Hans ten Have, from the collection of the author.

planes in dangerous missions, and jazz comedian Slim Gaillard was a member of the segregated squadron that flew on bomber escort duties. The navy, however, only recruited blacks as messmen. (Ironically black navy messman Dorie Miller was to become the first American war hero at Pearl Harbor.) Blacks enlisted at a rate "60 per cent above the proportion of the population."[19] Those who were selected were allocated to segregated units. In his 1941 "Uncle Sam Says" Josh White (cf. chapter 6) sums it all up:

> Well, airplanes flyin' 'cross the land and the sea,
> Everybody flyin' but a Negro like me.
> Uncle Sam says, "Your place is on the ground,
> When I fly my airplanes, don't want no Negro 'round."

The same thing for the navy, ships goes to sea,
All they got is a messboy's job for me.
Uncle Sam says, "Keep on your apron, son,
You know I ain't gonna let you shoot my big navy gun."

Got my long government letters, my time to go,
When I got to the army, found the same old Jim Crow.
Uncle Sam says, "Two camps for black and white,"
But when trouble starts, we'll all be in that same big fight.

If you ask me I think democracy is fine,
I mean democracy without the color line.
Uncle Sam says, "We'll live the American way";
Let's get together and kill Jim Crow today.

"Leadership is not imbedded in the negro race yet," Secretary of War Henry Stimson argued with the support of General George Marshall. He was convinced that desegregation would destroy morale.[20]

"Most big war plants had no blacks at all among their workers," James MacGregor Burns writes.[21] Your father might have given his life in Europe during World War I, but when you tried to find work in a defense factory you were told, "Black boy, nothing here for you." Bruce Bastin senses "the conscious hand of intellectual liberalism" in Josh White's 1941 "Defense Factory Blues,"[22] which he again cowrote with Waring Cuney (cf. chapter 6), but it expresses the painful reality:

Went to the defense factory, tryin' to find some work to do,
Had the nerve to tell me, "Black boy, nothing here for you."

My father died, died fighting 'cross the sea,
Mama said his dying never helped her or me.

I will tell you, brother, well it sure don't make no sense,
When a Negro can't work in the national defense.

I will tell you one thing: That bossman ain't my friend,
If he was, he'd give me some democracy to defend.

Mmm, mmm,
Mmm, mmm.

In the land of the free, called the home, home of the brave,
All I want is liberty, that is what I crave.

Uncle Sam had not called in vain. More than 3 million African Americans answered his call in 1940, and ultimately 1 million blacks served in the Second World War, "which approximated their ratio in the population as a whole."[23]

Uncle Sam had also called none too early. On 7 December 1941 Lt. Comdr. Mitsuo Fuchida's plans to surprise the United States Navy matured. Triumphantly he gave the secret signal: "Tora! Tora! Tora!"

The next month Leadbelly addressed himself to the "high authorities of the whole United States" in the unissued Library of Congress recordings "Dear Mr. President" & "President Roosevelt."

spoken: *Huddie Ledbetter, better known as Leadbelly, born in Louisiana.*
        And I'm talkin' directly, to the high authorities of the whole United States,
        Who's been tryin' to get Hitler and them to hesitate.
        And I wanna sing this song to the honorable, kind President Roosevelt.

        President Roosevelt been all over the United States,
        Tryin' to get Hitler to hesitate.

chorus: *About this war, yes, about this war!*

        President Roosevelt doin' all he can,
        Tryin' to get them Japanese to understand.

        President Roosevelt, he is mighty fine,
        Tryin' to get these Japanese, get that stuff off their minds.

        President Roosevelt said, "There will be no stormy weather,
        If everybody would stick together."

        President Roosevelt, he had the right mind,
        When he began to draft all these men, he was draftin' them in time.

        Was in nineteen hundred seventeen, it was awful mean,
        When they drafted mens, boys, there's some of them never been seen.

        President Roosevelt, he was mighty fine,
        Started draftin' these men, he was draftin' them just in time.

        If he hadn't started in time, he would have been behind,
        Everybody see now, that he had the right mind.[24]

PEARL HARBOR BLUES

Following Japan's occupation of French Indochina in July 1941, the United States put a full embargo on the sale of goods to Japan. This sanction was keenly felt because Japan imported 90 percent of its petroleum and gasoline from the United States.[1] In their search for alternative supplies, the Japanese turned their attention to the oil fields of the Dutch East Indies. On 16 October General Hideki Tojo became Japan's minister of war, army chief of staff and prime minister. A "hawk" like Tojo would never retreat from Indochina as the Americans demanded. Instead he prepared for a massive air attack on Pearl Harbor, the base of the American Pacific Fleet in Hawaii, commanded by Admiral Husband E. Kimmel and Lt. General Walter C. Short.

At 7:55 a.m. local time on 7 December 1941, the Japanese began "dropping bombs by the ton" as blues singer Peter "Doctor" Clayton (1898–1947) sang in his "Pearl Harbor Blues":

> December the seventh, nineteen hundred and forty-one,
> The Japanese flew over Pearl Harbor, dropping bombs by the ton.
>
> The Japanese is so ungrateful, just like a stray dog on the street,
> Well, he'll bite the hand that feeds him, soon as he get enough to eat.

> *Some say the Japanese is hard fighters, but any dummy ought to know,*
> *Even a rattlesnake won't bite you in your back, he will warn you before he strikes*
> *his blow.*

> *I turned on my radio, and I heard Mr. Roosevelt say,*
> *"We wanted to stay out of Europe and Asia, but now we all got a debt to pay."*

> *We even sold the Japanese brass and scrap iron, and it makes my blood boil in the*
> *vein,*
> *'Cause they made bombs and shells out of it, and they dropped them on Pearl*
> *Harbor just like rain.*

Clayton is outraged because of the unexpected nature of the attack and emphasizes the treachery by suggesting that the bombs that had killed the 1,177 Americans were made from scrap metal imported from the United States before the July embargo.

Clayton's song was a popular success, and was the basis of recordings made as late as 1961 by Sam "Lightnin'" Hopkins[2] and 1971 by Roy Dunn.[3] These artists were not the only ones to record blues about Pearl Harbor many years after the event. Ex-prize fighter "Champion" Jack Dupree, a blues pianist from New Orleans, recorded "Pearl Harbour Blues" in 1960 (the recording was made by British collector Francis Wilford-Smith, hence the English spelling of the title).

> *On December the seventh, in nineteen and forty-one,*
> *Well the Japanese bombed Pearl Harbor, and they used a Gatlin' gun.*

> *I remember so good, when I was walking down the street,*
> *When I heard the news, by people talkin' on the street.*

> *Well, I heard President Roosevelt, in his speech I heard what he say:*
> *"We're gonna hang on and fight back, until every man is free."*

> *Well, they started the draftin', from eighteen to forty-five,*
> *Lord, they caught me in between, and I never thought I'd ever be alive.*

> *But it didn't make no difference, didn't make no difference what people say,*
> *Yes, I had to go, I had to go 'most any day.*

> *I'm so glad, they won't have to use me today,*
> *They can do whatever they want, I'll be million miles away.*

Most Americans remembered where they were when the news of the attack on Pearl Harbor became known. Dupree says that he was walking in the street when he heard people talking about it. It is not surprising that Dupree's memory of the occasion was especially vivid, for Pearl Harbor would determine his life from 1941 to 1945, when he served in the United States Navy as a cook in the Pacific. He sings that he "was caught in between" when they were drafting "from eighteen to forty-five." Dupree is glad that the United States Army can't draft him anymore as he is now "million miles away." Largely to escape "Jim Crow," "Champion" Jack had settled in Europe in 1960, where he would stay until his death in 1992.

In February 1942 Lonnie Johnson recorded three songs about the draft on one day. One of these, "From 20 to 44,"[4] contains this stanza: "From eighteen to thirty-five, it didn't even cross my mind, but from twenty to forty-four, looks like everybody's got to go." The age limit for the draft had been extended when Pearl Harbor made a far greater number of servicemen necessary. Johnson was born in 1899, so the extension really did have an implication for him personally. In January 1942 Roosevelt ordered that the size of the army be increased to 3.6 million by the end of the year.[5]

Both Clayton and Dupree remembered the speech Roosevelt made in Congress the day after the attack. "Yesterday, December 7, 1941—a date which will live in infamy—the United States of America was suddenly and deliberately attacked by naval and air forces of the Empire of Japan," Roosevelt solemnly began after the applause had died down and he had slowly made his way towards the rostrum. Clayton remembers the president saying: "We wanted to stay out of Europe and Asia, but now we all got a debt to pay." In his momentous speech FDR reminded Congress that the United States was at peace with Japan and "was still in conversation with its Government." Dupree remembers Roosevelt saying: "We're gonna hang on and fight back, until every man is free." Dupree's paraphrase probably refers to the following line from the 8 December speech: "No matter how long it may take us to overcome this premeditated invasion, the American people in their righteous might will win through to absolute victory."[6]

The aftermath of Pearl Harbor was characterized by virulent anti-Japanese racism. The majority of the 127,000 people of Japanese descent living in America (many of them loyal American citizens) were placed in internment camps.[7] *Time* magazine instructed its readers in an article entitled "How to Tell Your Friends from the Japs,"[8] comic strips portrayed the Japanese as "teeth and spectacles," and schoolboys dreamed of fighting alongside John Wayne for the annihilation of "the murderous little ape-men."[9]

Before Pearl Harbor, there are no significant references to the Japanese in blues lyrics, but as a result of war fever they are often mentioned in the post-1941 period. In February 1942 Lonnie Johnson sang, "Every Jap I kill, there'll be peace for your poor little mind, I know I can't kill them all, but I'll give them a heck of a time."[10] Another Johnson song recorded the same day ended, "Baby, please wait for me, I'll soon be back to you, If I can't bring you a Jap, I'll bring you back a head or two."[11]

The Japanese attack seems to have made quite an impression on the members of the big band led by Lucky Millinder (1900–1966), who were playing for a dance, probably in New York's Savoy Ballroom, on the very Sunday when the news came through that Pearl Harbor had been bombed. On their live recording "Let Me Off Uptown," there is an Associated Press newsflash: "President Roosevelt decided today, after Japan's attack on Pearl Harbor and Manila, to call an extraordinary meeting of the cabinet for 8:30 p.m. tonight, and to have Congressional leaders of both parties join that conference at 9:00 p.m."[12] The most violently anti-Japanese lyrics were probably those sung in February 1942 by Trevor Bacon, one of the vocalists with the Millinder band. "We're Gonna Have to Slap the Dirty Little Jap" gives these black artists the chance to perpetrate some racist attitudes on their own account—an unfortunate but understandable reaction.

chorus: *We're gonna have to slap,*
           The dirty little Jap,
           And Uncle Sam's the guy who can do it.

           We'll skin the streak of yellow,
           From this sneaky little fellow,
           And he'll think a cyclone hit him when he's through it.

           We'll take this double-crosser to the old woodshed,
           We'll start on his bottom and go to his head.
           When we get through with him, he'll wish that he was dead,
           We've gotta slap the dirty little Jap.

           The Japs and all their hooey,
           Will be changed into chop suey,
           And the risin' sun will set when we get through it.

Their alibi for fighting is to save their face,
For ancestors waiting in celestial space.
We'll kick their precious face,
Down to that other place,
We've gotta slap the dirty little Jap.

We'll murder Hirohito,
Massacre that slob Benito,
Hang 'em with that Schicklgruber[13] when we're through it.

We'll search the highest mountains to the tallest tree,
To build us a hangin' post for the evil three,
We'll call in all our neighbors, let them know they're free,
We've gotta slap the dirty little Jap.

According to the Millinder band, the war hero "who slapped the Japs right down to their size" was General Douglas MacArthur. "Fightin' Doug MacArthur" was also recorded on 18 February 1942, five days before MacArthur was ordered by Roosevelt to break through the Japanese lines and escape from the Philippines he had tried to save. The lyricist clearly was not expecting this outcome, exhorting "Doug" to "dig in."[14]

In July 1941 MacArthur had become commander of the Philippines, a base from which Japan could be bombed after a Japanese attack. Only nine hours after Pearl Harbor, the Japanese destroyed more than half of MacArthur's air force. Roosevelt biographer Ted Morgan calls MacArthur's defeat in the Philippines "more crushing than Pearl Harbor, though never investigated."[15] Because of this defeat, the United States lost the Philippines, and the fall of British Malaya and Burma, and of the Dutch East Indies with its rich oil fields, became inevitable. Lucky Millinder's song shows how potent MacArthur's image as a war hero was. Roosevelt, aware of political realities, awarded him the Medal of Honor despite his defeat, but fired Commander Short and Commander Kimmel, making them the scapegoats for Pearl Harbor.[16]

In February 1941 the New York-based Selah Jubilee Singers recorded a song called "What a Time," which formed the basis of their May 1942 recording entitled "Wasn't That an Awful Time at Pearl Harbor." The song was composed by the tenors Thurman Ruth, John Ford and Nathaniel Townsley.

Wasn't that an awful time at Pearl Harbor? What a time, what a time!
When the Japs took us by surprise,

Three thousand men, children, lost their lives,
Wasn't that an awful time at Pearl Harbor? What a time, what a time!

chorus: *Just remember Pearl Harbor, all the time, all the time!*
When the Japs took us by surprise,
Three thousand men, children, lost their lives,
Just remember Pearl Harbor, all the time, all the time!

Well, stop, great God, and listen to me,
I wanna tell you 'bout a tragedy,
Read your papers and read them well,
You know the story I'm goin' to tell.
One Sunday morning 'bout seven o'clock,
They tell me Pearl Harbor did reel and rock.
The bombers came over and filled the sky,
The nation was angry, somebody had to die.
Enemy came in as a thief,
Left a many a heart in grief.
Men didn't have time to repent,
Souls went-a rushin' to judgment.

As the ships were struck and burst into flame,
Tell me men called on my God's name,
Cryin', "Ho, savior, don't pass me by,
Oh, Lord, well I hear you cryin',
Oh Lord, oh, someone's dyin',
Oh Lord, what will the punishment be?"

Well, they called on God, they called Him loud,
"Lord, have mercy, don't let me die."
God in the heaven had a man prepared,
His name was MacArthur, the chief of staff.
Like old Moses, in the days of old,
He'll stop the Japs, and stop them cold.
God in victory and you must win,
Don't stop fightin' until the end.[17]

Like Moses drowning the Egyptians in the Red Sea, the chief of staff will stop
the Japs with God's help. When the song was recorded in May 1942, MacArthur
had been in Australia since 11 March, after his painful defeat in and retreat from

the Philippines, but his popular image as a heaven-sent war hero had not been damaged.

An augmented version of the song was recorded as "Pearl Harbor—Parts 1 & 2" in June 1947 by the Chicago-based Soul Stirrers, with a superb gospel guitarist, Brother Willie Eason.

chorus: *Then, what a time (my Lord), oh, what a time (my Lord),*
          Eh, then, what a time, great God almighty, now, what a time!

> *Well, hello folks, how have you been?*
> *I've been away, but I'm back again.*
> *Been doing my bit in the gatherin' scraps,*
> *To buy a bond just to sink a Jap.*
> *I'm willing to have, eh, my sandwich little(r),*
> *By so doin' we did whip Hitler.*
> *Wake up, folk, and buy a bond,*
> *That-a will help the boys across the pond.*

> *Well, you read your papers and read them well,*
> *You'll know about the story that I'm going to tell.*
> *The year of nineteen forty-one,*
> *The Second World War had just begun.*
> *Old Hitler from Berlin stretched out his paw,*
> *Brought the European countries into war.*
> *Eh, Hitler himself he went out to plan,*
> *In some little place they call "No Man's Land."*
> *He told his men, said, "You need not fear,*
> *And I myself will be the engineer."*
> *Have a little patience, let me tell you the news:*
> *First thing he did, he put out the Jews.*
> *Next thing he did, to the European land,*
> *Took many small nations under his command.*
> *Then him and France, they began to fight,*
> *He taken beautiful Paris late one night.*

> *Eh, old Japan with the little sharp eye,*
> *Pretended that he wasn't on either side.*
> *He came over here, in the United States,*
> *So he and Mr. Roosevelt could communicate.*

He did not act like a man would argue,
He slipped around and bombed Pearl Harbor.

Well, great God almighty, what an awful sound,
Oh, how those bombs kept a-hittin' the ground.
The people didn't have time to repent,
Souls went a-leavin' in the judgment.
The women and the children began to cry,
"Lord, help me, don't let me die."
They called on God, called him loud,
Seemed as though a man came from the cloud.
The man who came, he was well prepared:
General Douglas MacArthur, the chief of staff.
He reminded me of Moses in the days of old,
He said, "Stop those Japs, we're knockin' 'em cold,
God's on our side, we gonna win,
We gonna keep on fightin' until the end."

Well, old Great Britain got troubled in mind,
Was sixty-five thousand on the firing line.
Old Great Britain sent out a cry,
For the United States to send supplies.
Our vessels got loaded and started across,
Next thing we heard our vessels were lost.
This caused America to get displeased,
Old Adolf Hitler tried to rule the sea.
An' we sent him a message right straight from home,
Said, "Man, you'd better leave our vessels alone."

When the war was on, I couldn't joyride,
They rationed my gas, rationed my tires.
Told me over thirty-five was against the law,
Had to save on my rubber, just to win the war.
Sweet in my coffee, wasn't sweet enough,
Men wearin' our pants, we couldn't have no cuffs.
Your ration books was numbered one and two,
They were covered with stamps, red, white and blue.
We had to count those points, count 'em every week,
If we would lose that book, we couldn't get no meat.

Well, nineteen hundred and forty-one,
The Second World War had just begun.
In nineteen hundred and forty-two,
They called for brothers and fathers too.
In nineteen hundred and forty-three,
They called for you and they called for me.
In nineteen hundred and forty-four,
That's when they called for more and more.
Nineteen hundred and forty-five,
I would tell you about it, but I don't wanna lie.
The war is over, the battle is won,
Those Japs couldn't take that Atomic Bomb.

This version borrows six couplets from the Selah Jubilee Singers recording, but adds no fewer than thirty-two new couplets, turning the song into a veritable history of the Second World War.

"Oh, What a Time" was recorded as late as 1961 by Philadelphia blues and gospel guitarist Blind Connie Williams (born c. 1915). Williams first sang twelve couplets borrowed from the Soul Stirrers, in which he wrongly identified Tojo as Roosevelt's guest. Japan is here personified by its prime minister from 1941 to 1944, General Hideki Tojo, although, contrary to the song, Tojo never visited the United States; before Pearl Harbor negotiations between the two countries were carried out by Secretary of State Cordell Hull and Ambassador Admiral Kichisaburo Nomura on behalf of the Japanese government. (Tojo resigned in 1944, was sentenced to death by the International Court for Important War Crimes in Tokyo and hanged on 12 November 1948.) The final ten couplets are of Williams's own making:

spoken: *What a time we was livin' in, when they bombed Pearl Harbor!*

chorus: *Well, what a time, well, what a time,*
           Well, what a time, great God almighty, tell me what a time!

           In the year of nineteen forty-one,
           Second World War had just begun.
           Hitler from Berlin stretched out his paw,
           Brought the other countries into the war.
           He himself went out to plan,
           In some old place they call "No Man's Land."

Told his men, said, "You need not fear,
Gonna be that engineer."

Won't you gather around? Tell you the news:
First thing he did, they got rid of the Jews.
Next thing he did, to the European land,
Took small countries under his command.
Germany and France began to fight,
Took beautiful Paris late one night.
Great Britain had trouble in mind:
Many men on the firing line.

Old Japan with a little sharp eye,
Pretended not to be on either side.
Tojo came to the United States,
Him and Mr. Roosevelt communicate.
He didn't act like a man would argue,
Snuck around and he bombed Pearl Harbor.
I don't know, but I've been told,
How Pearl Harbor's airbase got stole.
In and around the Pacific, boys,
Different men was declarin' our loss.
Some were high, some were low,
Some got sent a many mile or more.

Well, they did not fly that dreadful day,
But those old Japs stepped on their way.
What they did in the war was right,
Didn't have much of a chance to fight.
Some were smart and some were dumb,
That's how Pearl Harbor's base got bombed.
They bombed those ships right under their belt,
I could see what the captains felt.
Mother got the news, know she cried,
Wanted his letter, before he died.
We, true Americans, don't need to fear,
'Cause Jesus gonna be our engineer.
If you wanna help out Uncle Sam,
Save your pennies and buy defense stamps.[18]

As is also shown by Buster "Buzz" Ezell's August 1943 "Soldier Boy Blues,"
Roosevelt's tough political skills and strategic vision were held in high esteem by
the blues and gospel singers.

> The only way we can save our country, that is: let's go fight,
> And I declare, we'll do the thing that's right.
>
> I've got my questionnaire, it leads me in the war,
> If I'd be a murderer, I wouldn't break the county law.
>
> The airplanes crossin' the water, ninety-nine miles in the air,
> All these soldiers sure got to land over there.
>
> Now, bye, bye, mama and papa, don't you worry and cry,
> You always know, you know I was born to die.

spoken: Lordy, Lord!

> The only way we can save our country, that is: let's go fight,
> And I declare we'll do the thing that's right.
>
> Uncle Sam got a plenty money, if it all was stacked in piles,
> I believe to my soul, it would touch the skies.
>
> Roosevelt is a mighty Christian man, he's trying to do the things that's right.
> Old Hitler's slippin' 'round, trying to get to stealin' by night.
>
> He fought all of our fifth army, thought it was wishing us well,
> MacArthur's boys is ready to give him—, ha-ha-ha!
>
> Hitler, he's a mighty smart man, he thinks he knows it all,
> But when he come to find out, he'll be lowest of all.
>
> He's shootin' bombs and machine guns, makes a mighty loud sound,
> He's destroyin' a many people, miles and miles around.
>
> Now open up your schools and churches, let's go down in prayer,
> Could be hundreds and thousands, will be saved over there.[19]

Buster "Buzz" Ezell was an old, crippled guitarist from Georgia, who often
played with a harmonica fixed in a rack around his neck. He was the most frequent guest at a unique series of annual festivals of "old time music" organized
by Fort Valley State College, a black educational establishment founded in 1895.
Fort Valley State College had first organized a "Ham and Egg Show" in 1915.[20]

Ezell won several prizes and, in 1941 and 1943, nineteen recordings were made of him by the Library of Congress. Bruce Bastin reports that Ezell also played at the festivals of 1942, 1944, 1945, 1951, 1952 and 1955.[21] Bastin quotes the titles of songs Ezell sang on 30 March 1951 from one of the incomplete registration files: "The Story of Truman and Staff," "Great Things are Happening in Korea,"[22] "Boll Weevil the Farmers Trouble," and "A Robber of the First National Bank 1951," indicating that he had a strong penchant for topical and political song material.

Another example of Buster "Buzz" Ezell's 1943 Fort Valley performances is "Do Right By My Country," a religiously framed patriotic call to help "set this country free," which in passing calls attention to the rationing of meat and lard.[23]

One of the strangest titles ever given to a blues song is "Junian's, A Jap's Girl Christmas for His Santa Claus." The artist was Willie "61" Blackwell, who was recorded by Alan Lomax in Arkansas in July 1942. An account of the extraordinary circumstances under which Blackwell's song was recorded is given in Lomax's *The Land Where the Blues Began*. In order to make field recordings with the minimum of interference from the white establishment, Lomax had learned to pay formal calls on the mayor or the local music professor first. In Memphis in 1942, Lomax neglected to do so, and the Memphis police arrested the "nigger lover" who was associating with William Brown and Willie Blackwell. When Lomax was allowed to go, he returned to the two blues singers, and to keep out of trouble he took them with him to an Arkansas plantation, "across the river from Memphis." Lomax bought a jug of "country moonshine" and passed it around. Willie Blackwell, who had made eight commercial recordings for Victor in Chicago in July 1941,[24] was afraid to record as he believed he was still under contract to that company.

In his spoken preamble, Blackwell refers to the encounter with the Memphis police, and is indeed afraid that the Library of Congress recordings will cause difficulties when he tries to make a commercial record of the song (he never did have another commercial session, in the event).

spoken: *Well, I'm, I'm gonna sing, I'll tell you what I might sing. I might sing one of my little old favorite songs. Now, you tell me this won't give me no, no holdout. And, eh, it is just a record of my knowledge of, eh, the Japs, that I'm gonna sing now. But now I don't, now, look, I'm gonna look for you if. I might be just like the police was on you, if it be any hinder for this. 'Cause I'm gonna record it, you understand what I'm talkin' about? Well, all right.*

This is "Junior, A Jap's Skull Christmas for his Santa Claus."
'Cause I'm gonna record this number, you understand? But I'm just singin' this for
you. Is that all right now? I'm just gonna try this number just to see. It's the onliest
one that I am gonna try. But this is one of my recordings, because I'm an American
citizen.

Goodbye, I got to leave you, I've got to fight for America, you, and my boy,
Well, well, you can look for a Jap's skull Christmas, ooh, baby, for Junior's Santa
Claus.

If I just make it to our great general, Mr. MacArthur, the world knows he's a hero
of war,
That's where I will get my instructions, well, well, I'm sure that Junior will get his
Santa Claus.

Yes, when Junior starts to teethin', baby, please write to me,
Well, well, I'm gonna send him a Jap's tooth, so that he can cut his with ease.

When he start to setting lonely, teach him this for me,
To honor the land and laws of America, his dad is going to fight for his liberty.

spoken: *Well, all reet! Well, all reet then. What's to say brother?*

May be two or three summers, yes, and it may be two or three falls,
But if you no more see me, baby, just realize that I went down for America, you
and my boy.[25]

His soldier father will send Junior a Jap's tooth to ease the pains of teething
(presumably by sympathetic magic or "conjure"). The sending of a tooth probably refers to the practice of both Japanese and United States soldiers of extract-
ing gold teeth from enemy corpses.

The title of this song should probably be understood as "Junior, A Jap's Skull
Christmas for His Santa Claus." Here "Christmas" means "at Christmas time"
and "Santa Claus" is "a gift from Santa Claus."[26]

Many of the songs about Pearl Harbor discussed above also contain references to General MacArthur. For the president, MacArthur was "a potential
Mussolini" and "one of the most dangerous persons" in the United States.[27]
MacArthur, who had presidential aspirations himself, had criticized his "left-
wing" President in correspondence which Congressman Albert L. Miller made
public in April 1944.[28] In 1933 Roosevelt had warned the general in terms that
MacArthur would never forget: "Douglas, I think you are our best general, but

I believe you would be our worst politician."[29] For Willie Blackwell and many other blues singers, General MacArthur was simply the great American war hero who had pledged that he would return to the Philippines. Eddie James "Son" House (1902–1988), one of the most important Mississippi blues singers, knew that MacArthur was "not afraid." In his patriotic waltz "American Defense (This War Will Last You for Years)" House predicts that MacArthur will kill so many of the enemy that "it won't be enough Japs, to shoot a little game of craps."

> Mmm mmm, mmm, mmm.

chorus: No use to sheddin' no tears,
> No use to havin' no fears ,
> This war may last you for years.

> American defense,
> Will learn you some sense,
> Just how to take care of your boys.
> You must raise more produce,
> For more 'ssentially use,[30]
> Just to save all your worries and toils.

> Well, the red, white and blue,
> That represents you,
> You ought to do everything that you can.
> Buyin' war savin' stamps,
> Young men, go to the camps,
> Be brave and take a stand.

> Don't let troublesome times,
> All upset your minds,
> So you won't know just what to do.
> Keep pushin', keep shovin',
> Don't be angry: be lovin',
> Be faithful and honest and true.

> You can say, "Yes" or "No,"
> But we got to win this war,
> Because Gentle McCarthy's not afraid.
> It won't be enough Japs,

To shoot a little game of craps,
Because the biggest of them all will be dead.

This war sure do bother,
Our mother and father,
Our sisters and brothers too.
Dear friends and relations,
This war's in creation,
Don't let this worry you.

Douglas MacArthur did return to the Philippines; landing at Leyte on 20 October 1944, "The Lion of Luzon" liberated the Philippines.

When FDR suddenly died on 12 April, there was still a war to win, so Harry Truman certainly needed the support of all Americans. He had been vice president of the United States for only three months. FDR had seldom delegated any of his responsibilities to his vice presidents, who were expected to do little more than manage the Senate. Truman was the least prepared of them all.

A few weeks later, on 7 May 1945, the German army surrendered unconditionally, but the war with Japan was not over. In his 2 July 1945 "We Got to Win," Sonny Boy Williamson was convinced that the United States would "whip them Japanese too," even if General Douglas MacArthur, commander of the American forces in Southeast Asia, needed strong reinforcements to beat the Japanese. Given his age at the time, Williamson's second verse may well be autobiographical.

Now, the United States did it once, and I just knowed they was goin' to do it again,
Now, when the Germans first started the war, I just knowed them United States
was gonna win.

I didn't pass in the army, but I'm really doing everything I can,
Now, I just keep my fingers crossed, because the United States has just got to win.

I didn't mind going to the army, if that was all that we had to do,
Now, we have already whupped the Germans, and we have got to go and whup
them Japanese too.

You know, the president asked General MacArthur, "How many more ships do you
need?"
"You have to find me about a couple of more hundred ships, and just a few more
boys to be followin' after me."

Harry Truman had been president of the United States for only half an hour, when Secretary of State Henry Stimson handed him a memorandum that read: "Within four months we shall in all probability have completed the most terrible weapon ever known in human history, one bomb which could destroy a whole city."[31] Sonny Boy Williamson, less well informed, foresaw a long naval and land campaign. His recording was not issued at the time, because President Truman decided to drop atomic bombs on Japan. After Hiroshima and Nagasaki had been annihilated on 6 and 9 August, and the Japanese finally surrendered, the formal surrender took place aboard the U.S.S. *Missouri* on 2 September 1945, with MacArthur presiding.[32]

The blues from this period gives evidence of anti-Japanese racism. This phenomenon started immediately after Pearl Harbor and ended as soon as the war did. The need for image over reality, which is implicit in many of the recordings discussed in this chapter, was necessary to keep the home front motivated.[33]

HITLER AND HELL

When in 1933 Franklin Delano Roosevelt was inaugurated as president of the United States, Adolf Hitler became Reichskanzler of Germany. Twelve tumultuous years later, in April 1945, Roosevelt suffered a fatal stroke and Hitler committed suicide. The two most powerful men on earth never met, but they were clearly intrigued by each other's characters.

Classicist Eric Havelock analyzed the fact that their voices could now be heard all over the world: "Two political personalities totally opposed in temperament and values but both masters of myth-making played a key role in ushering in the new dimension of the spoken word. In their day Franklin Roosevelt and Adolf Hitler embodied power and persuasion over men's minds which was electronically transmitted and which proved functionally essential to the kind of political influence that they wielded. Their prototypes were the minstrels and reciters of the oral ages of the past, but their oral power now extended beyond the range of any previously imagined eloquence."[1]

Historians have noted the superficial similarities between the two leaders: "Both liked to talk, to dwell on old times with old friends, to act out roles, to be flattered, to play off friends as well as enemies against each other."[2] Both men had "vaulted to power on the wave of despair that accompanied the Great Depression. Both expressed the determination to lift their people out of the malaise of defeat and to restore the national will. Both made eloquent appeals to the emotions, both were daring gamblers."[3]

More significant, however, were the differences between them. Roosevelt had a Harvard education and came from an upper-class background. Hitler, whose father was a shoemaker, never completed his secondary education. They were antagonists in a battle between good and evil, one which took place on a scale the world had never witnessed before.

On 15 May 1933 Roosevelt sent an appeal for disarmament to fifty-four national capitals. It met with almost unanimous applause. Even Hitler called Roosevelt's message "a ray of comfort for all who wish to cooperate in the maintenance of peace." The world sighed in relief and Roosevelt thought he had averted the threat of war.[4]

Six years later, on 14 April 1939, with Germany armed to the teeth, and Austria and the Sudetenland "annexed," Roosevelt reminded Hitler in vain of his promise not to wage war.[5] The message from the White House made Mussolini and Göring speculate that Roosevelt's polio had led to a brain disorder.[6] A fortnight later, Hitler struck back in a sarcastic two-hour speech, which was broadcast by every major network in the United States. Hitler called Roosevelt's request for an assurance not to go to war "rank frauds and gross untruths" and recalled that Roosevelt "had stepped to the head of one of the largest and wealthiest States in the world. . . . I, who twenty-one years ago was an unknown worker and soldier of my people, have attained this, Mr. Roosevelt, by my own energy."[7]

One year later, in August 1940, after Germany had conquered France, Denmark, Belgium and the Low Countries, Huddie Ledbetter recorded "The Roosevelt Song" for the Library of Congress. The first questions were asked by Elizabeth Lomax, Alan's wife:

spoken: *I think, eh, the Roosevelt song next. Is that, eh, a political song, Huddie, or is it a blues, or what?*

I just made it. It's, it's not a blues, it's, eh, something like, eh, something like a political song.

Is that about President Roosevelt?

Well, it's a good one, it's just a few words about him, how he been traveling around through the world, trying to get peace, you know, amongst people, eh, President Roosevelt. Now this here's a little number I made about the war. And President Roosevelt is such a fine man and he's been giving advices, and going all through the world, trying to make peace. And so I made just these little few words, just to show you how times is:

President Roosevelt went all over the United States,
Trying to get Hitler and Germany to hesitate,
About that war, about that war.

President Roosevelt is a mighty fine man,
He's been trying to get Hitler and Germany to understand,
About that war, oh, about that war.

It's about that war (6x.)

Way 'cross the ocean, thought I'd find a job,
Nothing but them Germanies, sitting on a log,
About that war, oh, about that war.

Way 'cross the ocean, far as I can see,
All the United States people, trying to get some peace,
About that war, oh, about that war.

It's about that war (6x.)

This is the first version of a song that Leadbelly was to record again in January 1942 as "Dear Mr. President" & "President Roosevelt." The later version, discussed in chapter 12, expressed satisfaction with the effects of the president's early draft measures. In this version Leadbelly explains how President Roosevelt traveled the United States "trying to get Hitler and Germany to hesitate." Leadbelly's tribute to his president is the first blues in which Hitler is mentioned.

In November 1940 Ernest Blunt, an obscure blues singer known as "the Florida Kid," recorded eight sides in Chicago. Blunt's "Hitler Blues" contains a carpe diem appeal to his girlfriend:

Well, baby, have you heard about Hitler, honey, do you care?
May be on the way to our country, may heavy-hit us here.

chorus: *Because old Hitler he's a bad man, trying to take every country he know,*
Well, before he take this country, woman, please be my so-and-so.

I done warned, I done told you, more than once or twice,
To bring me plenty lovin', before Hitler takes our lives.

Well, Hitler say he was a man, from his feet to his chest,
He don't bar nobody, but God and Death.

Hitler got his just-right tanks, his planes and his ships,
He get over your town, he'll let his big bomb slip.

Hitler say some of our peoples are white, says, some are brown and black,
But Hitler says all Americans to him look just alike.

Well, you better mind how you get drunk, be careful how you clown,
You may wake up some of these mornings, Hitler be wreckin' your town.

Alongside the humorous use of geopolitics in the service of seduction, "the Florida Kid" has serious points to make about Hitler, whose racism and megalomania have not escaped him. As James MacGregor Burns writes, Hitler "had only hatred and contempt for Americans, half Judaized, half Negrified, and certainly not a warrior race."[8] The threat of a German invasion was considered a realistic one. Roosevelt had driven this lesson home in his eighteenth fireside chat broadcast on 11 September 1941. Wearing a mourning band around his arm for the death of his mother four days earlier, Roosevelt said that Hitler's "intention has been made clear. The American people can have no further illusion about it. No tender whisperings of appeasers that Hitler is not interested in the Western hemisphere, no soporific lullabies that a wide ocean protects us from him, can long have any effect on the hard-headed, farsighted, and realistic American people."[9] There was no time to lose, Roosevelt argued, for "when you see a rattlesnake poised to strike, you do not wait until he has struck before you crush him."[10]

In May 1941, Hitler was planning operation Barbarossa ("The Germans must be prepared to crush Soviet Russia in a quick campaign").[11] In those days blues guitarist Frank Edwards (b. 1909) was making his first recordings in Chicago. Edwards's lyrics tend to have elliptical structures, and his personal grammar and obscure diction make them hard to fathom. In his "We Got to Get Together," the United States is still neutral, but Hitler has "got blood in his eyes":

spoken:　*Lord, have mercy!*

　　　　　Hitler's troublin' the world, got 'em disturbed,
　　　　　Uncle Sam better decide. He got blood in his eyes.

chorus:　*You've got to get together, got to get together,*
　　　　　Got to closen up together, Germans hand in hand.

Mussolini jumped back, up in the sack,
Hitler kicked him out, so he couldn't get back.

spoken: *Blow it, boy, long time! Lord, have mercy.*

Sam called the men out name by name,
He ain't together, but they're ready just the same.

Uncle Sam need the champ, still wearin' the belt,
A well-trained band, when you leave Camp Shelby.

spoken: *Blow it, Mr. Longtime Man! I've got to. . . .*

Say, I left my woman, standing in the door,
Crying, "Lord, have mercy, man, please, don't go."[12]

The stanza about Mussolini is rather obscure, but it might refer to Italy's futile attempt to conquer Greece on 28 October 1940, which caused great irritation in Berlin. Edwards is saying that Uncle Sam badly needs an army of well-trained soldiers. The soldiers are not yet fully trained ("He ain't together"), but they are "ready just the same." "Uncle Sam need a champ, still wearin' the belt" seems to refer obliquely to black boxer Joe Louis, who was world champion when Edwards sang his song, and the stanza uses boxing as a metaphor for the impending battle between the United States and Germany; Louis had beaten German boxer Max Schmeling on 22 June 1938.[13]

Blues singer Peter "Doctor" Clayton had a solution to the German threat. "Let me sneak in Hitler's bedroom with a razor in my hand," he sang in his July 1941 "'41 Blues":

War is raging in Europe, on the water, land and in the air,
Ooh, if Uncle Sammy don't be careful, we'll all soon be right back over there.

The radios and newspapers, they all force me to believe,
spoken: *(Well, all right!)*
Yeah, Hitler and Mussolini, they must have the snatchin' disease.

Ain't gonna be no peace in Europe, till we cut off Hitler's head,
Ooh, Mussolini have heart failure, when he hears Stalin is dead.

I hope Hitler catch consumption, I mean the galloping kind,
And Stalin catch the leprosy, Mussolini lose his mind.

This whole war would soon be over, if Uncle Sam would use my plan:

spoken: *(Knock me out, man!)*
          Ooh, let me sneak in Hitler's bedroom, with my razor in my hand.

spoken: *Hey my!*

Clayton's perspective on the war is an isolationist one; Hitler had invaded Russia eight days previously, on 22 June 1941, and the Russian Bear was about to become an ally of Britain and would soon receive lend-lease aid from the United States, but Clayton has not yet become the warlike patriot of his later "Pearl Harbor Blues." When harmonica player Bill "Jazz" Gillum (1904–1966) recorded the song as "War Time Blues" two days before Pearl Harbor, the uncomplimentary reference to Stalin was omitted.[14]

In the American mind Hitler became synonymous with Hell. Rev. J. M. Gates, who had been pastor of Mount Calvary, Rockdale Park, in Atlanta, Georgia, since 1914, made his last recordings in Atlanta's Kimball Hotel on 2 October 1941. As we have seen, Gates had a knack for topical sermons, and on this day his mind was on the war. The first sermon he preached for the RCA microphones that Thursday morning was entitled "Hitler and Hell":

> *I want to speak to you this morning from this subject: "Hitler and Hell."*
>
> *And when I speak and think about Hitler,*
> *I can't help but thinkin' about hell: "Hitler and Hell."*
> *They tell me that he's a man who lives in a storm.*
> *And have his elevator service to go from one station to another in his palace.*
> *I'm tellin' you this morning that he is the dictator of Germany.*
> *Hitler, you must come down, you must come down.*
> *I'm sayin' to you as you sit back in your easy chair, while men is dying on the battlefield.*
> *You can easy be star as the devil on earth: "Hitler and Hell."*
> *You that speak the policies for your country: "Hitler and Hell."*
> *You say, "Go," men must go; say, "Come," then they must come.*
> *You, if you order them, their necks separated from their bodies, it must be done.*
> *Hitler, you must come down!*
> *You, you're too high: there only one God!*
> *And you must come down.*
> *I'm thinkin' now of innocent children and women dyin' all over the land and country as you come crushin' through like the demon of hell on earth.*
> *Hitler, you must come down, soon, sooner or later, you must answer at the judgment bar.*

Hitler, God got his eyes on you, (2x)
Well, he sees all you do,
And he hears every word you say,
Hitler, God got his eyes on you.

You is a standin' library for your peoples in Germany.
You is a walkin' and talkin' encyclopedia for your peoples in Germany.
You must come down!

Gates's final remarkable image is one of the totalitarian leader as the only source of approved ideas for his people.

Four days after the bombing of Pearl Harbor, Hitler declared war on the United States in an address to the Reichstag: "I will pass over the insulting attacks made by this so-called President against me. That he calls me a gangster is uninteresting. After all, this expression was not coined in Europe, but in America, no doubt because such gangsters are lacking here. Apart from this, I cannot be insulted by Roosevelt, for I consider him mad, just as Wilson was. . . . First he incites war, then falsifies the causes, then odiously wraps himself in a cloak of Christian hypocrisy and slowly but surely leads mankind to war, not without calling God to witness the honesty of his attack—in the approved manner of an old Freemason."[15]

Now that war had been declared, Leadbelly spoke out on Hitler. The result was his January 1942 Library of Congress recording, "Mr. Hitler":

spoken: *Now this here, is about Mr. Hitler. Mr. Hitler's been a tough man. People asked me*
           to make a song about Mr. Hitler, about three years ago, but I didn't. Mr. Hitler has
           been struttin' his stuff, I think, long enough. Now this is a song about Mr. Hitler:

spoken: *Yes, this is 'bout him.*

           Hitler started out in nineteen hundred and thirty-two,
           When he started out, takin' the homes from the Jews.

           That's one thing Mr. Hitler did do wrong,
           When he started out, drivin' them Jews from their homes.

chorus: *We gonna tear Hitler down (3x), someday!*
           We gonna bring him to the ground (3x), someday!

           He says if God rule heaven, he's gonna rule the world,
spoken: *(He thinks so!)*
           But the American people say he will be shot down just like a squirrel.

>   Mr. Hitler we gonna tear your playhouse down,
> spoken: (Yes, we is!)
>   You been flyin' mighty high, but you's on your last go-'round.
>
>   He ain't no iron, and he ain't no solid rock,
>   But we American people say, "Mr. Hitler is got to stop!"
>
>   Mr. Hitler, he think he is so keen,
>   But the American people, say he's the biggest ole liar you ever seen.
>
> spoken: Yes, he is!
>
>   Mr. Hitler, he's nothing but an agitator,
>   An' he put them Japs out, they ain't nothing but a syndicator.[16]

In the late thirties Leadbelly had become part of a growing group of left-oriented folksingers, of whom Woody Guthrie and Josh White were the most prominent. Their radical protest songs drew the attention of the FBI Leadbelly felt comfortable among his musical friends, and started to follow Communist Party lines. This may explain why Leadbelly refused to sing about Hitler in 1939. The sentiments among his friends would have discouraged a song about Hitler during the period of the Nazi-Soviet pact.[17]

Leadbelly sings that Hitler "started out in 1932, takin' the homes from the Jews." Hitler actually assumed power in 1933, but the rhyme takes precedence. We have seen in chapter 3 that the Nazis often insinuated that the American president was a Jew himself. Hitler called Roosevelt a "half-caste" who behaved like a "tortuous, pettifogging Jew."[18] The final line of the song refers to the Japanese attack on Pearl Harbor. Leadbelly thinks the agitator Hitler incited the Japanese on their path of bloodshed as his agents ("he put them Japs out").

On 22 June 1941 the German army invaded Russia. By March 1943, Willie Johnson, the leader and baritone voice of the famous Golden Gate Quartet, had composed a song in which the gospel quartet praised Stalin, denigrated Hitler, and recounted some of the events of the Russian campaign:

> chorus: Well, now Stalin wasn't stallin',
>   When he told the Beast of Berlin,
>   That they'd never rest contented,
>   Till they had driven him from the land.
>   So he called the Yanks and English,
>   And proceeded to extinguish,

Der Führer and his vermin,
This is how it all began:

Now the Devil he was readin', in the Good Book one day,
How the Lord created Adam, to walk the righteous way.
And it made the Devil jealous, he turned green up to his horns,
And he swore by things unholy, that he'd make one of his own.
So he packed two suitcases, full of grief and misery,
And he caught the Midnight Special, goin' down in Germany.
Then he mixed his lies and hatred, with fire and brimstone,
Then the Devil sat upon it, that's how Adolf was born.
Now Adolf got the notion that he was the master race,
And he swore he'd bring new order, and put mankind in its place.
So he set his scheme in motion, and was winnin' everywhere,
Until he upped and got the notion for to kick that Russian bear.

Yep, he kicked that noble Russian, but it wasn't very long,
Before Adolf got suspicious, that he had done something wrong.
'Cause that Bear grabbed der Führer, and gave him an awful fight,
Seventeen months he scrapped der Führer, tooth and claw, day and night.

Then that bear smacked der Führer, with a mighty armored paw,
And Adolf broke all records, runnin' backwards to Kharkov.
Then Goebbels sent a message to the people everywhere,
That if they couldn't help the Führer, God, don't help that Russian Bear.[19]

Then this Bear calls on his buddy, the noble fightin' Yank,
And they set the Führer runnin', with their ships and planes and tanks.
Now der Führer's having nightmares, 'cause der Führer knows darn well,
That the Devil's done wrote the welcome, on his residence in—.

"The lyrics of 'Stalin Wasn't Stallin'' should help divest gospel of its unearned Uncle Tom image," Tony Heilbut comments.[20] Johnson's composition certainly is quite ingenious. The Bear was stronger than the Beast and gave the Führer an awful beating that lasted for "seventeen months." When Marshall Paulus capitulated after the battle of Stalingrad on 3 February 1943, twenty months had elapsed since the German invasion. As the Russians had needed a few months to prepare their counteroffensive, a period of seventeen months is quite accurate for the smacking with the "mighty armored paw."

War worker receiving training in the machine-shop practice at a National Youth Administration work center, Brooklyn, New York, August 1942. Photo by Fritz Henle, reproduced from the collections of the Library of Congress.

The same day that the Golden Gate Quartet recorded their accomplished tribute to Stalin in New York City, the Library of Congress set up recording equipment at Fort Valley State College. They had already recorded Buster "Buzz" Ezell (cf. chapter 13) at the 1941 Festival of Old Time Music. Ezell now sang a long ballad about "Roosevelt and Hitler." *Life* magazine quoted seven lines of its lyrics in an article about food production by Negro farmers:[21]

Part One

spoken: *Buster Ezell: "The story of Roosevelt and Hitler and the war fight, nineteen and*
              forty-two":

chorus: *Strange things are happening in this land, (2x)*
              The war is going on, causing many hearts to mourn,
              There's strange things a-happening in this land.

              You may read the Holy Bible, where Matthew does record,
              There are pestilences, earthquakes, and also rumors of war,
              There you can see,

The Bible do fulfil,
There's strange things a-happening in this land.

Nations against nations, are rising in this land,
Kingdoms against kingdoms, you just can't understand,
But you need not to be surprised,
For the time is drawing nigh,
There's strange things a-happening in this land.

We have read also of famines, shall come in this land,
If you notice closely, you'll see and understand,
Provisions are so high,
Till we can't hardly buy,
There's strange things a-happening (in this land).

Roosevelt with Hitler, he tried to live in peace,
But old Hitler he's destroying, every vessel he can see,
He's treating us so mean,
With his dreadful submarines,
There's strange things a-happening in this land.

Hitler, he is fighting, he is making every charge,
Trying to win this victory, so the land might be enlarged,
He's fighting everywhere,
On the land and in the air,
There's strange things a-happening (in this land).

Some said Roosevelt was a coward, they said he would not fight,
But he was just only was a-waiting, till he got things fixed up right,
When he made it up in his mind,
He got on the firing line,
There's strange things a-happening in this land.

Hitler tried to fool the Negroes, by saying they ought not to fight,
Said, "You have no home in the country, no flag and equal rights,"
But the niggers they knewed the best,
Their deeds did prove the test,
There's strange things a-happening . . .

Part Two

When Uncle Sam called to them, they answered, "Here are we,
To perform a soldier's duty, whenever we may be,"

They answered true and brave,
If the trenches makes their grave,
There's strange things a-happening in this land.

Hitler called these Japanese, they could not help from crying,
Said, "If you go up against that race, you're coming out behind,
If you try to take their place,
You cannot keep from dying,"
There's strange things a-happening in this land.

Hitler told his wife at the supper table, he dreamt a mighty dream,
Said, "If I cut out these submarines, I'll save a many a men,
But if I fight and if I win,
I will gain a many a frien',"
There's strange things a-happening in this land.

Now, sinners, God's power, you just can't understand,
Whole world will tremble, from the doing of His hand,
It's beyond the human sight,
But all He does is right,
There's strange things a-happening in this land.[22]

According to Ezell the war had been predicted in the Bible. He bases his assumption on the eschatological words of Jesus in Matthew 24:6–7: "And ye shall hear of wars and rumours of wars: see that ye be not troubled: for all *these things* must come to pass, but the end is not yet. For nation shall rise against nation, and kingdom against kingdom: and there shall be famines, and pestilences, and earthquakes, in divers places." For Ezell "the time is drawing nigh"; the end of the world is near. By quoting Hitler, who is supposed to have said that blacks "have no home in the country, no flag and equal rights," Ezell has found a neat way to make his point to white Americans while remaining patriotic. Ezell even pictures Hitler at the supper table with his "wife" (Hitler married his mistress, Eva Braun, one day before their joint suicide on 30 April 1945).

Buster Ezell uses the original chorus and the second verse of a song that harked back to the Great War, a version of which was collected c. 1920–22.[23]

After Mussolini had failed in Greece and North Africa, the Allied forces invaded Italy on 11 July 1943. A fortnight later the king of Italy dismissed Mussolini, who was taken prisoner. "Mussolini got scared and cut out, didn't he?"

harmonica blower Sonny Boy Williamson asked in his December 1944 "Check Up on My Baby":

> I've got to check up on my baby, I've got to see how my baby been gettin' along,
> Now, and I'm goin' and fight now for our country, that'll keep Mussolini from treatin'
> my baby wrong.

spoken: *Mussolini got scared and cut out, didn't he?*

> Now, don't you know what Hitler told President Roosevelt?
> Said: "We made the fastest airplane in the world."
> Ah, President Roosevelt said, "I think you're telling a lie, brother,"
> Said, "We got a airplane that's built up like a squirrel,
> And I sent my boys to check up on their baby, you know,
> Ah, my boys must see how their baby been gettin' along,"
> He said, "If you help me win this war, that'll keep Hitler from treatin' your baby
> wrong."

> Now, don't you know, my baby, she can't even write, and my baby can't even send
> no telegram,
> I've got to check up on my baby, I know my baby wanna know just where I am.
> And I've got to go and check up on my baby, I've got to see how my baby been
> gettin' along,
> Well, now we just got to win this war, I swear because they don't mean my baby no
> harm.

spoken: *Oh, yeah!*

> Well, now, and I've got something to tell you, baby, that I know you really, really
> can't do,
> I know you can't love me, and you wanna love some other man too.
> But I've got to go and check up on you, baby, I've got to see, baby, how you've been
> gettin' along,
> Well, now and if you help me, baby, I swear I won't never do you no harm.[24]

Williamson recorded three songs about the war in which airplanes play an important part. The first of these is "War Time Blues," in which he imagines himself the pilot of a war plane spying for guns hidden in the wood (see chapter 12). The second is "Win the War Blues." Sonny Boy's plane is now identified as a *Thunderbolt*[25] and the enemy are the Japanese "who are so rotten, that I just love to see them die." In this song, Sonny Boy wants to use the machine gun hidden in the woods himself "to show old man Hitler, that Sonny Boy don't mean him no good."[26] "Check Up on My Baby" was the third. With pilots like Sonny Boy, and airplanes like the *Thunderbolt*, Hitler does not stand a chance.[27]

In this chapter several examples of outbursts against Hitler by singers whose names were known dramatically illustrate the point that he (like Mussolini and, earlier, the kaiser) was one of the very few whites whom it was safe for blacks to criticize. "Hitler Toast" is the most outspoken such black tirade on record; the toaster understandably had to remain anonymous.

> *Gettin' a little tight! Here's to Hitler and his . . .*
> *In his last hitch,*
> *We's after his ass, the son of a bitch.*
> *We're gonna cut off his dick,*
> *And split his bag,*
> *Gonna wipe our asses with his own flag.*
> *We're gonna bang-hole his wife and cuss his luck,*
> *For not havin' no women for us to fuck.*
> *We're gonna eat his bread and drink his gin,*
> *Gonna fuck every woman in old Berlin.*
> *We're gonna skin his dick like a rotten banana,*
> *Till his asshole whistle "Star Spangled Banner."*
> *We're gonna walk in his palace and shit on his floor,*
> *Hang "Old Glory" up over his door.*
> *So here's to Hitler and his last hitch,*
> *May his ass rot off with the seven-years' itch.*
> *When the war is over, we'll sail back en masse,*
> *And tell all the boys how Hitler kissed our ass.*

That a toast with an abusive text like this was recorded at all in 1942 is remarkable. The toaster even says that black soldiers will humiliate and castrate Hitler (something that whites normally did to blacks) and will get away with raping his wife and all the (white) women in Berlin! Even white Americans would have found this rather disturbing in 1942, although they hated Hitler as well. To an African American, ideally with a drink in his hand, a toast often provided a way to vent frustration by the use of abusive language in rhyme, more often than not loaded with sexual references.[28]

Blacks were no longer willing to postpone their demands until the end of the war, as W. E. B. Du Bois had done in the Great War. In the Second World War, they tried to achieve a "double *v*": victory over the Nazi foe abroad and victory over racism at home. The 14 March 1942 issue of the *Chicago Defender* shows a full-page advertisement of a blindfolded Justitia and a large *V*: "Remember Pearl Harbor . . . and Sikeston Too!" Japan and Sikeston ("a capital in the last, foul stronghold of barbarism in the U. S. A.") both must fall (an African American was lynched after an alleged attempted attack on a white woman in Sikeston, Missouri, in January 1942). In Europe the black soldiers fought the racist foe, but there was hardly any integration of the black forces and white forces in their own American army. Only when infantry shortages became dramatic in the winter of 1944–45 did General Eisenhower allow some volunteer replacements in white units. Back home after the war black soldiers refused to accept discrimination any longer. There was no going back: blacks' participation in the United States Army in World War II meant the end of segregation.

WIN THE WAR

Pick up the newspaper: it's war . . . all over," Rev. J. M. Gates preached in October 1941. We "dream about the war," and "our daily thought is on war." In his recording "When the War Is Over," he speculated about what would happen next.[1] "The worst war is the war in the home," Gates observed. When the war is over "the union shall be back in the old home again." Families had been disrupted and love relationships had been broken because of the war. Many blues songs were recorded which lament (or celebrate) the absence of a large part of the male population during the Second World War.[2] However, Roosevelt also needed "manpower" at home during this time. In the thirties he had struggled to find "jobs for workers," now he had to find "workers for jobs."[3]

Following the attack on Pearl Harbor, America armed itself to the teeth. In his State of the Union address, delivered to Congress on 6 January 1942, Roosevelt unfolded his plans for wartime production in 1943: 125,000 planes, 75,000 tanks, 35,000 anti-aircraft guns and 10,000,000 tons of shipping.[4] To complete this program massive amounts of aluminium, steel, rubber and petroleum were needed, which would inevitably lead to a severe shortage at home.

Anthropologist Margaret Mead wrote that one of the nation's greatest strengths was in the American character: "To win this war, we need the impassioned effort of every individual in this country. . . . The government must mobilize people not just to carry out orders but to participate in a great action and to assume responsibility."[5] Roosevelt wholeheartedly agreed. In his fireside chats he appealed to the people, and the people responded.[6] The American people were led to believe that their response was part of a fight for freedom, liberty and democracy. However, as Jerome Bruner concluded in a study of American popular attitudes, those were not the real reasons why America had entered the war: "We went to war because our security demanded it."[7]

In his 28 April 1942 fireside chat Roosevelt made "a call for sacrifice": "First, we must, through heavier taxes, keep personal and corporate profits at a low reasonable rate. Second, we must fix ceilings on prices and rents. Third, we must stabilize wages. Fourth, we must stabilize farm prices. Fifth, we must put more billions into war bonds. Sixth, we must ration all essential commodities which are scarce. And seventh, we must discourage installment buying, and encourage paying off debts and mortgages."[8]

In March 1942 singer Muriel Nicholls, better known as "Wee Bea Booze," recorded "War Rationin' Papa," one of the first blues songs about the rationing of "all essential commodities" in World War II. As we have seen, this theme was also used in songs about World War I.

> War rationin' papa, you are stingy as you can be,
> You are so connivin', you take every nickel from me.
>
> You rationed my sugar, my coffee ain't sweet,
> But I'm gonna cut out, baby, if you ration my meat.
>
> Oh, war rationin' papa, you's mean as you can be,
> You keep everything for yourself, but you hold out on me.
>
> You make me cook your cornbread, and cabbage without a speck of grease,
> A hard-working woman like me, ought to call the chief of police.
>
> You made me cut my liquor, to one little drink a day,
> But as soon as you get drunk, you give everything away.

As so often, a political issue has been turned into a sexual metaphor. Another example of a "Ration Blues" that can also be experienced as a sexual metaphor was recorded in October of the same year by Louis Jordan, who would become known as "the global GI favorite." Jordan's recordings were among those issued on the V (Victory) Discs and as a result "he developed a solid following among all branches of the US armed forces."[9]

Baby, baby, baby, what's wrong with Uncle Sam?
He's cut down on my sugar, now he's messin' with my ham.

chorus: *I got the ration blues, blue as I can be,*
          Poor me, I've got those ration blues.

I gotta live on forty ounces of any kind of meat,
Those forty little ounces got to last me all the week.
I gotta cut down on my jelly, it takes sugar to make it sweet,
I'm gonna steal all your jelly, baby, and rob you of your meat.

I like to wake up in the morning, with my jelly by my side,
Since rationing started, baby, you just take yourself and hide.
They reduced my meat and sugar, and rubber's disappearin' fast,
You can't ride no more with papa, 'cause Uncle Sam wants my gas.

There are several blues and gospel songs that refer to wartime rationing.[10] Some of these were discussed in chapter 13.[11] Rationed goods mentioned in various lyrics include: clothes (coats, cuffs, pants, shoes), drink (liquor), groceries (butter, coffee, sugar), meat (ham, grease, lard), oil (automobiles, gas, nylons), rubber (chewing gum, tires), and tobacco (cigarettes).

In a September 1943 Gallup Poll the American public was asked: "Aside from food, what things that you need very much right now for your home or family would you buy if you could get them?" The goods mentioned, in order of frequency, are tires and tubes, stockings, refrigerators, automobiles, washing machines, electric irons, shoes, hairpins, stoves, kitchen utensils, electric articles, radios, and safety pins.[12] Four items are to be found in both the blues lyrics and the Gallup lists: tires, stockings, automobiles and shoes.

In January 1945 a Gallup Poll asked: "What one product that is now rationed do you find it hardest to cut down on or get along without?" The answers were: 20 percent sugar, 19 percent butter, 19 percent meat, 10 percent gasoline, 5 percent shoes, 2 percent canned foods, 1 percent fuel oils and 24 percent others. Women were more inclined to mention sugar and butter, whereas a greater number of men mentioned meat and gasoline.[13]

The rationing of rubber presented the greatest difficulties for the Roosevelt administration. The shortage of rubber led to a reduction in the use of automobiles, which in turn helped relieve the shortage of gasoline. Efforts to produce synthetic rubber were not very successful,[14] so Roosevelt made a radio call to persuade the nation to turn in scrap rubber. Within a month 450,000 tons of old tires, rubber raincoats, garden hoses, rubber shoes, bathing caps and gloves

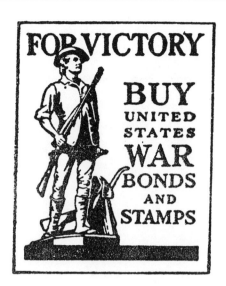

FOR VICTORY

BUY
UNITED
STATES
WAR
BONDS
AND
STAMPS

Advertisement for war bonds and stamps
printed on the sleeves of 78 rpm records.

were handed in at the nearest filling station.[15] This made people feel patriotic,
but was not nearly enough to meet the needs of wartime.

Coupons were needed for the purchase of rationed goods like meat, shoes,
fats and coffee. The quota for each family was determined by local rationing
boards.[16] How the system worked is shown in a stanza of "Pearl Harbor"
by the Soul Stirrers (discussed in chapter 13). All scarce goods were given a
number of points. A monthly ration book contained forty-eight points. The
shopkeeper used the points to buy new stock. Lost ration books were not
replaced.[17]

The "unavoidable inequity"[18] that was the result of the preferential treatment
practiced by some local rationing boards in the distribution of the ration stamps
was not in accordance with the "three high purposes for every American"
outlined by Roosevelt in a February 1942 fireside chat in which he tried to fight
defeatism:

1. We shall not stop working for a single day. If any dispute arises we shall keep
on working while the dispute is solved by mediation or conciliation, or arbitration—
until the war is won.

2. We shall not demand special gains or special privileges or special advantages
for any one group or occupation.

3. We shall give up conveniences and modify the routine of our lives if our
country asks us to do so. We will do it cheerfully, remembering that the common
enemy seeks to destroy every home and every freedom in every part of our land.[19]

Buster "Buzz" Ezell, whose career was discussed in chapter 13, offered advice in his "Obey Your Ration Laws" in August 1943:

spoken: *Buster Ezell is giving you the subject: "1943, Obey your ration laws."*

Go get your grocery card, obey your ration laws,
Tell everybody, don't violate this law.

I know this makes you feel glad, to obey your ration laws,
It'd be mighty sad, if we didn't have no boss.

You throwed away your horse and buggy, you went to buyin' automobiles,
Now you can't hardly buy you, a decent peck of meal.

You had meat in your smokehouse, you had tubs full of lard,
Now I catch you hangin' around, some white man's backyard.

spoken: *Tryin' to get something, see?*

You had corn in your corn crib, fodder by the load,
Now they catch you trampin', all up and down the road.

spoken: *Ain't got nothing, obey your ration laws!*

You had good shoes on your feet, big, ample clothes to wear,
Now you haven't got money enough, to pay a barber to cut your hair.

spoken: *Poor boy now, obey your ration laws!*

My 'mobile gives me trouble, it left me on the road,
I've got no money, nothing to pay my board.

I want you to loan me half a dollar, I wants to buy me some gas,
All this trouble, by livin' in the world too fast.

spoken: *Lord, Lord, obey your ration laws!*

My home's in Alabama, all around Birmingham,
I makes my money, workin' on the old mill dam.

spoken: *Obey your ration laws! Beat it out now, boy!*[20]

If the ration laws are not obeyed we "have no boss" (i.e., there is no authority) in the country. The president had asked Americans "to give up conveniences" and Ezell supports him. He thinks people are "livin' in the world too fast."

In April 1941 Roosevelt set up the Office of Price Administration and Civilian Supply. The OPA was to become one of the "most unpopular agencies."[21] In January 1942 Roosevelt authorized the OPA to set maximum prices, and as a result the first head of the OPA, Leon Henderson, froze all prices in March. The Price Control Act passed Congress in October.[22] Businessmen were irritated because they thought the prices set were too low, and consumers were annoyed by the resultant decrease in the quality of the goods. The only ones who thrived were salesmen of items on the black market. Here a pair of nylon hose could be had for five dollars, and five-dollar shoes cost seven dollars.[23]

In 1945 blues singer and washboard player Ann Sorter-McCoy[24] recorded a song called "Tell It to The O.P.A."[25]

> When I had no money during depression, my icebox was filled with meat,
> Well, now that I've plenty of money, can't find nothing to eat.
>
> How well do I recall, the words my grocery said to me,
> He said, "I know just how you feel, you may have my sympathy."
>
> Now, I stared at the meat counter, my mouth watered for a slice of ham,
> But there was a sign which read: "All meat reserved for Uncle Sam."
>
> I said, "No, Mr. Grocery Man, please don't treat poor me this way,"
> He gave me a sad story, sayin', "Tell it to the O.P.A."
>
> Now I pretends to be dyin', from missed meal cramps,
> He said, "If you get hungry, you can eat your ration stamps."
>
> I says, "Oh, Mr. Grocery Man, please don't treat poor me this way,"
> He say, "I know your destiny is pitiful, tell it to the O.P.A."
>
> Again I looked at the meat, the grocery looked me in the eye,
> He say, "The day you snatch that meat, it will be your turn to die."
>
> I cried, "No, Mr. Grocery Man, what hard words to say,
> 'Cause I was only thinkin', of how to jive the O.P.A."

In his March 1944 "You Can't Get That No More," Louis Jordan, "the king of the jukeboxes," sang about the OPA in similar terms.

> I went out to get some groceries the other day,
> From my neighborhood grocery store,
> And before I could open my mouth,
> The grocery man said, "No!"

"You can't get that no more," that's what he said,
"You can't get that no more."
He said, "I sold all I had the other day,
It ain't me, Mr. Jordan, it's the O.P.A.,
You just can't get it, you got to do with what you got,
Ain't gonna have no more for the duration, you gotta be careful with your food,
                                                                         son."

The hep cats used to stand on the corner in their zoot suits,
And them long chains hangin' down, all lookin' cute,
But things is very different now,
Since Uncle Sam has got some Japs to shoot.
Uh, huh, they can't do that no more,
No, sir, they can't do that no more,
No more standin' on the corners day and night,
'Cause Uncle Sam says that you got to work or you got to fight,
So they can't do that no more, no, you can't do that no more.

You know the glamor gals has stopped glamorizin',
They're workin' in defense plants, wearin' slacks,
And some of the fine chicks is cuttin' out every day,
Joinin' the WAVES and the SPARs and the WACs.[26]
Now, fellers, you can't get that no more,
I'm tellin' you, fellers, you just can't get it,
You can't jive these girls like you used to do,
'Cause some of 'em is makin' more money than you,
I'm telling you, boys, you just can't get that no more,
No, you can't get that no more.

You know, the girls used to wake up every morning and say,
"Lord, send me a handsome man, one that's physically fit,"
But Uncle Sam has got all of them now,
And the gals has got to take just what they can get.
Girls, you can't get that no more,
Ain't no need of gigglin', girls, you just can't get it no more, that's all,
Girls, you can't be particular, you got to take what's left,
Either them worn out 3-As or them beat-up 4-Fs,
That's all, you just can't get it no more, no, you can't get that no more.[27]

There were enough 4-Fs around, for in his last hundred days Roosevelt asked Congress "for legislation to use the services of the four million 4-Fs."[28] A medical grading used in the United States Army, 4-F stands for "unfit for service." However, there were more meanings attached to the term. In January 1945 dancer and singer Henry "Rubberlegs" Williams (1907–1962) alluded to them in his "4-F Blues." The singing is quite exuberant, because Charlie Parker, who played alto saxophone at the session, had dropped three Benzedrine tablets into Rubberlegs's coffee.[29]

> Girls, what you gonna do, when Uncle Sam takes your boy-man to war?
> Some of you gonna drink muddy water, sleep in a hollow log.[30]
>
> Took your good soldier's money, give it to your 4-F man,
> Now, Mr. Roosevelt has passed a bill, and brought out a brand new plan.

spoken: Get it! Open it up! Open it up! Put destruction on it!

> I used to love you, mama, but it's all over now,
> I've come to the conclusion, you never loved me no how,
> I'm goin' away, baby (3x), just to worry you off my mind.

In his dictionary of jazz and blues recordings Eric Townley suggests another interpretation of the term "4-F Man": "The second meaning is a reference to men chasing girls and is known as 'the four F's', an abbreviation for 'find 'em, fool 'em, fuck 'em, and forget 'em'."[31]

In the second couplet Rubberlegs Williams mentions a bill that Roosevelt "passed" and a brand new plan he "brought out." Did Williams perhaps have in mind yet another set of "4Fs," Roosevelt's "Four Freedoms" speech, delivered before Congress on 6 January 1941? Roosevelt's four essential human freedoms were: freedom of speech and expression, freedom of every person to worship God, freedom from want and freedom from fear.[32]

Lyrics that contain references to the buying of war bonds and defense stamps were examined in chapter 13. The idea of selling war bonds to the American public came from Secretary of State Henry Morgenthau, who wanted "to use bonds to sell the war, rather than vice versa."[33] All in all there were seven war loan drives from December 1942 to the end of the war. The various drives were accompanied by insistent presidential appeals in the fireside chats. In his 8 September 1943 chat Roosevelt said: "Every dollar that you invest in the third war loan is your personal message of defiance to our common enemies—to the ruthless savages of Germany and Japan—and it is your personal message of faith and good cheer to our allies and to all the men at the front. God bless them!"[34]

The fifth war loan was introduced by a fireside chat that had the launching of this drive as its main purpose: "And every one—every man or woman or child—who bought a war bond helped—and helped mightily! There are still many people in the United States who have not bought war bonds, or who have not bought as many as they can afford. Everyone knows for himself whether he falls into that category or not. In some cases his neighbors know too. To the consciences of those people, this appeal by the President of the United States is very much in order. . . . I urge all Americans to buy war bonds without stint. Swell the mighty chorus to bring us nearer to victory!"[35]

Eventually the grand total sum of $135 billion was raised in this way. Polls showed that the real reasons for the success of the war bonds involved not enthusiasm for the New Deal or the four freedoms but the safety of an investment made to help relatives in the army or to ensure postwar purchases.[36]

In March 1945 vocalist Johnny McNeil sang an "End O' War Blues" accompanied by Charles Brown with Johnny Moore's Three Blazers: "If you buy plenty war bonds and stamps, ooh, Lord, we'll soon be back from over there." The lyrics are clearly an updating of Doctor Clayton's "'41 Blues" (cf. chapter 14).

> War is raging in Europe, on the sea, land and in the air,
> Friends, if you buy plenty war bonds and stamps, ooh, Lord, we'll soon be back from
> over there.
>
> Here come Uncle Sam, painted in red, white and blue,
> Hitler and Tojo just as well to throw up their flag, ooh, Lord, ain't nothing else for
> them to do.
>
> Uncle Sam done crossed, over old Tojo's line,
> And Hitler had heart failure, ooh, Lord, he lost his no-good mind.
>
spoken: Drive 'em on down, boy!
>
> Friends and mothers, wives and sweethearts too,
> You don't have to worry, ooh, Lord we'll soon be marching home to you.

Just before the recording, on 23 February 1945, the American flag had been planted on the tiny island of Iwo Jima, a turning point in the fight against the Japanese.

One of the most effective means of reaching the public on the issue of the war bonds was the popular song. Some of the wartime blues 78s are stored in brown paper sleeves, which carry a drawing of an armed soldier and the text: "For Victory—Buy United States War Bonds and Stamps." One blues singer, pianist Cecil Gant (1913–1951) was discovered during a bonds sale: "The Treasury Department was staging a massive campaign to sell war bonds, and one day in L.A. Pvt. Gant found himself watching a bond rally at 9th and Broadway. During an intermission he asked if he might come on to the platform and play the piano."[37] The result was such a success that Gant was recorded as "Pvt. Cecil Gant, The G.I. Sing Sation." Gant became one of the hottest sellers of 1944, and had an extensive recording career until his death (though the military rank was dropped when it was no longer topical).

The 78 records were made of shellac, a product rationed during the war. In July 1942 James Caesar Petrillo, president of the American Federation of Musicians from 1940 to 1958, banned all recording out of fear of the effect of jukeboxes on the demand for live music; consequently the studios were virtually closed for the next two years.[38] Because of the withdrawal of the dime store labels, the wartime shellac rationing and the Petrillo ban, the number of blues and gospel 78s had dropped from about 450 in 1937 to about 288 in 1941 to about 131 in 1942—as few as in 1933, in the depths of the depression.[39] Consequently the majority of the recordings from the "Petrillo era" analyzed in this study were made by the noncommercial Library of Congress.

An important exception was Louis Jordan, who did not stop recording during the Petrillo ban. This was possible because he was playing "music for the morale of a fighting America," as it was advertised.[40] His recordings from the period were mainly made for AFRS (Armed Forces Radio Service) and V-Disc (Victory Disc). The resulting transcriptions were broadcast to the armed forces. In August 1943 Jordan recorded "The Infantry Blues" for the AFRS:

spoken: *Let's go, guys!*

I got those "Gee my feet are killin' me since I'm in the infantry blues,"
I walk so doggone much, I can't get my poor feet out of my shoes.

I got those "Roll two blankets in my pack don't know when I'm coming back blues,"
The blankets ain't so tough, but what gets me is that extra pair of shoes.

I got to hike every morning, hike every night,
Come back on the weekend, go out and get tight.
Yes, yes, but I can't help it I guess.
You've got to take it like a soldier,
When you get those infantry blues.

That the "morale of fighting America" was really boosted by Jordan's lyrics is made clear by the audience's enthusiastic reaction to the song on this live recording. In early 1943 Jack Kapp of the Decca recording company had bought the World Broadcasting System. In the autumn Kapp made a deal with the AFM whereby previous and new recordings made by World could be released. Commercial recording resumed in 1944, but this maneuver gave Decca nearly a year's head start over other companies.[41]

"G.I. Jive"[42] was one of Louis Jordan's biggest hits, reaching number one on the *Billboard* chart. The topical song about army jargon received much airplay from disc jockeys and stayed on the charts for twenty-five weeks.[43] The song pokes effective fun at the forest of abbreviations that soldiers and sailors had to put up with.

Huddie Ledbetter, who also recorded for AFRS and V-Disc, sang "Army Life"[44] for Folkways records in May 1944. Like Louis Jordan's songs, it provided relief from wartime tension for the soldiers by mildly ridiculing army discipline and logistics. These songs were composed by white songwriters—"G. I. Jive" by Johnny Mercer and "Army Life" by Irving Berlin.

To win the war, sacrifices had to be made by the civilian population: essential commodities were rationed, prices were controlled, and people were urged to invest in war loans. Wartime rationing is mildly ridiculed in blues lyrics, and there are some nationalistic calls for investment in the loans. The OPA seems to have been unpopular on a more serious level. However, there is no criticism of the president as the leader of his country's war effort.[45]

TELL ME WHY YOU LIKE ROOSEVELT

n June 1944 as FDR was running for reelection to an unprecedented fourth term, a Gallup Poll asked the American population: "What would you say are the two main arguments for voting for Franklin Roosevelt?" The answers can be summarized thus: "He has a wider firsthand knowledge of the war situation than his opponent and is therefore better fitted by experience to handle it. The middle of the war is no time to change administrations." The people were also asked the main arguments for voting against FDR: "His domestic policies have been wastefully and inefficiently carried out, with too much bureaucracy, red tape, and assertion of dictatorial power not only over the people, but over Congress. No man should hold public office for as long as Roosevelt has. It is high time for a change."[1] Thomas Dewey, the governor of New York, had succeeded Wendell Willkie as the Republican presidential candidate. Dewey did not have Roosevelt's charisma and was beaten by the incumbent, although the difference between them was a mere 3 million votes.

Henry Wallace, Roosevelt's vice president since 1941, had been ousted. His successor was Harry S. Truman, the senator from Missouri. During the war years Truman had distinguished himself by a sensible investigation of the organization of the army camps and a thorough investigation of defense production. Roosevelt and Truman were rarely seen together. At a White House lunch on 18 August 1944 future Vice President Truman was shocked to notice the president's physical condition; his hands were shaking so much that more cream fell into the saucer than into the cup of coffee. On one occasion FDR told his vice president not to travel by airplane, "because it was important that one of them stay alive."[2]

One blues artist who sang that he had voted for FDR in 1944 was the obscure harmonica player James "Jack of All Trades" McCain. Early in 1945 he recorded "Good Mr. Roosevelt" for J. Mayo Williams's small label, Chicago; Williams was evidently interested in topical songs, as he also recorded the 1945 blues by Ann Sorter-McCoy discussed in chapter 15, and the songs by Big Joe Williams and the Evangelist Singers that are discussed in this chapter.

chorus:　*Oh yeah, now I've got plenty confidence in President Roosevelt,*
Well, I said we've just got to win this war, now, people, because this country haven't
never failed.

Well, I said I just knowed, I just knowed, now, people, you know that President
Roosevelt was gonna win,
Because me and my wife—that is Lee—you know, we voted him back in his chair
again.

spoken:　*Play it a while, Slim!*

Well, I said, now, Mr. President Roosevelt's been trying, people, you know, the very
best that he can,
The reason he ain't been doing no better, you know, President Roosevelt is kind of
short on his men.[3]

Early in January 1945 Roosevelt had indeed sent a "work or fight bill" to Congress, intended to achieve total mobilization.[4]

Two days after his fourth inauguration on 20 January 1945, Roosevelt left for Yalta to meet Stalin and Churchill. Charles Wilson, Churchill's doctor, wrote in his diary that "the President appears a very sick man. He has all the symptoms of hardening of the arteries of the brain in an advanced stage, so that I give him only a few months to live."[5] On 12 April 1945 Roosevelt suffered a massive, fatal cerebral hemorrhage in Warm Springs, Georgia.

A shock wave went through the world: hardly anyone had realized how bad Roosevelt's health had really been. In New York, record producer Joe Davis, always alert for a marketing opportunity (although no doubt sincerely moved as well), immediately contacted the blues pianist whom he had had under contract for just two weeks, ex-boxer "Champion" Jack Dupree. Only six days after the president's death, Dupree recorded both a tribute to the deceased president and a salute to his successor. Dupree's "F.D.R. Blues" was advertised as "a new sensational timely blues record" in *The Billboard* of 28 April.[6]

> I sure feel bad, with tears runnin' down my face,
> I've lost a good friend, was credit to our race.
>
> FDR was everybody's friend,
> Well, he helped everybody, right unto the end.
>
> May God in heaven, have mercy on his soul,
> And may the angels, ooh, well, well, take him right unto the fold.

spoken: Yes, we lost a good friend. Good man, credit to our race. Yes, yes!

> I know I can speak, for my friends if I choose,
> 'Cause he went away and left me, and I've got the FDR Blues.

To Dupree, Franklin Delano Roosevelt was a "credit to our race," a term commonly applied to distinguished black Americans. Dupree, taking the view that great men of all races are equally deserving of respect, enrolls FDR as an honorary black man. Although Roosevelt was "everybody's friend," he had made an indelible impression especially on the black population.

After his death Roosevelt was virtually canonized by black Americans. In "His Spirit Lives On" Big Joe Williams compares FDR's achievements to Christ's healing of the crippled and the blind:

> Well, you know the President Roosevelt, he was awful fine,
> He helped the crippled, boys, and almost healed the blind.

chorus: Oh, yeah, gonna miss President Roosevelt.
> Well, he's gone, he's gone, but his spirit will always, will go on.
>
> He traveled out east, he traveled on over the west,
> But after all the presidents, President Roosevelt was the best.
>
> President Roosevelt went to Georgia, boys, and he was reeling round and round,
> I just can imagine he seen that pale horse, when it was trailing him down.
>
> Well, now he traveled by land, and he traveled by sea,
> He helped the United States, boys, and also helped Chinee.
>
> Well, now the rooster told the hen, "I wants to go crow,"
> Said, "Now President Roosevelt is gone, can't live in this shack no more."

Big Joe Williams and the author at the American Folk
Blues Festival dressing room, Concertgebouw, Amsterdam,
12 October 1968, from the collection of the author.

Williams sees Roosevelt's death as such a shocking event that even the animal kingdom is moved. He had used similar imagery before, as we saw in chapter 5; in his "Providence Help the Poor People," the hen cannot "lay no more." In the last line of his song Williams may express fear that he will even lose his home now that the president is no longer there to care for him.

On 13 April Roosevelt's mortal remains were carried from the Little White House in Warm Springs, Georgia, to the White House in Washington, D. C. As the train crossed the Georgia countryside, it passed "four black women at the edge of a cotton field, kneeling with their hands clasped."[7] The next day the coffin was drawn to the White House by six white horses and a seventh serving as outrider (Williams's "pale horse," however, is drawn from the book of Revelation). President Franklin Delano Roosevelt was buried on 15 April 1945 in Hyde Park, his hometown on the Hudson River in upstate New York.

Big Joe Williams had not forgotten his president when he rerecorded his memorial tribute fifteen years later as "President Roosevelt." Williams's prediction that the president's spirit would always "go on" was true for him and many other African Americans.[8]

To the black population President John Fitzgerald Kennedy was in many ways the natural successor to President Roosevelt. When Kennedy was murdered, parallels were drawn with both FDR and Abraham Lincoln. For Big Joe Williams history had repeated itself. His December 1963 memorial tribute to President Kennedy, "A Man Amongst Men,"[9] was simply a revision of "His Spirit Lives On."

The foremost tribute to Roosevelt in black music was paid by a Miami disc jockey called Otis Jackson. His two-part composition "Tell Me Why You Like Roosevelt" was recorded at least seven times between 1946 and 1972. The song was first recorded, again on the Chicago label, in April 1946, one year after the president's death, when Jackson was a member of the male vocal group called the Evangelist Singers. The next year both the Reliable Jubilee Singers and the Soul Stirrers recorded cover versions of the song. Otis Jackson rerecorded the song in September 1949 with the National Clouds of Joy. This version follows:

Part One

chorus: *Tell me why you like Roosevelt? Wasn't no kin.*
Huh, God Almighty; was a poor man's friend.

In the year of nineteen and forty-five,
A good president laid down and died.
I knew how all of the poor people felt,
When they received the message we have lost Roosevelt.
In his life there were all indication,
At Warm Springs, Georgia, he received salvation.
Listen, boys, and don't you rush,
Elizabeth Shoumatoff, she grabbed a brush,
Dipped it in water and began to paint,
She looked at Pres and began to think.
She never painted a picture for him at night,
And she knew that the President didn't look right.
The time of day was twelve o'clock,
Tell me that Elizabeth had to stop,
Great God Almighty, she started too late,
That is why that they called that unfinished portrait.
A little bit later, about one-thirty,
Had a cerebral hemorrhage, and the world looked muddy.
They called Atlanta, Washington too,

Just like zigzag lightning, the call went through.
Called long distance to notify the wife,
Doctor Bruenn said he died at three thirty-five.
And great God almighty, wasn't no bell to tone,
But in less than thirty minutes, the world was in mourn.

Other presidents' administration, Congress assembled,
Great God almighty, the poor folks trembled.
The rich would ride in the automobile,
Depression made poor people rob and steal.
I looked next door to our beloved neighbor,
Wasn't getting anything for their hard labor.
Great God almighty, there were moonshine stilling,
Brought about a crime wave robbing and killing.
After other presidents had made us mourn,
Roosevelt stepped in, gave a comfortable home.

Part Two

Only two presidents that I ever felt:
Abraham Lincoln and Roosevelt.
Way back yonder in those olden days,
There was Abraham Lincoln, freein' the slaves.
The Roosevelt's administration, Congress assembled,
The first time in history, appointed a Negro general:
General Benjamin O. Davis, I'm trying to relate,
First Negro general of the United States.
After Dorie Miller had shown the skill,
Kept sending him to sea, until he got killed.
This Roosevelt said, "I'll back the attack,"
Appointed a Negro captain, over white and black:
This qualified man was Hugh Mulzac.
Racial prejudice he tried to rule out,
Invited Negro leaders into the White House.
Advocated the fair practice of labor,
To let the poor man know, he was our emancipator.
Made Madame Bethune, first lady of the land,
And made a part of his will to Mr. Prettyman.
Endorsed inventions of Doctor Carver,

This is why that I say, he was an earthly father.
'Cause he took my feet out of the miry clay,
Haven't had to look back at the WPA.

I have told you the history of Roosevelt's life,
Now he's done with his grievin' and strife.
Great God almighty, but he left a sweet wife,
Hadn't been so worried since she were a girl,
But after Roosevelt's death, what will become of the world?
And she notified his sons, across the sea,
"Don't you all get worried about poor me,
Just keep on fighting for victory.
Well, your father is dead, but you all were grown,
I wouldn't worry about your father, but the world's in mourn."

Well, great God almighty, look what a time,
England asked Churchill to resign.
After workin' through the European war so hard,
Put him out in the hands of the almighty God.
His successor was Attlee,
Great God almighty, what history.
Wish Roosevelt could have lived to see,
"Old Glory" wavin' over Germany.
But God almighty knew just what was best,
He knew that the president he needed a rest.
The battle done fought, victory done won,
Our problem have just begun.
When your burden get heavy, don't know what to do,
You call on Jesus, he's a president too.[10]

"Tell Me Why You Like Roosevelt" is probably the most important song about Roosevelt, as it eloquently summarizes FDR's achievements as perceived by the black population. Otis Jackson's magnum opus is divided into five parts, separated by a chorus in which the president is characterized as a man who did not set himself above others, but who identified with the common people. In the first part, the circumstances surrounding the president's death are described. The second part shows what an improvement FDR's presidency was as compared to "other presidents' administrations." The third part compares Roosevelt to Abraham Lincoln. Various examples are given to show that, just like

Lincoln, Roosevelt liberated the black man. In the fourth part Jackson worries about the future now that the "good president laid down and died." The fifth and final episode expresses regret that Roosevelt did not live to see Germany being defeated. The song shows how Roosevelt advanced Negroes in different fields and explains how the Roosevelt myth arose. The various characters in this Roosevelt epic are identified as follows:

Elizabeth Shoumatoff was the last of many portrait painters commissioned by Roosevelt. The day the president died she was sketching in the room.[11]

Dr. Howard G. Bruenn was a cardiac specialist who had been a commander in the navy. A year before Roosevelt's death he had been appointed to stay close to the president.[12]

Brigadier General Benjamin O. Davis, Sr., was the first black general in the United States Army. He was appointed on 16 December 1940. His son, General Benjamin O. Davis, Jr., became the first black general in the United States Army Air Corps in 1954.[13]

Dorie Miller was a messman on the USS *Arizona* and was awarded the Navy Cross. At Pearl Harbor, Miller manned a machine gun and brought down four Japanese planes.[14] Messman was one of the lowly jobs routinely allocated to blacks in the United States Navy. Miller died in action in the South Pacific in 1943.

Captain Hugh Mulzac was appointed as the first black captain of a merchant ship, the *Booker T. Washington*, which was launched at Wilmington, Delaware, in 1942.[15]

Mary McLeod Bethune may have been the president's most important Negro adviser. She was the only woman in the so-called "Black Cabinet" of the thirties. She had founded a small black college in Florida, patterned after the ideas of Booker T. Washington, and worked in the National Youth Administration (NYA) from 1935 to 1943. As a close friend of Mrs. Eleanor Roosevelt, she had easy access to the president.[16] In 1934 Mrs. Bethune visited FDR for the first time. Eloquently she pleaded for full citizenship for 14 million Americans. In a 1949 *Ebony* article Mrs. Bethune remembered the president's emotional reaction: "When I had finished, I saw that tears were coursing down President Roosevelt's cheeks. He leaned across the table and grasped my hands in both of his. 'Mrs. Bethune', he said, 'I am glad I am able to contribute something to help make a better life for your people. I want to assure you that I will continue to do my best for them in every way'. He choked a little. Tears flowed from his eyes." A fortnight later Mrs. Bethune was offered the

Mary McLeod Bethune, founder and director of the Division of Negro Affairs of the National Youth Administration, Daytona Beach, Florida, January 1943. Photo by Gordon Parks, reproduced from the collections of the Library of Congress.

post of administrator of the Office of Minority Affairs of the NYA, the first such post created for a Negro woman in the United States.[17] In August 1955 Otis Jackson made a memorial recording about her with the Dixie Humming-birds.[18]

Arthur Prettyman was Roosevelt's black valet, who carried the president from his wheelchair to his bed.[19] From Otis Jackson's song we learn that a grateful Roosevelt remembered Prettyman in his will.

Dr. George Washington Carver, born a slave, was head of the Department of Research at Tuskegee Institute and one of the most distinguished agricul-tural chemists of his generation. Carver's inventions, especially the products he derived from peanuts and soybeans, revolutionized the economy of the South.[20]

The circumstances surrounding Roosevelt's death have often been recounted. In analyzing the myths that have arisen, we should try to distinguish fact from fiction. There were three people, all of them women, present in the room when the end came: Margaret Suckley, Lucy Rutherford and Elizabeth Shoumatoff.

Margaret Suckley was Roosevelt's cousin and friend.[21] Lucy Rutherford-Mercer had been FDR's social secretary. In 1918 Eleanor Roosevelt had read letters which "proved beyond a doubt" that her husband "had been having an affair" with Lucy.[22] This relationship always stood between Franklin and Eleanor. On the day of Roosevelt's death at Warm Springs, Mrs. Roosevelt was unaware of Lucy's presence there.

Society painter Elizabeth "Mopsy" Shoumatoff was a friend of Lucy's, who had commissioned her to paint a portrait of her beloved president.[23] In 1990 Mrs. Shoumatoff published her memoir, F.D.R.'s Unfinished Portrait. In it she refutes the claims of some historians which have been perpetuated in the myth. On the morning of 12 April 1945, the president was signing some papers presented to him by William D. Hassett, his press secretary. Hassett later claimed that he was irritated by Mrs. Shoumatoff's "measuring the President's nose," which interrupted the paperwork.[24] Mrs. Shoumatoff writes that it was never her practice to measure her models' noses.[25] When she had set up her easel and board, the president was seated behind a card table covered in mail. Mrs. Shoumatoff, who naturally was studying the president's face intently, was struck by his "exceptionally good color" (ironically a sign of the approaching catastrophe). While Lucy and Margaret were sitting on the sofa at the other end of the room, Elizabeth talked to the president about stamps (Roosevelt's hobby). Margaret brought in a green drink meant "to increase the appetite" and the Filipino butler set the table for lunch. "We have fifteen minutes more to work," the president told him. Mrs. Shoumatoff is certain that these were Roosevelt's last words. Suddenly the president raised his right hand to his head, and, without uttering a sound, collapsed unconscious in his armchair. Mrs. Shoumatoff never heard the president say "I have a terrific headache," the words reported in virtually every account of the tragedy published since 1945.[26] Arthur Prettyman carried the president to his bed, and when Dr. Bruenn, who had been having lunch, came to the bedside, the president was injected with amyl nitrate and adrenalin. The heavy breathing of a man in agony resounded through the house. Roosevelt's face turned purple; he was pronounced dead by his cardiac specialist at 3:35 p.m. Central War Time.[27]

In Elizabeth Shoumatoff's unfinished watercolor, the president's searching eyes, with the dark bags of a very tired man under them, still seem to look into eternity.

The second part of Otis Jackson's Roosevelt saga starts with a reference to the administration(s) of "other presidents" who had made the poor people "rob and steal." This interesting phrase has been self-censored by the omission of a name, but the subsequent reference to the horrors of the depression leaves no doubt about the only possible candidate. In his 1947 version, Willie Eason had clearly sung "During the Hoover's administration Congress assembled." Blind Connie Williams, who based his 1961 version on the Soul Stirrers record, also mentioned Hoover by name.

The fourth part of Jackson's song is unique in blues and gospel music, as it presents one of only two references to the first lady. In Jackson's song she is pictured as a "sweet wife, hadn't been so worried since she were a girl." The public was not aware that Franklin and Eleanor had a marriage of convenience. Eleanor was shocked to hear that FDR's favorite female companion, Lucy Rutherford, had been present at her husband's death. Their daughter Anna, who had kept Lucy's presence to herself, was confronted with a frustrated mother who had a hard time controlling her intense emotions.[28] In her memoirs of the White House years Eleanor concluded: "I was one of those who served his purposes."[29]

The fifth part refers to 26 July 1945, the day when Churchill's Conservative Party lost the general election. The new prime minister was Clement Attlee. The singer expresses amazement at this turn of history: "England asked Churchill to resign, after workin' through the European war so hard." Even greater is Jackson's regret that Roosevelt had not lived to see "Old Glory wavin' over Germany." Problems continue for black people, and Jackson does not expect the new president to be as helpful to them. He concludes his Roosevelt memorial with orthodox Christian advice, containing, however, a remarkable implied estimate of Roosevelt's qualities: "When your burden get heavy, don't know what to do, you call on Jesus, he's a president too."[30]

Joseph Goebbels heard the news of Roosevelt's death on the steps of his propaganda ministry immediately after an air raid. He called for champagne and telephoned Hitler in his bunker: "My Führer! I congratulate you. Roosevelt is dead."[31] The Allied forces' war effort was too far advanced for Roosevelt's death to make any difference, however, and seventeen days later Adolf Hitler committed suicide.

Less than an hour after Roosevelt's death a black limousine stopped at the door of the White House. Harry Truman took the elevator to Mrs. Roosevelt's second-floor study. Gently she laid her hand on Truman's shoulder and said, "Harry, the president is dead." "Is there anything I can do for you?" he asked.

Mrs. Roosevelt shook her head. "Is there anything we can do for you? For you are the one in trouble now."[32]

When "Champion" Jack Dupree recorded his Roosevelt in memoriam six days later, he also sang a salute to the incoming president. "God Bless Our New President!" was the other side of the record.[33]

> May God bless our new president!
> Because I believe he was heavenly sent.
>
> He sure got a tough job, and it is on his hand(s),
> To try to bring peace, brotherly love to our land.
>
> Stand behind our President Truman, each and every one of you,
> 'Cause you know that's what, FDR would want us to do.
>
> It is our duty, put our shoulders to the wheel,
> Harry Truman would be our friend just as I feel.
>
> Oh, it's a hard thing, to fill FDR's shoes,
> But if we all would help, ooh, well, well, I swear we cannot lose.[34]

CONCLUSION

"Once we were Republicans, but now we're Democrats," Ethel Waters (1896–1977) sang in the 1933 film *Rufus Jones for President.*[1] In the immediate aftermath of Roosevelt's election a political revolution was beginning to take place. African-American opinion was largely ignored in the thirties and forties, and as a result historians have not been able sufficiently to establish the reasons for the seismic shift from the Republican to the Democratic Party that took place at that time. This study has aimed, through an analysis of the era's blues and gospel lyrics that contain more or less direct social and political comment, to shed some light on the question of why Roosevelt was so popular among blacks.

Blues songs were not political in an organizational sense. They contain little expression of conventional political ideology or advocacy of programs and solutions. The songs do, however, deal with the effects of events, policies and personalities on the singer's life and physical needs. When Ida Cox sings in 1939 that "Uncle Sam started chopping, cutting thousands off the WPA," she does not criticize the president, but describes how she has "propped" herself at her front door waiting for the "long white envelope" with the pink dismissal note coded "304."

All this suggests a sense of alienation from the political process and a lack of formal participation. The subject most frequently involving advocacy is World War II, significantly the least controversial topic, as virtually all Americans were in agreement about it.

The preceding chapters contained examinations of 128 blues and gospel lyrics that contain references to the social and political situation of black people in the United States in the period from 1901 (the assassination of William McKinley) to 1945 (the death of Franklin Roosevelt). Some of the other 221 texts, which are referred to in the notes but have not been analyzed, are unissued and un-available (17 percent) or are alternative versions of the songs under discussion (28 percent). Others contained lyrics the content of which was either dupli-cated by the songs quoted, or which were considered to be less relevant to the present purpose (55 percent). The following diagram presents the relation between the total number of "political" blues and gospel songs (grey) and those selected for analysis (black).

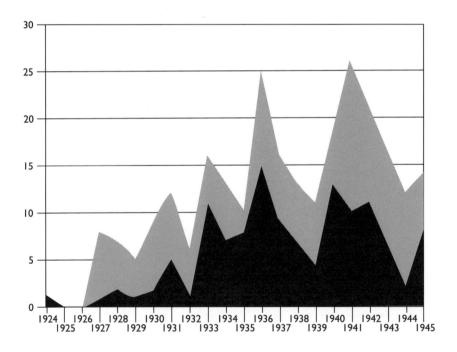

The peaks in the diagram coincide with the hard times of the Hoover days (1928, 1930 and 1931), the first relief efforts through Red Cross stores (1933), the CWA (1934), the bonus payment and the PWA (1936), the WPA projects (1937), the draft (1940), the approach of war (1941), Pearl Harbor (1942), wartime rationing (1943) and FDR's death (1945).

The total number of blues and gospel records issued each year as represented by Robert Dixon and John Godrich[2] fell dramatically after the Wall Street crash. A comparison with the chart above shows that the depression, which was responsible for the decrease in the total number of blues and gospel recordings, occasioned a rise in "political" recordings about the hard times. In 1933, when only some 140 records (280 sides) were issued, no fewer than fifteen blues songs about the Red Cross stores and the hard times were recorded. It would appear that blues and gospel songs with social comment provided some much-needed temporary relief for the unemployed black community, which was able to identify with the singers.

Forty-one percent of the lyrics were recorded in Chicago and 25 percent in New York City. This is not a guide to the origins of the artists, who sometimes had to make extensive journeys to reach the recording studios of the big cities. However, the majority of the artists lived in one of those cities, although they very often hailed from the country originally. The twenty-two noncommercial recordings (15 percent) were often made on location. Fortunately the origins of some 60 percent of the singers are known. They were all born in the southern states. Of the approximately one hundred singers, thirteen came from Mississippi, nine from Georgia, eight from Arkansas, seven from Louisiana, seven from Tennessee and four from Texas.[3]

Some artists recorded more than one song with political comment. If we count different versions of the same song only once, the following artists recorded most political blues and gospel songs: (seven) John Lee "Sonny Boy" Williamson (1914–1948), William "Big Bill" Broonzy (1898–1958), Josh White (1915–1969), Bill Gaither (1910–1970); (six) Huddie "Leadbelly" Ledbetter (1889–1949), Lonnie Johnson (1889–1970); (five) Rev. J. M. Gates[4] (c. 1884–c. 1942), Louis Jordan (1908–1975); (four) "Champion" Jack Dupree (1910–1992), Charley Jordan (c. 1890–1954), Buster "Buzz" Ezell (18??–195?). The political songs of these eleven artists constitute 23 percent of the total in the period covered. All except Buzz Ezell and Charley Jordan had extensive recording careers, though many others with such careers (Tampa Red, Washboard Sam, etc.) recorded little political material.

Of the 128 songs selected 118 were sung by seventy-three men; only ten (8 percent) were sung by nine women. Some of these women (Lucille Bogan, Wee

Bea Booze, Lil Johnson and Billie McKenzie) commented on social conditions as they affected their men and, in turn, themselves. The women's lyrics are assertive in their outspokenness, and although they are fewer in number, they are certainly not less direct than the men's.

Many of the topical themes in blues songs are related to the man-woman relationship, a subject that inevitably ensured a higher sales potential. However, the noncommercial recordings are often more strictly topical and less concerned with sex. The collectors of noncommercial recordings sometimes requested songs with outspoken political comment, and the artists felt less inhibited when they had been assured that the recordings served no commercial purpose.

Of the 128 songs selected, only twelve were sung by seven gospel artists or groups. The gospel artists are of the opinion that "the world is in a hell of a fix" because "men have turned their backs on Christ" (Black Billy Sunday). To them Roosevelt is an earthly father. Although "the whole world trembles because of sin," "God is workin' through Roosevelt" (Rev. J. M. Gates). They are convinced that evil will be conquered as "Jesus is a president too" (Otis Jackson). The very nature of the black sermon, with its impromptu exchanges between pulpit and pew, affords a unique view of political developments as they affected everyday life. Members of the congregation freely discussed with their pastor the ways in which their lives were influenced by politics.

Only four of the seven presidents from the period 1901 to 1945 were mentioned in the songs. Theodore Roosevelt's dinner with Booker T. Washington was the subject of Gus Cannon's recording twenty-six years after the event. Although Roosevelt's attitude towards blacks has been called contradictory and paternalistic,[5] Gus Cannon's song shows that Washington's visit was an important emancipatory event that had not been forgotten after a quarter of a century. Booker T. Washington's visit to the White House must also have been an important reason why many blacks, including fourteen recorded blues singers, were named after President Theodore Roosevelt.

The songs about World War I were all recorded many years after the war, in the period from 1925 to 1961, although some unrecorded songs were also collected and published by folklorists. Woodrow Wilson was seen as a king on his throne who had segregated the army that liberated Europe. Blind Willie Johnson censored his own line about the president whom he dared not attack explicitly. Wilson was also criticized by Leadbelly because he started the draft too late. As a result many insufficiently trained soldiers were unnecessarily wounded or killed.

Herbert Hoover was looked upon as the personification of the depression. He continued segregation, and the black population felt reduced to gambling and bootlegging. People starved in so-called "Hoovervilles." The blues singers ignored him as much as he tried to ignore their people. Most of the recorded songs from this period date from 1930 to 1932, and they are the first commercial recordings to reflect contemporary issues.

While Wilson and Hoover received hardly any attention from the blues and gospel singers, Taft, Harding and Coolidge were ignored altogether. In sharp contrast many songs were devoted to Franklin Delano Roosevelt beginning in 1933. Why this sudden change?

As most of the 78s can be dated with great accuracy, certain historical events from 1928 onwards can be followed from day to day on the basis of these recordings. Data as they appear in the lyrics are generally remarkably accurate; how had the blues and gospel singers acquired the detailed knowledge of topical political events? Some of them (e.g., Amos Easton, Sonny Boy Williamson and Leadbelly) were literate and read the newspapers. References to headlines appear in these singers' lyrics. Probably black newspapers like the *Chicago Defender* and *The New York Age* were those most often read. Some who were illiterate may have been read the news by friends or relations.

Betty Houchin Winfield describes how "when the dishes had been washed, average Americans went to one of their small neighborhood theaters to relax and enjoy." Here, for twenty-five cents, they saw newsreels, an early form of televised news. They could see the fireside chats they had already heard on the radio. The newsreels emphasized the president's travels, his personality and human-interest situations and thus provided an image of an energetic President.[6]

The radio was the major source of information. Several songs paraphrase lines from the fireside chats and other presidential speeches broadcast by radio. In this way FDR reached a mass audience. The famous Pearl Harbor speech about "the day that will live in infamy" was heard by 62,000,000 listeners, "the largest audience for a single radio program up to that time."[7]

As is the case with expensive modern audiovisual machines, the ownership of radios bore no relation to income. When Roosevelt came to the White House in 1933 there were 19 million households with radios (63 percent). When he died in 1945, the number had risen to 33 million (88 percent).[8] Basing his information on a study by Arthur F. Raper,[9] Paul Oliver has argued that radios were scarce among blacks in rural areas.[10] However, we have seen that most of the artists who recorded topical songs had moved from the rural South to the urban areas in the North. Here electrification provided easy access to radio waves.

When FDR entered the White House, this politicians' politician consciously created an image of himself that served as a beacon of light for the black population. How was this image created and sustained through four terms of office? In her *FDR and the News Media* Betty Houchin Winfield argues that Roosevelt "loved the dramatic and the unusual." He made "shrewd use of his own expressive features" and let the photographers know that "proper poses only" were allowed and that "no candid pictures were to be taken in the White House." This resulted in a gentlemen's agreement between the president and the press, whereby "the greatest sin was to depict the president's legs or reminders of his lameness."[11] The rarest of all FDR photos are those of him being helped from a car or seated in a wheelchair. Many people did not even realize that their president could not walk. There are in fact only two pictures of him in a wheelchair among the 125,000 in the Roosevelt library.[12]

The Roosevelt style was built around his appearance and his immediately recognizable voice. With his smile, his pince-nez and his cigarette holder, the president made a dashing impression, and provided the nation with a father figure during the post-1932 depression and the Second World War. Like all master politicians, Roosevelt was a superb actor who often held his public spellbound. The black minority was comforted by the hope he radiated.

What then, did the blues and gospel singers think of Roosevelt's policies? They were complimentary about his reorganization of relief distribution. In the New Deal fight against unemployment some of the president's alphabetical agencies, such as the CWA and the PWA, were hailed enthusiastically. Regarding the war, Roosevelt had organized the draft in time, and reacted convincingly to the attack on Pearl Harbor. To the blues singers he was the ideal wartime leader.

Not all agencies met with applause. The NRA, the WPA and the OPA were the targets of some criticism. The fate of the "Scottsboro boys" proved how limited even this president's influence could be.

In some cases FDR successfully managed to stay away from the limelight. Thus the bonus payments were generally lauded in spite of the president's veto, and Douglas MacArthur could be admired as a national war hero in spite of his White House ambitions, which were scarcely noticed by the people. Roosevelt's image was so powerful that the usually observant blues and gospel singers were sometimes manipulated. However, such times were exceptions, and the singers usually were keenly aware of what was going on in the White House.

Altogether, a remarkable number of blues and gospel songs were devoted to Franklin Roosevelt and his presidency. This was partly the result of circumstances; political and social blues became more common in the thirties as economic conditions got worse, and in the forties the nation was at war. The wartime lyrics show that black people hoped for a "double v"—an American victory over the Germans and the Japanese and a resultant victory in terms of black emancipation. Since blacks had again proved their fighting spirit when the nation was in distress, they hoped that discrimination in the army would end and that the black minority would be accepted as equals after the war.

Blues lyrics also show that the New Deal was an epoch-making event in American history. For the first time since Reconstruction, the black population saw some point in engagement with the political process. In the New Deal era, unemployment had been fought in a revolutionary way. In spite of the scarcity of trustworthy data about the economic impact of the New Deal on blacks, Nancy Weiss writes about "a significant reduction in black unemployment" because of the New Deal projects.[13] In January 1931 unemployment among black males in Chicago was 43.5 percent. In March 1940 unemployment among nonwhite males had fallen to 16.7 percent in the Windy City.[14]

The blues and gospel singers who sang about the bonus payments had not always received one themselves, and neither had those who sang about the war always fought in it, but from behind their masks they voiced the emotions their people had in common. The blues and gospel lyrics provide evidence for the reasons behind the black switch from the Republican to the Democratic Party in the Roosevelt era. The New Deal measures had raised the status of black Americans, and the personal charisma of Franklin Roosevelt had inspired confidence.

Versions of the forties songs in which FDR was compared to Christ would also be sung in praise of John F. Kennedy in the sixties. Kennedy had the same flair for style and communication Roosevelt had. He too radiated hope. He too died an unexpected death.

FDR had not freed the "Scottsboro boys," nor did JFK get the civil rights bill through Congress. Still, the personalities of both presidents had caught the imagination of black America. Next to the pictures of Christ and Martin Luther King, photos of Roosevelt and Kennedy were still hanging on the walls of black people's homes many years after the two presidents' deaths.

NOTES

Introduction

1. Bruce Harrah-Conforth, sleeve notes for *Nobody Knows My Name: Blues from South Carolina and Georgia*, one of the three albums with Lawrence Gellert field recordings, Heritage HTLP 304, Great Britain, 1984.

2. The three Lawrence Gellert albums are *Negro Songs of Protest*, Rounder LP 4004 (= Timely TILP 112), 1973, *Cap'n You're So Mean*, Rounder LP 4013, 1982 and *Nobody Knows My Name*, Heritage HTLP 304, 1984.

3. Wolfe and Lornell, p. 106.

4. Lomax, p. 143.

5. Gallup, p. 36.

6. Weiss, pp. 205–6.

7. Sitkoff, p. 96.

8. Quoted in Badger, pp. 219–20.

The President, Sittin' on His Throne

1. "Uncle" Bob Ledbetter, "Cleveland Campaign Song," unissued Library of Congress recording, Oil City, Louisiana, 10 October 1940 and "Uncle" Ben (Collins), "When McKinley Was Shot," unissued Library of Congress recording, Smyrna, Delaware, 5 June 1941.

2. Blues singers named after Theodore Roosevelt were: Roosevelt "Baby" Brooks, Roosevelt Charles (b. 1919), Theodore "Teddy Roosevelt" Darby (b. 1906), "Blind" Roosevelt Graves, Roosevelt Holts (b. 1905), Roosevelt Lee (b. 1930), Roosevelt Marks, Roosevelt May (1915–1978), Roosevelt Scott (b. 1907), Roosevelt Sykes (1906–1983), Theodore Roosevelt "Hound Dog" Taylor (1917–1975), Roosevelt Wardell, Roosevelt Thomas "Grey Ghost" Williams (1903–1996).

3. Oliver (1984), pp. 125–26.

4. Cf. Gatewood, chapter 2.

5. Theodore Roosevelt, *Autobiography* (New York: Da Capo Press, 1985).

6. Sitkoff, p. 20.

7. Mullen, pp. 46–47.

8. W. C. Handy, "Those Draftin' Blues," rejected by Columbia, 25 September 1917. Wilber Sweatman, "Those Draftin' Blues (Intro. Somebody's Done Me Wrong)," Columbia A-2645, New York City, 17 August 1918.

9. Jimmy Rushing, "Draftin' Blues" (composer credit: "Pinkard"), OKeh 5897; reissued on CBS LP 53973, New York City, 30 October 1940.

10. Yack Taylor with Skeets Tolbert, "Those Draftin' Blues," Decca 8516, New York City, 17 December 1940.

11. Joe Calicott, "War Time Blues" (composer credit: "J. Calicott"), Blue Horizon LP 7-63227, Memphis, Tennessee, 21 July 1968.

12. John (Big Nig) Bray, "Trench Blues" (93-A), Document DOCD 5411, near Morgan City, Louisiana, 17 October 1934. Other versions of this song by Bray are 92-A and 242-A-3.

13. "Kingfish" Bill Tomlin, "Army Blues" (composer credit: "Tomlin"), Paramount 13034; reissued on Document DOCD 5193 with notes by Howard Rye, Grafton, Wisconsin, November 1930.

14. Pink Anderson, "The Boys of Your Uncle Sam," Folkways LP 3588, Spartanburg, South Carolina, 14 August 1961.

15. Pink Anderson, "The Kaiser," Spartanburg, South Carolina, Bluesville LP 1071, 14 August 1961.

16. Charlie Oaks, "The Kaiser and Uncle Sam," Vocalion 15104 and 5073, New York City, 4 August 1925. The song was also recorded by the white artists Ernest V. Stoneman ("Uncle Sam and the Kaiser," OKeh 40430, New York City, 27 May 1925) and Henry Whitter ("The Kaiser and Uncle Sam," OKeh 40229, New York City, 10 December 1923).

17. Tracy, pp. 52–58.

18. Kid Coley, "War Dream Blues," Victor 23369; reissued on RST JPCD 1504-2, Louisville, Kentucky, 15 June 1931.

19. William and Versey Smith, "Everybody Help the Boys Come Home," Paramount 12505; reissued on Document DOCD 5045, Chicago, August 1927. The tune was later recorded, with a religious text, by Sister Cally Fancy as "Everybody Get Your Business Right," Brunswick 7110; reissued on Document DOCD 5313, Chicago, 15 August 1929.

20. John P. Davis, p. 621.

21. Sister Cally Fancy, "Death is Riding Through the Land—Parts 1 & 2," Vocalion 1663; reissued on Document DOCD 5313, Chicago, 28 October 1931.

Another World War I blues composition is Little Brother Montgomery, "This War

Got Everybody Troubled," Magpie unissued, Herstmonceux, Sussex, England, 26 August 1960. Cf. discography by Francis Wilford-Smith in *Blues & Rhythm* 75, January 1993, p. 8.

Unrecorded World War I songs were published in books by Niles and Odum. Occasional items are to be found in 1920s folklorist compilations by Scarborough, Newman White, etc.

22. Schulte Nordholt (1991), p. 100.

23. Lynn Abbott and Doug Seroff, "America's Blue Yodel," *Musical Traditions* 11 (1993): 5.

24. Whistler and His Jug Band, "Jail House Blues" (composer credit "Whistler"), Gennet 5614; reissued on RST JPCD 1501-2, Richmond, Indiana, 25 September 1924.

25. Earl McDonald's Original Louisville Jug Band, "She's in the Graveyard Now" (composer credit: "McDonald"), Columbia 14255-D; reissued on RST JPCD 1502-2, Atlanta, Georgia, 30 March 1927.

26. Jim Jackson, "He's in the Jailhouse Now," Vocalion unissued, Chicago, 10 October 1927 and "He's in the Jailhouse Now," Vocalion 1146; reissued on Document DOCD 5114, Chicago, 22 January 1928.

27. Pink Anderson, "He's in the Jailhouse Now," Riverside LP 12-611, Charlottesville, Virginia, 29 May 1950. Anderson also recorded this song as "In the Jailhouse Now," Bluesville LP 1051; reissued on Folkways LP 3588, New York City, 1961.

28. Weiss, pp. 87–90.

29. Ibid., p. 89.

30. For a discussion of William L. Dawson as a politician, see James Q. Wilson, "Two Negro Politicians: An Interpretation," in *Negro Politics in America*, ed. Harry A. Bailey, Jr. (Columbus, Ohio: Charles E. Merrill Books, 1967).

31. Jimmie Rodgers, "In the Jailhouse Now" (composer credit: "Rodgers"), Victor 21245; reissued on Victor LPM 2634, Camden, New Jersey, 15 February 1928.

32. Jimmie Rodgers was also overdubbed by Hank Snow's Rainbow Ranch Boys, "In the Jailhouse Now No. 2," Victor 20-6092; reissued on Victor LPM 2564, Nashville, Tennessee, 18 March 1955.

33. Memphis Jug Band, "He's in the Jailhouse Now" (composer credit: "Burt Murphy"), Victor 23256; reissued on Document DOCD 5023, Memphis, Tennessee, 21 November 1930.

34. Billy Mitchell, "In the Jailhouse Now," Bluebird B6651; reissued on Document DOCD 5388, Chicago, 4 April 1936.

35. John Jackson, "He's in the Jailhouse Now," Rounder LP 2032, 22 March 1982. An earlier unissued version of the song was recorded for Arhoolie Records in Fairfax, Virginia, 8 December 1967.

36. William Charles Sallis, "The Color Line in Mississippi Politics, 1865–1915," (Ph. D. diss., University of Kentucky, 1967), p. 330, quoted in McMillen, p. 48.

37. C. E. Johnson to James Weldon Johnson, 19 April 1920, box C-388; NAACP, quoted in McMillen, p. 55.

38. Oliver (1991), pp. 190–91.

39. McElvaine, p. 22.

40. Ibid., p. 39.

41. Bertha "Chippie" Hill, "Hard Time Blues," OK unissued, Chicago, 16 December 1927.

Other "hard time" blues from the Coolidge era are:

Burl C. "Jaybird" Coleman, "Times Gettin' Hard—Work's Been Gettin' Scarce," Gennett unissued, Birmingham, Alabama, c. 27 August 1927. This might be the same song as:

Lucious Curtis, "Time Is Gittin' Hard," Library of Congress unissued; issued on Matchbox SDMLP 230, Natchez, Mississippi, 19 October 1940.

Bessie Smith, "Poor Man's Blues" (composer credit: "Smith"), Columbia 14399-D; reissued on Columbia CGLP 30450, New York City, 24 August 1928.

Big Bill Broonzy, "Starvation Blues," Paramount 12707; reissued on Document DOCD 5050, Chicago, October 1928. In the Roosevelt era a second part was recorded:

Big Bill Broonzy, "Starvation Blues" (composer credit: "William Broonzy"), Bluebird B5706; reissued on Document DOCD 5051, Chicago, 23 March 1934.

Hard Time in Hooverville

1. Blacks were not appointed to federal positions, educational grants were reserved for whites, a racist appointment to the Supreme Court was effectuated and pleas for investigations in discriminatory practices were ignored (Sitkoff, p. 28).

2. Johnson, p. 239.

3. A "duck" is a cigarette butt.

4. An earlier recording is Eugene "Buddy" Moss, "Chesterfield," Columbia unissued, Nashville, Tennessee, 4 May 1966. The name "Chesterfield" was first registered by Drummond of St. Louis in 1896. The present owner of the trademark, Liggett Group Inc. from Durham, NC, has no information on the Buddy Moss song: letter from Mary B. Bell, consumer relations supervisor, to the author, 10 December 1993.

5. Chris Smith reports that John Jackson, who played second guitar on some songs at the concert where Moss recorded "Chesterfield," sang a fragmentary and garbled version of the song at the Gloucester Blues Festival in 1994.

Cf. Walter "Furry" Lewis, "The President," Ampex LP 10140, New York, August 1971.

Cf. David Evans, "The Toast in Context," *Journal of American Folklore* 90 (1977): 129–48.

6. Hugh Brogan, *Longman History of the United States of America* (London: Longman, 1985; reprint, London: Book Club Associates, 1993), p. 518.

7. According to Wentworth and Flexner, "to mooch" can mean to beg or to steal.

8. Keith Summers, review of 504 LP 20, "Religious Recordings from Black New Orleans," *Keskidee* 3 (summer 1993): 57.

9. Washington Phillips, "The World Is in a Bad Fix Everywhere," Columbia unissued, Dallas, Texas, 2 December 1929. For Washington Phillips and his "novelty instrument," the dolceola, cf. Guido van Rijn, "Denomination Blues," a paper presented at the International Conference on African-American Music and Literature ("Religion Versus Secularity in African American Cultural Traditions") at Liège University, Belgium, 24–26 October 1991.

10. Cf. "Sleepy" John Estes, "Hobo Jungle Blues," Decca 7354; reissued on Document DOCD 5016, New York City, 3 August 1937.

A version of Short's song was later recorded by Lane Hardin, "Hard Time Blues," Bluebird B6242; reissued on Document DOCD 5036, Chicago, 28 July 1935. Hardin may also have recorded this song as "Bluebird Blues" under the pseudonym "Leroy Simpson," Modern unissued, Arkansas (?), 1952.

A blues song about a bluebird who visited the president in Washington is Sonny Boy Williamson, "Blue Bird Blues—Part 2," Bluebird B7979; reissued on Document DOCD 5056, Aurora, Illinois, 17 December 1938.

11. Samuel B. Charters, *The Legacy of the Blues* (New York: Da Capo, 1977), p. 21.

12. Leuchtenburg (1963), p. 2. See also the photo of a New York "Hooverville" opposite p. 172.

13. Dixon and Godrich (1970), pp. 104–5.

14. Guido van Rijn and Hans Vergeer, sleeve notes to Charley Jordan, "It Ain't Clean," Agram ABLP 2002, The Netherlands, 1978.

15. Bob Hall and Richard Noblett, "A Handful of Keys: A Man Trying to Get Away—Charlie Spand," *Blues Unlimited* 117 (January/February 1977): 22–23.

16. Richard Sterner, *The Negro's Share: A Study of Income, Housing and Public Assistance* (New York: Harper and Brothers, 1943), pp. 157, 159.

17. Oliver (1984), p. 132.

18. Furry Lewis, "The Panic's On," Vocalion unissued, Chicago, 20 April 1927.

19. Robert "Barbecue Bob" Hicks, "Bad Time Blues," Columbia 14461; reissued on Document DOCD 5047, Atlanta, Georgia, 27 October 1928.

20. Charlie "Specks/Black Patch" McFadden, "Times Are So Tight," Bluebird B5203; reissued on Blues Documents BDCD 6041, Chicago, 2 August 1933.

21. Mack Rhinehart and Brownie Stubblefield, "The Panic Is On," ARC unissued, Chicago, 26 October 1936.

22. Jimmy McCracklin, "The Panic's On," Modern 926; reissued on Ace CHCD 216, Oakland, California, 1954.

23. L. V. Conerly, "High Water," Flyright LP 512, Franklinton, Louisiana, 26 August 1966.

24. Further depression songs from the Hoover era are:

Andy Chatman, "Hard Times on Me Blues," Brunswick 7185; reissued on Document DOCD 5337, Chicago, 1 July 1930.

Charley Jordan, "Tough Times Blues," Vocalion 1568; reissued on Document DOCD 5097, Chicago, 4 November 1930.

Ed Bell, "Starvation Moan," Columbia unissued, Atlanta, Georgia, 4 December 1930.

Elder Curry, "Hard Times," OKeh 8879; reissued on Blues Documents BDCD 6035, Jackson, Mississippi, 16 December 1930.

Skip James, "Hard Time Killin' Floor Blues," Paramount 13065; reissued on Document DOCD 5005, Grafton, Wisconsin, February 1931.

Kid Wesley Wilson, "Hard Times," Columbia 14588-D, New York City, 10 February 1931.

Clara Smith, "Unemployed Papa—Charity Workin' Mama" (composer credit: "Burns and Razaf"), Columbia 14619-D; reissued on Document DOCD 5337, New York City, 4 August 1931.

Francis "Scrapper" Blackwell, "Hard Time Blues," Champion 16361; reissued on Blues Documents BDCD 6029, Richmond, Indiana, 24 November 1931.

King Solomon Hill, "Times Has Done Got Out of Hand," Paramount 13125 (not found), Grafton, Wisconsin, January 1932.

Carrie Edwards, "Hard Time Blues," OKeh 8938; reissued on Document DOCD 5337, New York City, 17 February 1932.

Leroy Carr, "The Depression Blues," Vocalion 1693; reissued on Document DOCD 5137, New York City, 16 March 1932.

Josh White, "Bad Depression Blues," Banner 32437; reissued on Document DOCD 5194, New York City, 11 April 1932.

Blind Arthur Blake, "Depression's Gone From Me Blues," Paramount 13137; reissued on Document DOCD 5027, Grafton, Wisconsin, c. June 1932.

Frank James, "Depression Blues," Champion unissued, Richmond, Indiana, 22 September 1932.

Eugene "Buddy" Moss, "Hard Times Blues," Banner 32736; reissued on Document DOCD 5123, New York City, 19 January 1933.

FDR and Blacks

1. Morgan, pp. 76–77.

2. Traum, p. 8.

3. Morgan, p. 259.

4. Buhite and Levy, p. 15.

5. *Financial Analysts Journal,* as quoted in *NRC Handelsblad,* 31 October 1992.

6. Big Joe Williams, BBC interview, Crawford, Mississippi, 1976, as quoted in Oakley, p. 171.

7. C. R. Smith interview, 6 February 1978, Eleanor Roosevelt Oral History Project, Franklin D. Roosevelt Library, quoted in Weiss, p. 123.

8. Cf. "Blacks on Blacks," *Time*, 27 April 1936, pp. 10–11 and "Elks & Equality," *Time*, 12 August 1935, pp. 9–10.

9. Cf. Weiss, p. 252 and Schulte Nordholt (1956), p. 193.

10. *Time*, 12 August 1935, p. 9.

11. *Ebony*, May 1948, p. 26.

12. Weiss, p. 41 n. 18 (Sara Roosevelt was born on 21 September 1854).

13. *Louisiana Weekly*, 24 November 1934, clipping in Roosevelt Administration Scrapbooks, vol. 2, microfilm reel 16, Schomburg Center for Research in Black Culture. Quotation from Weiss, p. 41, reference in Weiss p. 42 n. 21.

14. The Fisk University Quartette recorded for Victor (1909 and 1911), Edison (unknown date), Columbia (1915, 1916, 1919, 1920, 1924 and 1926) and Rainbow (1935).

15. Kirk, p. 117.

16. Broughton, p. 13. For an alternative view of the processes at work, see Doug Seroff, "The Original Fisk Jubilee Singers and the Spiritual Tradition," *Keskidee* 2 (1990): 9.

17. Goreau, pp. 61–62.

18. Weiss, p. 187. Cf. Ralph D. Casey, "Republican Propaganda in the 1936 Campaign," *Public Opinion Quarterly* 1 (April 1937): 35.

19. Sheldon Harris, p. 472.

20. Sheldon Harris, obituary for Viola Wells, *Living Blues* 64 (March/April 1985): 70. Harris mistakenly gives "1940" as the date of the 20 January 1941 inauguration.

21. Lornell (1989), p. 68.

22. Sheldon Harris, p. 556. FDR's fourth inauguration took place on 20 January 1945.

23. Eleanor Roosevelt, "Some of My Best Friends Are Negro," *Ebony* (February 1953): 23.

24. Eleanor Roosevelt is only mentioned in Annie Brewer's 1937 "Roosevelt Blues" and in Otis Jackson's 1949 "Tell Me Why You Like Roosevelt."

25. "At the White House," *Crisis* (July 1933): 160.

26. "Hampton Quartet aboard Roosevelt band wagon on N.Y. State tour," photo of quartet and caravan in the *Afro-American*, 17 October 1936.

27. Cf. photo from the event in *Norfolk Journal and Guide*, reproduced in Lornell (1989), p. 83.

28. Weiss, p. 38.

29. Chilton (1972), p. 162.

30. Seminole Syncopators, OKeh 40228; reissued on Collectors Items LP 006, New York City, April 1924 and Atlanta, Georgia, 30 August 1930.

31. Basie, p. 126.

32. Elizabeth McDuffie, "FDR Was My Boss," *Ebony* (April 1952): 73.

33. "Little 'Little White House': FDR's favorite musician builds replica of President's home," *Ebony* (May 1948): 25–26.

34. Interview with Graham W. Jackson, Atlanta, 10 June 1977, quoted in Weiss p. 38.

35. Tully, p. 369. For a touching photograph of Graham Jackson playing the accordion with tears streaming down his face, see Lippman or *Life*, 23 April 1945, p. 24.

36. Haskins and Mitgang, p. 222.

37. The film is on *Times Ain't Like They Used To Be: Early Rural & Popular American Music,* Yazoo video 512, Newton, New Jersey, 1992. A photo of the event is in Kirk, p. 243.

38. Kirk, p. 230.

39. David Evans, letter to the author, 24 May 1994. Evans thinks the information was given him by Sam Chatmon (1897–1983), a member of the Mississippi Sheiks.

40. Heilbut, p. 76.

41. Weiss, p. 276.

42. Ibid., pp. 218–19.

43. Stanley Green, pp. 166–67.

44. Weiss, p. 219.

45. The following cover versions of "F.D.R. Jones" were recorded by black and white, American and European artists in 1938 and 1939:

Artist	Record	Reissue	Date
Cab Calloway	Vocalion 4498	Tax MLP-8006	11/2/38
Jack Teagarden		Aircheck 24	11/16/38
Van Alexander	BlueBird B-10092		12/27/38
Mills Brothers	Brunswick A 820[?]	Ace of Clubs ACL 1242	2/?/39
Teddy Stauffer	Telefunken A2974	Teldec 628665	3/28/39
Van Straten	Parlophone F-1505		7/3/39
Carroll Gibbons	Columbia FB-2268	World SH 167/8	7/20/39
Jack Harris	HMV BD-5515		7/20/39
Geraldo (vcl George Elrick)	HMV BD-5510		7/21/39
Ivor Moreton and Dave Kaye	Odéon A 272225		7/28/39
Harry Roy	Par F-1523		8/18/39
Lew Stone (vcl Sam Browne)	Decca F-7185		8/28/39
Glenn Miller		RCA NL 42010	10/6/39
Billy Cotton (vcl Alan Breeze)	Rex 9650		10/16/39
Joe Loss	RZ MR-3188		11/18/39
Jack Hylton (vcl Arthur Askey)	HMV BD-781		11/28/39

46. Rainer E. Lotz, sleeve notes to *Charlie and His Orchestra: German Propaganda Swing, 1941–1942*, Harlequin HQCD 03.

47. For a fictional allusion to this phenomenon cf. Himes, p. 155. For historical information cf. Herzstein.

48. Charlie and His Orchestra, "F. D. R. Jones," Berlin, January 1942; reissued on Harlequin HQCD 03.

I Got to Go to That Red Cross Store

1. Dulles, p. 270.

2. Oliver (1991), pp. 222–23.

3. William Alexander Percy to Oscar Johnston, 11 February 1937, box 45, DPL, as quoted in McMillen, p. 148.

4. Dulles, p. 272.

5. John Cowley, "Shack Bullies and Levee Contractors: Black Protest Songs & Oral History," *Juke Blues* 3 (December 1985): 6–12 and *Juke Blues* 4 (spring 1986): 9–15, revised and expanded from an article in *John Edwards Memorial Foundation Quarterly* 16, no. 60 (winter 1980). A fine general introduction is Daniel.

6. Nan Elizabeth Woodruff, *As Rare As Rain: Federal Relief in the Great Southern Drought of 1930–31* (Urbana and Chicago: University of Illinois Press, 1985), p. 138.

7. Roberta Morgan, "Social Implications and the Human Side," *The Journal of the Birmingham Historical Society* 1, no. 1 (January 1960): 14–15.

8. Jim Baggett, assistant archivist, Birmingham Public Library, letter to the author, 28 July 1994.

9. *The Birmingham News*, 4 November 1932, p. 27.

10. Lucille Bogan, "Groceries on the Shelf," Banner 32904; reissued on Document BDCD 6037, New York City, 19 July 1933. For the lyrics of the song see Lucille Bogan, "Women Won't Need No Men," Agram Blues ABLP 2005, The Netherlands, 1979. The artist who first recorded this song in November 1929 was Charlie "Specks" McFadden (Paramount 12928).

11. Roland wants to go to "Hill," so this line does not make sense.

12. Frank "Springback" James, "New Red Cross Blues," Bluebird B6824; reissued on Document DOCD 5289, Chicago, 21 December 1936.

13. Others are:

Unknown artist "Negro Songs of Protest," "Red Cross Store," Lawrence Gellert unissued; Rounder LP 4013, Georgia(?), 1933.

Pete Harris, "The Red Cross Store," Library of Congress unissued; Document DOCD 5231, Richmond, Texas, May 1934.

Speckled Red, "Welfare Blues," Bluebird B8069; reissued on Document DOCD 5205, Aurora, Illinois, 17 December 1938.

14. The first verse of the song was used by One String Sam in his "I Need a Hundred Dollars," J.V.B. 40; reissued on Document DOCD 5223, Detroit, c. 1956.

15. David Evans, "The Bubba Brown Story," *Blues World* 21 (October 1968): 9 and "Bubba Brown: Folk Poet," *Mississippi Folklore Register* 7, no. 1 (spring, 1973): 15–31.

16. "Boogie" Bill Webb, "Red Cross Store" (two versions), unissued David Evans recordings, New Orleans, Louisiana, 27 August 1970 and "Red Cross Store," Flying Fish LP 506, February 1986.

17. Don Kent, "Marshall Owens," obituary in *Living Blues* 26 (March/April 1976): 7.

18. Roy Dunn, "Red Cross Store," Trix LP 3312, Covington, Georgia, 20 August 1972.

19. *Polk's Birmingham (Jefferson County, Ala.) City Directory, 1934*, vol. 47, Birmingham, Alabama, 1934, p. 355.

20. *1932 Annual Report of the Jefferson County Chapter of the American National Red Cross.* "Birmingham, Alabama."

21. Barnett said Scott's real name was "Sonny" or "Babe" Scarborough, and that he had died shortly before World War II in Shubuta, Mississippi, where he was survived by his sister and a "so-called son." Gress Barnett, interviewed by Gayle Dean Wardlow, as published in *78 Quarterly* 5 (1990): 95.

22. Forrest City Joe, "Red Cross Store," Atlantic LP 1352, Hughes, Arkansas, August 1959.

23. John A. Lomax, "Notes on the Songs of Huddie Ledbetter ('Leadbelly')," c. 1935. Xeroxed by John Cowley from microfilm of Library of Congress field notes etc.—Music 442. Unpublished.

24. Wolfe and Lornell, p. 222.

25. The final stanza is part of "How Do You Know," a song that Leadbelly recorded in New York City on 23 April 1944. It was issued on Asch 331-2 and was reissued on Document DOCD 5228.

26. Oliver (1960; 1991), pp. 219–21.

27. Information from Sylvester Oliver, supplied by David Evans, letter to the author, 20 August 1994.

28. The other four versions of the song McDowell recorded are:

Mississippi Fred McDowell, Red Cross Store Blues, Heritage LP 302, Como, Mississippi, 22 April 1962.

Mississippi Fred McDowell, Red Cross Store Blues, Arhoolie LP 1027, Como, Mississippi, 2 May 1965.

Mississippi Fred McDowell, Red Cross Store Blues, Revival LP 1001, Como, Mississippi, August 1967.

Mississippi Fred McDowell, Red Cross Store, Capitol LP 409, Jackson, Mississippi, 8/10 September 1969.

29. Josh White, "Welfare Blues," Banner 33024; reissued on Document DOCD 5195, New York City, 6 March 1934.

30. John Cowley, unpublished notes prepared for "I'm in the Highway Man," the Flyright album on which the song was issued in 1980 (FLYLP 542).

31. Badger, p. 164.

32. Louisiana Johnny, "Charity Blues," Vocalion unissued; issued on Document DOCD 5331, Chicago, 19 October 1934.

33. Other relief blues are:

Zeke Bingham, "People's Relief Blues," ARC unissued, Hattiesburg, Mississippi, 24 July 1936.

Floyd "Dipper Boy" Council, "I Don't Want No Hungry Woman," Vocalion 04643; reissued on Document DOCD 5168, New York City, 9 February 1937.

Other songs about the American Red Cross are:

Rev. Moses Mason, "Red Cross the Disciple of Christ Today," Paramount 12601; reissued on Document DOCD 5165, Chicago, c. January 1928.

Joel Hopkins, "Thunder in Germany, Red Cross on My Own," Heritage LP 1001; reissued on Collectors Issue LP 5530, Dickinson, Texas, 12 June 1959. (This may be the most mistitled blues song ever: what Hopkins actually sings is "Soldiers dyin' in Germany, Red Cross on my arm.")

CWA, You're the Best Pal We Ever Knew

1. Blind Willie McTell, "Hillbilly Willie's Blues," Decca 7117; reissued on Document DOCD 5008, Chicago, 25 April 1935. This song was based on "NRA Blues" by white country singer Bill Cox. Cf. Tony Russell, pp. 73–74.

2. Hoover, p. 107.

3. Townley (1976), p. 285 offered the outrageous suggestion that in this song RFC stood for "Real Fine Cunt."

4. Leuchtenburg (1963), pp. 72–73.

5. Hoover, pp. 264–65.

6. Bastin (1986), p. 169.

7. The song that was later recorded by Kid Prince Moore, "Pickin' Low Cotton," ARC unissued; issued on Document DOCD 5180, New York City, 8 April 1936 seems to have a musical relationship to White's song, but has different and nonpolitical lyrics.

8. Nathan Miller (1983), p. 339.

9. Kenneth S. Davis (1986), p. 310.

10. Leuchtenburg (1963), pp. 121–22 and Miller, pp. 339–40.

11. Badger, p. 198.

12. For Pullum's biography cf. Guido van Rijn and Hans Vergeer, sleeve notes to *Black Gal*, a Joe Pullum reissue album, Agram ABLP 2012, The Netherlands, 13 February 1986.

13. McElvaine, p. 153.

14. In February 1937 this song would be recorded as "Working for the PWA" by Black Ivory King (see chapter 8).

15. Morgan, p. 409.

16. Bob Groom, sleeve notes to Walter Roland, *Complete Recorded Works in Chronological Order—Volume 2, 1934–35*, a compact disc with Walter Roland reissues, Document DOCD 5145, Austria, 1993.

17. From Roosevelt's third fireside chat of 24 July 1933, as quoted in Buhite and Levy, pp. 34–35.

18. For details on Walter Vinson, see Guido van Rijn and Hans Vergeer, sleeve notes to *Rats Been on My Cheese*, a reissue album of Vinson's prewar work, Agram Blues ABLP 2003, The Netherlands, 1978.

19. Morgan, pp. 401–2.

20. Kenneth S. Davis (1986), p. 258 n.

21. Morgan, pp. 404–5.

22. Group, "Toasts" (6647-A-3), Library of Congress unissued, Sherard (?), Mississippi, 4 August 1942.

23. Dusky Dailey (vocal by Tommy Hicks), "Pension Blues," Vocalion 04977; reissued on Document DOCD 5391, Dallas, Texas, 16 June 1939.

Got a Job on the WPA

1. McElvaine, p. 265.

2. Nathan Miller (1983), p. 367.

3. Henry H. Adams, p. 73.

4. Leuchtenburg (1963), p. 126.

5. McElvaine, p. 183.

6. Ibid., p. 266.

7. "F.D. asked to okey higher WPA wage," *Baltimore Afro-American*, 29 August 1936, p. 7.

8. Broonzy and Bruynoghe, p. 96.

9. "Big Boy" Teddy Edwards, "W-P-A Blues," Decca 7184; reissued on Document DOCD 5440, Chicago, 15 May 1936.

10. Big Bill Broonzy, "W.P.A. Blues," ARC 6-08-61; reissued on Document DOCD 5127, Chicago, 27 May 1936.

11. Merline Johnson, "Working on the Project," ARC 7-10-64; reissued on Document DOCD 52926, Chicago, 30 July 1937.

12. As quoted in Jim O'Neal, sleeve notes to *OKeh Chicago Blues*, Epic EGLP 37318, c. 1983.

13. Howard, p. 130.

14. Ibid., p. 126

15. McElvaine, p. 297.

16. Ibid., p. 298.

17. Henry H. Adams, p. 129 (Farm Security Administration, National Youth Administration and Civilian Conservation Corps).

18. This line is not part of the verse. My correction.

19. At this point Yannick Bruynoghe mistranscribed Big Bill's letter: "While I play this WPA Rag" should be part of the verse and Bruynoghe gave "where" instead of "while" (my correction).

20. Broonzy and Bruynoghe, p. 93.

21. Ibid., p. 94.

22. Big Bill Broonzy, "WPA Rag" (composer credit: "Broomzy"), Vocalion 04429; reissued on Document DOCD 5129, Chicago, 15 September 1938.

23. Morgan, p. 417.

24. Broonzy and Bruynoghe, p. 27.

25. Calvin Frazier, "This Old World's in a Tangle," Detroit, Michigan, 15 October 1938 and "Welfare Blues," Detroit, Michigan, 16 October 1938, Library of Congress unissued; issued on Flyright FLYLP 542.

26. Sitkoff, p. 71.

27. Howard, pp. 257–58.

28. Ibid., p. 258 n. 1. Time 35, no. 26 (24 June 1940): 60.

29. According to Wentworth and Flexner the pink slip is "a discharge notice; notification to a worker that he has been dismissed. Common since c1925. From the traditional printed notice, usu. put in an employee's pay envelope."

30. Harrison, p. 72.

31. McElvaine, p. 308.

32. Raymond Randall to Dear Sir, 6 January 1936, WPA Papers, Box 2; as quoted in Weiss, p. 42.

33. The New York Age: National Negro Weekly 48, no. 31 (7 April 1934): 1.

34. "WPA offered plans to end relief bias," New York Amsterdam News, 30 November 1935, p. 1.

35. "WPA Chief tells of racial problem in giving out relief," Pittsburgh Courier, 7 December 1935.

36. Townley (1976), p. 64.

37. Tad Jones, "Professor Longhair Interview," Living Blues 26 (March/April 1976): 20.

38. Bastin (1986), p. 324.

39. Ibid., p. 323.

40. Cf. "Fighting Josh aims to tumble walls like namesake," Ebony (March 1946): 6–7.

41. Morgan, p. 664.

Guitarist Bill Gaither recorded four songs that briefly mention the WPA:

"L & N Blues," Decca 7246; reissued on Document DOCD 5251, Chicago, 20 October 1936.

"Racket Blues," Decca 7818; reissued on Document DOCD 5253, New York City, 29 June 1939.

"Lazy Woman Blues," Decca 7668; reissued on Document DOCD 5254, Chicago, 13 September 1939.

"New So Much Trouble," Decca 7690; reissued on Document DOCD 5254, Chicago, 22 October 1939.

Other songs that refer to the WPA are:

"Negro Songs of Protest," "Gonna Leave Atlanta," Lawrence Gellert unissued; issued on Rounder LP 4013, Georgia (?), possibly late thirties.

Rosetta Howard, "Stay on It," Decca 7459; reissued on Document DOCD 5273, New York City, 21 April 1938.

Gene Gilmore, "Charity Blues," Decca 7671; reissued on Document DOCD 5444, Chicago, 29 September 1939.

"Champion" Jack Dupree, "All Alone Blues," OK 06642; reissued on Columbia CK 52834-2, Chicago, 27 November 1941.

Sam "Lightnin'" Hopkins, "I Just Don't Care (Candy Kitchen)," Aladdin unissued; issued on Imperial LP 9211, Houston, Texas, February 1948.

Sam "Lightnin'" Hopkins, "Candy Kitchen," RPM 378; reissued on Kent LP 9008, Houston, Texas, 1949/50.

Sam "Lightnin'" Hopkins, "Candy Kitchen," Arhoolie LP 1097, Berkeley, California, 26 November 1961.

Sylvester and His Mule Blues

1. Nathan Miller (1983), p. 346.

2. Paul Garon and Beth Garon, p. 253.

3. Elizabeth McDuffie, "FDR Was My Boss," *Ebony* (April 1952): 74.

4. Headquarters of the Democratic National Committee, "Roosevelt, the Humanitarian," *The Crisis* (October 1936): 298.

5. Graham, p. 267.

6. "Negro Farmer Phones President Roosevelt to Save his Home," *The New York Age: National Negro Weekly* (10 March 1934): 1.

7. Kenneth S. Davis (1986), p. 289.

8. Wolters, pp. 26–27.

9. McDuffie, p. 74.

10. Weiss, p. 226 n. 57, gives three Sylvester Harris references from the Roosevelt Administration Scrapbooks, vol. 1, microfilm reel 16, Schomburg Center for Research in

Black Culture that I have not yet seen: *New York Sun*, 30 October 1934 (?), unidentified Associated Press dispatch, 30 April 1935 and interview with Ida Wood, New York City, 25 October 1976.

11. "Sylvester Vows to Hold on to Farm As Long As He Lives," *Ebony* (March 1957): 93–94.

12. Bob Campbell, "Starvation Farm Blues," Vo 02798; reissued on Story of Blues CD 3528-2, New York City, 1 August 1934.

13. Weiss, p. 55.

Don't Take Away My PWA

1. Leuchtenburg (1963), p. 121.
2. Wolters, p. 195.
3. Leuchtenburg (1963), p. 133.
4. Wolters, p. 198.
5. "Interview with Sterling Tucker," Washington, D. C., 23 March 1977, as quoted in Weiss, p. 53.
6. Myrdal, pp. 1104–5.
7. Ibid., p. 206. On his 29 September 1939 recording "Brown Skin Woman" (Decca 7671; reissued on Document DOCD 5444), Gene Gilmore sang the following verse about FDR's 1936 election: "Well, it takes a plenty money, to get you way up there, like it took the voters to put Mr. Roosevelt in his chair."
8. "20,000 Harlemites Hi de Ho for Roosevelt," *Baltimore Afro-American*, 26 September 1936, pp. 1–2. Elder Lightfoot Solomon Michaux recorded for Victor in 1933–34.
9. Dave "Black Ivory King" Alexander, "Working for the PWA," Decca 7307; reissued on Document DOCD 5278, Dallas, Texas, 15 February 1937.
10. McElvaine, p. 297.
11. Leuchtenburg (1963), p. 257.
12. Kenneth S. Davis (1993), p. 138.
13. Ibid., pp. 421–22.
14. Sitkoff, p. 69.

Some "hard time" blues and interviews from this period not discussed here are:

Charley Jordan, "Tight Time Blues," Decca 7065; reissued on Document DOCD 5098, Chicago, 24 August 1934.

Daddy Stovepipe, "35 Depression," Bluebird B6023; reissued on Document DOCD 5166, Chicago, 26 February 1935.

Lonnie Johnson, "Hard Times Ain't Gone No Where," Decca 7388; reissued on Blues Documents BDCD 6024, Chicago, 8 November 1937.

Rowena Knight/Liberty High School Quartet, "Hard Times," Library of Congress unissued, Newton, Texas, 16 May 1939.

Ida Cox, "Hard Times Blues," Vocalion 05298; reissued on Affinity AFSCD 1015, New York City, 31 October 1939.

Harriet McClintock, "Monologue on Hard Times and Family," Library of Congress unissued, Sumterville, Alabama, 29 October 1940.

Josh White, "Hard Times Blues," Key 516; reissued on Document DOCD 5405, New York City, 1941.

Ollie Shepard, "Hard Times Is on Me," OKeh 06409; reissued on Document DOCD 5435, New York City, 2 May 1941.

Bill "Jazz" Gillum, "Down South Blues," Bluebird B9004; reissued on Document DOCD 5199, Chicago, 5 December 1941.

The Sales Tax Is on It

1. McElvaine, p. 23.
2. Ibid., p. 24.
3. Ibid., p. 57.
4. Hoover, p. 468.
5. Myrdal, p. 1270.
6. Ibid., p. 334.
7. Hoover, p. 138 n. 2.
8. Badger, p. 55.
9. Kenneth S. Davis (1986), p. 138.
10. Ratner, p. 467.
11. Leuchtenburg (1963), p. 154.
12. A sexual blues punning on the poll tax is Monkey Joe, "Taxes on My Pole," Vocalion 04471; reissued on Document DOCD 5412, Chicago, 8 September 1938.
13. McElvaine, pp. 260–63.
14. Advertisement in the *Chicago Defender*, 11 April 1936, p. 32.
15. Old Ced Odom, "It's Your Yas Yas Yas," Decca 7247; reissued on DOCD 5388, Chicago, 30 September 1936.
16. Leuchtenburg (1963), p. 154.

When the Soldiers Get Their Bonus

1. Waters and White, pp. 284–88.
2. Morgan, p. 356.
3. McElvaine, p. 93.

4. Kenneth S. Davis (1986), p. 78 n. The date in Davis's note is incorrect; it should be the summer of 1932 (not 1933).

5. Hoover, p. 361.

6. Ibid., pp. 225–32.

7. Morgan, p. 357.

8. Nathan Miller (1983), p. 273.

9. Coit, p. 436.

10. Nathan Miller (1983), p. 359.

11. Joe Pullum, "Black Gal No. 4," Bluebird B5947; reissued on Document DOCD 5393, San Antonio, Texas, 29 January 1935.

12. Waters and White, p. 286.

13. Kenneth S. Davis (1986), p. 513.

14. Ibid., p. 617.

15. Morgan, p. 407.

16. Guido van Rijn, Hans Vergeer and Cor van Sliedregt, sleeve notes to *Black Gal*, Joe Pullum's first reissue album, Agram ABLP 2012, Haarlem, The Netherlands, 13 February 1986.

17. This is take 2. An unissued take 1 was issued on Document DOCD 5307.

18. According to Wentworth and Flexner, the slang word "hinkty" or "hincty" that Wheatstraw uses in the song means "snobbish."

19. Advertisement in the *Chicago Defender*, 1 February 1936, p. 3. Other Ford dealers aimed their *Chicago Defender* ads at the bonus veterans as well: "Veterans! Buy your new or used Ford" (13 June 1936) and "Make your bonus $$ go farther! A brand new Ford for as low as $150 down" (20 June 1936).

20. Red Nelson, "What a Time I'm Havin' (Off the Soldiers' Bonus)" (composer credit: "Nelson"), Decca 7185; reissued on Old Tramp OTCD 06, Chicago, 18 April 1936.

21. Bob Groom pointed out "this group may have some connection with the town of Edgewater on the outskirts of Mobile, Alabama." Hattiesburg, Mississippi, where they recorded, is only about a hundred miles from Mobile along US 98. See "Blues Forum," No. 172, column in *Blues World* 28 (March 1970): 12.

22. Five years later this song was recorded by Bill "Jazz" Gillum with Big Bill Broonzy on guitar:
Bill "Jazz" Gillum, "My Big Money," BlueBird 34-0707; reissued on Document DOCD 5199, Chicago, 30 July 1942.

23. Robert Lee McCoy, "I Have Spent My Bonus," Bluebird B7303; reissued on Wolf WBCD 002, Aurora, Illinois, 11 November 1937.

24. Kenneth S. Davis (1986), pp. 663–65.

25. Leuchtenburg (1963), p. 147.

26. Hoover, p. 469.

27. Davis (1986), p. 665.

28. Lash, pp. 366–67.

Further songs that mention the bonus issue are:

B. K. "The Black Ace" Turner, "Bonus Man Blues," ARC unissued, Fort Worth, Texas, 5 April 1936.

Frank Busby, "'Leven Light City," Decca 7295; reissued on Document DOCD 5252, Chicago, 6 April 1937.

Cedar Creek Sheik, "Jimmy Shut His Store Doors," Bluebird B6634; reissued on Old Tramp OTCD 03, Charlotte, N.C., 15 June 1936.

There is even a post-World War II bonus song, possibly referring to the 1944 GI Bill of Rights:

Eddie "Cleanhead" Vinson, "Bonus Pay" (composer credit: "Vinson"), Mercury 8039; reissued on Trip TLP 5590, c. spring 1947.

The "Scottsboro Boys"

1. Carter, p. vii.

2. Ibid., p. 5.

3. The "Scottsboro boys" were Olen Montgomery (age unknown), Clarence Norris (seventeen), Haywood Patterson (nineteen), Ozie Powell (seventeen), Willie Roberson (sixteen), Charley Weems (twenty), Eugene Williams (thirteen), Andrew Wright (nineteen) and Leroy "Roy" Wright (thirteen).

4. Badger, p. 288.

5. Allen K. Chalmers, "Scottsboro Boys," in *The Thirties: A Time to Remember*, ed. Don Congdon (New York: Simon and Schuster, 1962), p. 172.

6. *The New York Age: National Negro Weekly*, "Scottsboro Trial Opens in Decatur with Counsel for Defense Scoring Heavily in Motion to Quash Indictments," 1 April 1933, p. 1.

7. Carter, p. 186.

8. Ibid., p. 213.

9. Ibid., p. 215.

10. Ibid., p. 238.

11. Ibid., p. 84.

12. "Scottsboro Once More on Trial: Alabama Now Hopes for an End to this Case," *Life*, 19 July 1937, pp. 30–31. Reprinted in Goodman between pp. 274 and 275.

13. Goodman, p. 271.

14. Carter, p. 249.

15. Chalmers in Congdon, p. 172.

16. *Afro-American*, 2 December 1933.

17. Carter, p. 307.

18. Orville Gilley was a white witness for the prosecution who claimed to have witnessed the whole affair.

19. Louis McHenry Howe to Attorney General Homer Cummings, 22 June 1934 and Randolph Preston, memorandum of 3 July 1934 as quoted in Carter, p. 392 n. 55.

20. "Mac" is Lizzie's husband, Irvin McDuffie, who had to leave the White House due to alcohol-related problems in 1939.

21. Elizabeth McDuffie, "FDR Was My Boss," *Ebony* (April 1952): 81.

22. Carter, pp. 322, 324.

23. Ibid., p. 379

24. Ibid., p. 383.

25. Allan Knight Chalmers to Forney Johnston, 11 November 1938, as quoted in Carter, p. 392.

26. Franklin Delano Roosevelt to Bibb Graves, 7 December 1938, as quoted in Carter, p. 394.

27. Carter, p. 394.

28. Bibb Graves to Franklin Delano Roosevelt, 27 December 1938, as quoted in Carter, p. 397 n. 67.

29. Wolfe and Lornell, p. 207.

30. Ibid., p. 208.

31. Ibid.

32. Ibid., p. 222.

33. Handbill of Apollo Theatre, in Scottsboro Administrative File 2, NAACP Papers, as quoted in Carter, p. 385 n. 38.

34. Wolfe and Lornell, p. 59.

35. Ibid., pp. 70–87.

36. Ibid., pp. 99–121.

37. Carter, pp. 411–13.

38. Max Roach Quartet, "Scott Free," Soul Note SNCD 1103, Milano, Italy, 31 May 1984.

Uncle Sam Is Calling

1. Sara Martin, "Uncle Sam Blues," OKeh 8085; reissued on Document DOCD 5395, New York City, c.17 July 1923.

2. Cf. 1923 versions by Edna Hicks, Clara Smith and Tudie Wells.

3. Buhite and Levy, p. 150.

4. Kenneth S. Davis (1993), p. 493.

5. Pen Bogert, *Hidden History: The Story of Blues in Louisville*, forthcoming. Extract

published as notes to Bill Gaither (Leroy's Buddy), *Complete Recorded Works in Chronological Order, Volume 1*, Document DOCD 5251, Austria, 1994.

6. "The FDR Tapes: Secret Recordings Made in the Oval Office of the President in the Autumn of 1940," *American Heritage* 33 (February/March 1982): 23–24.

7. Weiss, p. 277.

8. Blum, p. 188.

9. The same theme was used by guitarist Brownie McGhee in his "Million Lonesome Women," OKeh 06329; reissued on Columbia CD 475700-2, Chicago, 22 May 1941.

10. Kenneth S. Davis (1993), p. 604.

11. Leuchtenburg (1963), p. 308.

12. For a photograph of the event see Freedman, p. 137.

13. Further patriotic calls to defend the country were:

Yank Rachell, "Army Man Blues," Bluebird B8840; reissued on Wolf WBCD 007, Chicago, 3 April 1941.

Leroy Williams, "Uncle Sam Done Called," Library of Congress unissued, issued on Flyright FLYLP 541, Lake Cormorant, Mississippi, c. 24–31 August 1941.

Eva Taylor, "Uncle Sammy Here I Am," Bluebird B11368, New York City, 22 October 1941.

Big Bill Broonzy, "In the Army Now," OKeh 06601; reissued on Document DOCD 5133, Chicago, 2 December 1941.

Jimmy Rushing, "For the Good of Your Country," Columbia 36685; reissued on CBS LP 54163, 27 July 1942.

14. Dixon and Snowden, p. 54.

15. Ibid., p. 55.

16. Haskins (1986), p. 35.

17. Nat "King" Cole, "Gone With the Draft" (composer credit: Earl Dramin-Wesley Prince-Nat King Cole), Decca 8535, Los Angeles, 6 December 1940.

18. Other songs that deal with the training camps are:

Ollie Shepard, "Army Camp Blues," OKeh 06409; reissued on Document DOCD 5435, New York City, 2 May 1941.

Nora and Delle, "Army Camp Blues" (composer credit: "King-Merridy"), Decca 7852, New York City, 10 June 1941.

19. Blum, p. 184.

20. Ibid., p. 185.

21. Burns (1971), p. 54.

22. Bastin (1986), p. 324.

23. Mullen, p. 52.

24. This Leadbelly recording comprises matrices 6407-A-1 (spoken introduction) and 6407-A-2 (song). It had been recorded before Pearl Harbor as "The Roosevelt Song,"

Library of Congress unissued; issued on Document DLP 612, Washington, D. C., 23 August 1940 (see chapter 14).

Other songs on the draft are:

Tampa Red, "You'd Better Be Ready to Go," Bluebird B8890; reissued on Document DOCD 5212, Chicago, 24 June 1941.

Harmon "Peetie Wheatstraw" Ray (issued as by Joe McCoy), "Got to Go Blues," Bluebird B8956; reissued on Blues Documents BDCD 6020, Chicago, 30 January 1942.

Pearl Harbor Blues

1. Morgan, p. 574.
2. Sam "Lightnin'" Hopkins, "December 7, 1941," Avco Embassy AVELP 33006, Houston (?), Texas, 1961. Hopkins only uses stanza one of the Clayton original.
3. Roy Dunn, "Pearl Harbor Blues," Trix LP 3312, Covington, Georgia, 2 July 1971. Dunn uses stanzas 1, 3 and 4 of the Clayton original.
4. Lonnie Johnson, "From 20 to 44," Bluebird B8980; reissued on Blues Documents BDCD 6025, Chicago, 13 February 1942.
5. Burns (1971), p. 246. Johnson's year of birth has mistakenly been quoted as 1889 and 1893 (cf. Samuel B. Charters, notes to Lonnie Johnson, "The Complete Folkways Recordings," Smithsonian Folkways SFCD 40067).
6. Roosevelt's speech is quoted in Burns (1971), pp. 165–67.
7. Blum, p. 161.
8. *Time*, 22 December 1941.
9. Blum, pp. 46–47.
10. Lonnie Johnson, "Baby, Remember Me," Bluebird 34-0714; reissued on Blues Documents BDCD 6025, Chicago, 13 February 1942.
11. Lonnie Johnson, "The Last Call," Bluebird B8980; reissued on Blues Documents BDCD 6025, Chicago, 13 February 1942.

Some further songs that refer to the Japanese are:

Wee Bea Booze, "Uncle Sam Come and Get Him" (composer credit: "Grainger"), Decca 8619; reissued on Wolf WBJCD 007, New York City, 19 March 1942.

David Edwards, "The Army Blues," Library of Congress unissued; issued on Indigo OGOCD 2003, Clarksdale, Mississippi, 20 July 1942.

Oran "Hot Lips" Page, "Uncle Sam's Blues (Uncle Sam Ain't No Woman)," V-Disc 191, New York, 8 March 1941. "Uncle Sam Blues," Associated Transcriptions, New York, 8 June 1944. "Uncle Sam's Blues" take 3, Savoy 520; reissued on Foxy LP 9007 and take 6, Savoy 755; reissued on Savoy LP 2208. New York City, 14 June 1944. "Uncle Sam Blues," unissued (?), Voice of America Concert, New York, c. 1944–45.

William "Lawyer/Soldier Boy" Houston, "In the Army Since 1941," Atlantic unissued; issued on Atlantic LP 7226, Dallas, Texas, 1950.

Arthur Weston, "Uncle Sam Called Me (I Got to Go)," Testament TLP 2209; reissued on Testament TCD 5012, East St. Louis, September 1964 and Adelphi ADLP 1012, East St. Louis, September 1969.

12. Lucky Millinder, "Let Me Off Uptown," Alamac 2425, possibly Savoy Ballroom, New York City, 7 December 1941, as quoted by Howard Rye in *Blues & Rhythm* 6 (February 1985): 40.

13. "Schicklgruber" was the original name of Adolf Hitler's father.

14. Lucky Millinder, "Fightin' Doug MacArthur" (composer credit: "Buck Ram"), Decca 4261; reissued on Classics CD 712, New York City, 18 February 1942.

15. Morgan, p. 623.

16. Ibid., p. 624.

17. This version of the song was also collected by Frank C. Brown. It was sent in by a teacher in the Durham High School for Negroes in September 1944. Transcript in *Folk Ballads from North Carolina*, vol. 2 of *The Frank C. Brown Collection of North Carolina Folklore*, ed. Newman Ivey White (Durham, N. C.: Duke University Press, 1957), transcription 241, p. 553.

The following unissued recording may well be a version of the Selah Jubilee song:

New York, Georgia Singers, "Pearl Harbor," Library of Congress unissued, Fort Valley, Georgia, June/July 1943.

18. Other versions of "What a Time" are:

Hixson Harmony Five, "What a Time (Pearl Harbor)," unissued field recordings by Byron Arnold, 10 July 1947.

Percy Wilborn, "Oh, What a Time (A History of World War II)," 77 LALP 12-3, Retrieve State Farm, Snipe, Texas, 12 March 1951. Wilborn uses twenty-two couplets from the Soul Stirrers version, but adds three original ones about the dropping of the atomic bomb.

After President Kennedy's assassination Brother Thurman Ruth and the Harmoneers used the song for a reflection entitled "That Awful Day in Dallas," Savoy 4208, 29 November 1963. As a member of the Selah Jubilee Singers, Ruth had been one of the three composers of the 1941 original.

The most recent version of "What a Time" was recorded by the Harps of Melody in Memphis on 30 November 1985. This unissued High Water recording borrows some stanzas from the Soul Stirrers version, but it also contains an original appraisal of black hero Dorie Miller (cf. chapter 16). The lead singer who claims to have composed the lyrics is Ruth Youngblood.

19. This is the final and complete version of the song that Ezell had twice tried to record earlier in the session as "Let's Go Fight" (7042-A and 7042-B).

20. A photo taken at one of the shows was published in Cohn, p. 204.

21. Bruce Bastin, "Fort Valley Blues," *Blues Unlimited* 111 (December 1974/January 1975): part 1; 112 (March/April 1975): part 2; and 113 (July/August 1975): part 3.

22. Georgia blues guitarist John Lee Zeigler (b. 1929), who was Ezell's neighbor, clearly remembers Ezell playing this song. Zeigler thinks Ezell died in the late fifties (interview with John Lee Zeigler, Utrecht, The Netherlands, 18 November 1995).

23. Buster "Buzz" Ezell, "Do Right By My Country" (7046-A), Library of Congress unissued, Fort Valley, Georgia, 1 August 1943. Also at Fort Valley was Buster Brown (1911–1976), who was later to achieve fame as a popular rhythm and blues artist with his hit recording "Fannie Mae." The following recording he made in 1943 is of interest for its wartime lyrics:

Buster Brown, "War Song," Library of Congress unissued; reissued on Matchbox SDMLP 250, Fort Valley, Georgia, 5 March 1943.

Of similar interest is Deacon Sam Jackson, "Tear Tokyo Down," Library of Congress unissued, Fort Valley, Georgia, June/July 1943.

24. All eight 1941 Willie "61" Blackwell recordings were reissued on Document DOCD 5229.

25. In his *The Land Where the Blues Began* (London: Methuen, 1993), p. 10, Alan Lomax tries to reconstruct the event from a fifty-two-year old memory:

Willie B. came blundering from the bar. "Nuff of them old wore-down songs," he muttered. "We gotta put this in high. Give it a modern kick. Now listen," he said, turning his drunken gaze on me. "You pretty nice white man. Least I believe you are. And I'm gonna give you my latest composin for your record. But don't you put it on no radio. Do, and I'll be on you like that Memphis cop was on Brown here." Willie laughed and the others looked embarrassed. "'Member how that was? Well, this is a record of my knowledge of the Japs. The title is A Jap Girl for Next Christmas from Santy Claus." He began in his broken voice:

Goodbye, goodbye, I got to leave, girl, Uncle Sam done call,
I got to fight for you, America and God,
I got to fight for you, America and God,

"This is one of my recordings because I'm an American citizen . . . I am an American citizen," he muttered, glaring around. "These Memphis cops call me vagrant, but I'm a musician. I'm a recording artist for the Vict'ry company. Known all over the world. But these Southern laws don't recognize a man by his talent. They just think a . . . ." He paused and brought his face close to mine. "You ain't from round here. You don't play no part in all this mess goin round here. You don't know nothing about it, and I, Willie B., better known as 61, because I rambles 61 Highway from Chicago clean down to New Orleans with my guitar for my buddy, I am going to tell you. . . ."

26. The first writer who correctly heard "skull" instead of "girl," thus solving this riddle, is Jim O'Neal; see "BluEsoterica," *Living Blues* 114 (April 1994): 128. Another example of grisly souvenirs is to be found in Inez Washington, "Soldier Man Blues,"

Cincinnati 2301, 1945, which contains the line: "I know good old Uncle Sam, will send my man back to me: I'll know he'll bring me souvenirs, I hope it's Tojo and Hitler's ears."

27. Lisio (1974), p. 285.

28. Morgan, p. 731.

29. MacArthur, pp. 96–97.

30. Garbled line, probably intended to be "for more essential war use."

31. Margaret Truman, p. 238.

32. Geoffrey C. Ward, "Douglas MacArthur: An American Soldier," *National Geographic* 181, no. 3 (March 1992): 54–83.

Fifty years after the Japanese attack on Pearl Harbor Bob Groom wrote an article about the attack and its aftermath as reflected in blues and gospel recordings. See "Tiger in the Night," *Blues & Rhythm* 66 (January 1992): 12–15. The article proved a useful source of reference in the preparation of this chapter.

33. Some "the war is over" blues are:

John "Shifty" Henry, "Hypin Women Blues," Enterprise 106, Los Angeles, California, c. 1945.

"Big" Jim Wynn, "Shipyard Woman," Gilt Edge 527; reissued on Whiskey, Women, And . . . LP 703, Los Angeles, California, 1945.

Pleasant Joseph, "Post War Future Blues," Philo 118, New York City, 5 October 1945.

Louis Jordan, "Reconversion Blues," Decca 18762; reissued on Charly CDX-7, New York City, 15 October 1945.

Duke Henderson, "G.I. Blues," Globe 108, Los Angeles, California, 1946.

Turner Willis, "Re-enlisted Blues," Trilon 1058, Oakland, California, 1946.

Joe Turner, "I Got My Discharge Papers," Savoy unissued; issued on Savoy LP 2223, Los Angeles, California, 23 January 1946.

Pleasant Joseph, "Desperate G.I. Blues," Savoy 5526; reissued on Savoy LP 2224, New York City, 13 February 1946.

Huddie "Leadbelly" Ledbetter, "Defense Blues," Disc 5085; reissued on Document DOCD 5311, New York City, c. June 1946.

Charles Brown, "Sunny Road," Exclusive 233, Los Angeles, California, late 1946.

Al "Stomp" Russell, "World War 2 Blues," Queen 4162, Los Angeles, California, December 1946.

Walter Davis, "Things Ain't Like They Use To Be," Victor 20-2335; reissued on Document DOCD 5287, Chicago, 5 February 1947.

Huddie "Leadbelly" Ledbetter, "National Defense Blues," Folkways LP 2941, New York City, October 1948.

A 1949 song about President Truman is:

Harmon "Peetie Wheatstraw" Ray, "President's Blues," Decca 48107; reissued on Wolf WBJCD 007, New York City, 20 May 1949.

Some blues about the atomic bomb are:

Homer Harris, "Atomic Bomb Blues," Columbia unissued; issued on CBS CD 467249 2, Chicago, 27 September 1946.

"Memphis" Willie Borum, "Overseas Blues," Bluesville LP 1034; reissued on Original Blues Classics CD 573, Memphis, Tennessee, 12 August 1961.

Hitler and Hell

1. Havelock, p. 31.

2. Burns (1971), p. 67. Cf. J. A. Garraty, "The New Deal, National Socialism, and the Great Depression," *American Historical Review* 78, no. 4 (1973): 907–44.

3. Nathan Miller (1983), p. 418.

4. Kenneth S. Davis (1986), pp. 125–27.

5. Sherwood, p. 116.

6. Kenneth S. Davis (1993), p. 437.

7. Ibid., p. 439.

8. Burns (1971), p. 174.

9. Franklin Delano Roosevelt, fireside chat 11 September 1941 (in Buhite and Levy, p. 193).

10. Ibid., p. 194. Perhaps this quotation inspired Doctor Clayton when he wrote his "Pearl Harbor Blues" (cf. chapter 13).

11. Burns (1971), p. 68.

12. Eight years later Edwards recorded the song as "Gotta Get Together," New York, Savoy LP 16000, August 1949.

13. For an analysis of blues recordings about Joe Louis see "Joe Louis and John Henry," chapter 5 in Oliver (1968).

14. Bill "Jazz" Gillum, War Time Blues (composer credit: "W. Gillum,") Bluebird B8943; reissued on Document DOCD 5199, Chicago, 5 December 1941.

15. Burns (1971), p. 174.

16. A later version of this song, with less comprehensive lyrics, is Huddie "Leadbelly" Ledbetter, "Mr. Hitler," Folkways LP 2034; reissued on Document DOCD 5310, New York City, c. May 1944.

17. Earlier Leadbelly had composed a campaign song for Wendell Willkie, the Republican Presidential candidate of 1940. In "He Was the Man," Folkways LP2942, New York City, October 1948, Leadbelly had "imagined the night of victory for the candidate." Leadbelly made his living singing songs people wanted to hear and in this way he could please both Republicans and Democrats (cf. Wolfe and Lornell, p. 209–10).

18. Burns (1971), p. 309.

19. This line is an adaptation from the 1904 "coon song" "The Preacher and the Bear."

20. Tony Heilbut, sleeve notes for "The Gospel Sound," the album on which the song was reissued in 1972.

21. "Ham and Egg Show: Negro Farmers Vie for Prizes, Learn How to Produce More Food," *Life* (22 March 1943): 21.

22. A later version of Ezell's song is Buster "Buzz" Ezell, "Roosevelt and Hitler," Library of Congress unissued, Fort Valley, Georgia, 1 August 1943. It has not been issued due to technical faults, but it contains verses 1 and 5–12 of the c. 5 March original. The same tune may have been used for the unrecorded "Great Things are Happening in Korea" that Ezell sang in 1951 (cf. chapter 13).

23. Will "Shorty" Love, "Strange Things Wuz Happening," c. 1920–22, transcript in *Folk Ballads from North Carolina*, vol. 2 of *The Frank C. Brown Collection of North Carolina Folklore*, ed. Newman Ivey White (Durham, N. C.: Duke University Press, 1957), transcription 240, p. 553. Brown later recorded Love, "who was a colored janitor for many years on Duke University East Campus," singing his song: Will ("Shorty") Love, "Strange Things Was A-Happening," Library of Congress unissued, Durham, North Carolina, 9 December 1939.

Other recordings based on the "strange things" refrain are:

"Blind" Joe Taggart, "Strange Things Happening in the Land," Paramount 13094; reissued on Document DOCD 5154, Grafton, Wisconsin, c. December 1929.

Rev. A. W. Nix, "Strange Things Happening in the Land," Vocalion 1634, Chicago, 28 March 1931.

John Handcock, "There is Mean Things Happening in this Land," Library of Congress unissued, Washington, D. C., 9 March 1937.

Sister Rosetta Tharpe, "Strange Things Happening Every Day," Decca 8669; reissued on Document DOCD 5335, New York, 22 September 1944.

Sister Rosetta Tharpe, "Strange Things Are Happening," Savoy MGLP 14224, c. 1969.

24. Echoes of this song can be found in Otis "Lightnin' Slim" Hicks, "G.I. Slim," Excello 2169; reissued on Excello LP 8000, Crowley, Louisiana, 1960.

25. The P-47 *Thunderbolt* was one of the single-engined monoplanes that had become the most effective fighter bombers.

26. Sonny Boy Williamson, "Win the War Blues," Bluebird 34-0722; reissued on Document DOCD 5058, Chicago, 14 December 1944.

Blues pianist Roosevelt Thomas "Grey Ghost" Williams (1903–1996) recorded a "Hitler Blues" on an acetate that was sent to Alistair Cooke of the BBC for a 1940 wartime broadcast.

27. Cf. Frank A. Young, "Brown America Takes the Air: The Story of the First Negro Fliers in the United States Air Corps," *Chicago Defender*, 13 June 1942, p. 23.

28. Cf. David Evans, "The Toast in Context," *Journal of American Folklore* 90 (1977), in which references to key works on the subject can be found.

Win the War

1. Rev. J. M. Gates, "When the War Is Over," Bluebird B8851, Atlanta, Georgia, 2 October 1941.

2. One example, which is not discussed here, is Billie Hayes, "Man Shortage Blues," Beacon 5001; reissued on Krazy Kat KKLP 802, New York City, 1945.

3. Burns (1971), p. 334.

4. Ibid., p. 190.

5. Margaret Mead, *And Keep Your Powder Dry*, 1942, pp. 161, 167 and 174, as quoted in Burns, p. 272.

6. Cf. Charles "Cootie" Williams, "Gotta Do Some War Work," Hit 8090; reissued on Affinity AFSLP 1031, New York City, 4 January 1944.

7. Jerome S. Bruner, *Mandate from the People*, 1944, pp. 27–29, as quoted in Burns, p. 467.

8. Franklin Roosevelt, fireside chat of 28 April 1942, as quoted in Buhite and Levy, p. 224.

9. Chilton (1992), p. 121.

10. One example not discussed here is Seth "Skoodle Dum Doo" Richard and [?] Sheffield, "Gas Ration Blues," Regis S107; reissued on Flyright CD 45, prob. Newark, New Jersey, c. late 1943.

11. See "Pearl Harbor" by the Soul Stirrers and "Do Right By My Country" by Buster "Buzz" Ezell in chapter 13.

12. The Gallup Poll, 29 October 1943.

13. Ibid., 17 February 1945.

14. Blum, pp. 132–33.

15. Burns (1971), pp. 258–59.

16. Ibid., p. 227.

17. Goodwin, p. 356.

18. Blum, p. 227.

19. Franklin Roosevelt, fireside chat of 23 February 1942, as quoted in Buhite and Levy, p. 215.

20. Ezell recorded two more versions of this song that day, both called "Obey the Ration Laws" (7052-A and 7052-B). All three versions consist of the same nine couplets and there are hardly any differences in the choice of words. These recordings are still unissued because of technical faults.

21. Blum, p. 222.

22. Ibid., pp. 227–28.

23. Ibid., p. 97.

24. This singer had recorded as Ann Sortier and accompanied Robert Lee McCoy on washboard in 1940. As Amanda Porter/Sorter/Sortier (=Saucier?) she had played

washboard on recordings by Joe McCoy and harmonica blower Bill "Jazz" Gillum in 1941.

25. Paul B. Sheatsley, "O.P.A.," *Blues Unlimited* 91 (May 1972): 20.

26. WAC stands for "Women's Army Corps," WAAC for "Women's Army Auxiliary Corps," and WAVES for "Women Accepted for Volunteer Emergency Service." The SPARs are the Women's Auxiliary of the Coast Guard; the name is adapted from the Coast Guard motto *semper paratus* (always prepared).

27. This song had earlier been recorded for V-Disc 237B; reissued on Official LP 6061, Los Angeles, 22 November 1943. Songwriter Sam Theard ("Lovin' Sam From Down In 'Bam") was an old comedian whose compositions were favored by Louis Jordan.

28. Burns (1971), p. 560.

29. Ross Russell, p. 192.

30. This verse was sung by Blind Lemon Jefferson in his "Wartime Blues," Paramount 12425; reissued on Document DOCD 5017, Chicago, c. November 1927.

31. Townley (1976), p. 392.

32. Burns (1971), pp. 34–35.

33. Blum, p. 17.

34. Franklin Roosevelt, fireside chat of 8 September 1943, as quoted in Buhite and Levy, p. 271.

35. Franklin Roosevelt, fireside chat of 12 June 1944, as quoted in Buhite and Levy, pp. 304–5.

36. Burns (1971), p. 20.

37. Tony Russell, notes to "Rock Little Baby," a reissue album of Gant's work, Flyright LP 4710, 1974.

38. Cf. Dixon and Godrich (1970), p. 99.

39. Ibid., pp. 104–5.

40. Chilton (1992), p. 91.

41. Sanjek and Sanjek, pp. 80–81.

42. Louis Jordan, "G.I. Jive" (composer credit: "Johnny Mercer"), Decca 8659; reissued on Juke Box Lil LP 602, New York City, 15 March 1944.

43. Chilton, p. 106.

44. Huddie "Leadbelly" Ledbetter, "Army Life," Folkways LP 2034; reissued on Document DOCD 5310, c. May 1944. A few months before his death Leadbelly recorded the song live at the University of Texas: "I Don't Want No More of Army Life," Playboy LP 119, Austin, Texas, 15 June 1949.

45. Some other recordings about the war effort are:

Ollie Shepard, "Navy Blues," OKeh unissued, New York City, 6 January 1942.

Bill "Jazz" Gillum, "Woke Up Cold in Hand," Bluebird B9042; reissued on Document DOCD 5199, Chicago, 30 July 1942.

Tell Me Why You Like Roosevelt

1. The Gallup Poll, 10 July 1944.

2. McCullough, p. 327.

3. It used to be thought that James "Jack of All Trades" McCain was a pseudonym for Sonny Boy Williamson. The lyrics, however, give evidence to the contrary: Sonny Boy's wife's name was Lacey Belle, not Lee. McCain also identifies his pianist as "Slim." Memphis Slim (1915–1988) confirmed to Mike Rowe that he had played piano on this recording, and that, although McCain was indeed an uncanny Sonny Boy imitator, he was definitely a different artist. Cf. Mike Rowe, "*Bluebird Blues* by Wolfgang Lorenz," *Blues Unlimited* 148/9 (winter 1987): 56.

4. Burns (1971), p. 560.

5. Moran, p. 226.

6. Bastin (1990), p. 144.

7. Morgan, p. 767.

8. Big Joe Williams, "President Roosevelt," Arhoolie LP 1002, Los Gatos, California, 5 October 1960.

9. Big Joe Williams, "A Man Amongst Men," Testament LP 01; reissued on Testament TCD 5007, Chicago, c. December 1963.

10. Other versions of this Roosevelt saga are:

Evangelist Singers, "Tell Me Why You Like Roosevelt—Parts 1 & 2," Chicago 116, Chicago, April 1946.

Reliable Jubilee Singers, "Tell Me Why You Like Roosevelt—Parts 1 & 2," Apollo 131, c. February 1947.

Soul Stirrers with Willie Eason, "Why I Like Roosevelt—Parts 1 & 2," Aladdin 2018; reissued on Imperial LMLP 94007, Chicago, 2 June 1947.

"Brother" Willie Eason, "Roosevelt a Poor Man's Friend—Parts 1 & 2," Regent unissued, Atlanta, Georgia, 30 April 1951.

Blind Connie Williams, "Tell Me Why You Like Roosevelt," Testament TLP 2225; reissued on Testament TCD 5024, Philadelphia, Pennsylvania, 5 May 1961.

Perry Tillis, "Tell Me Why You Like Roosevelt," Flyright LP 537, Elba, Alabama, 1972.

11. Cf. Shoumatoff.

12. Gunther, p. 415.

13. Ploski and Kaiser, p. 934.

14. Ibid., pp. 610–11.

15. Ibid., p. 577.

16. Kirby, 1992, pp. 110–12 and Ploski and Kaiser, pp. 871–72.

17. Mary McLeod Bethune, "My Secret Talks with FDR," *Ebony* (April 1949): 43–51. The quotation is from p. 46.

18. Otis Jackson, "The Life Story of Madame Bethune—Parts I and II," Peacock 1753, August 1955.

19. Morgan, p. 763.

20. Ploski and Kaiser, pp. 727–28. See also "Slave-born Negro Scientist Is Honored In Alabama," *Life* (22 March 1937): 37–38.

21. Morgan, p. 709.

22. Ibid., p. 201.

23. Ibid., p. 762.

24. Ibid., p. 763.

25. Shoumatoff, p. 115.

26. Ibid., pp. 116–18.

27. Franklin D. Roosevelt, Usher Books, card 64, FDR Library, Hyde Park, New York, microfiche Roosevelt Study Center, Middelburg, The Netherlands.

28. Morgan, p. 769.

29. Eleanor Roosevelt (1949), p. 349.

30. This image is also used in the Southern Bell Singers, "The Tragedy of Kennedy," Vee Jay 934, late 1963. Cf. Guido van Rijn, "Jesus Is a President Too: Actuele Blues en Gospel songs over de moord op John F. Kennedy," in *Amerikanisten: Werk in Uitvoering* (Groningen, The Netherlands: Groningen Universiteitsdrukkerij, 1995).

31. Burns (1971), p. 601.

32. Margaret Truman, pp. 208–9.

33. Whereas two of the Dupree 78s of this session sold five thousand copies each, "F.D.R. Blues/God Bless Our New President!" was bought by only 420 people. Cf. Bastin (1990), p. 155.

34. A very late reference to Roosevelt's death, in a song protesting a police crackdown on the numbers racket, occurs in Arbee Stidham, "Mr. Commissioner," Checker 751; alternate take issued on Chess CHD4CD 9340, Chicago, 22 March 1952.

Conclusion

1. Roy Mack, director, *Rufus Jones for President*, Vitaphone, 1933.

2. Dixon and Godrich (1970), pp. 104–5.

3. The other states of origin are South Carolina (three), Kentucky (two), Florida (two), Virginia (one), Alabama (one), Maryland (one), North Carolina (one) and Oklahoma (one).

4. In "President Roosevelt is Everybody's Friend," a 1934 sermon analyzed in this study, Gates claims he is "now a half a century of age." His cousin Emmett Gates told Pete Lowry that Gates died "in Atlanta c. 1940 . . . his funeral was the biggest ever until Martin Luther King's" (see *Living Blues* 16 [spring 1974]: 45). Gates made his last recordings in Atlanta on 2 October 1941.

5. Miller (1992), p. 363.

6. Winfield, pp. 117–18.

7. Sterling and Kittross, p. 206.

8. Ibid., p. 533.

9. Cf. Raper.

10. Oliver (1985), "Sales Tax on It: Race Records in the New Deal Years," in *Nothing Else to Fear*, p. 200.

11. Winfield, pp. 111–14.

12. Sidey, p. 55.

13. Weiss, p. 299.

14. Sterner, pp. 362–63.

BIBLIOGRAPHY

Adams, D.K. *Franklin D. Roosevelt and the New Deal*. London: The Historical Association, 1979.

Adams, Henry H. *Harry Hopkins: A Biography*. New York: Putnam, 1977.

Badger, Anthony J. *The New Deal: The Depression Years, 1933–1940*. Basingstoke, Hampshire, England: The MacMillan Press, 1989. Reprint, London: MacMillan, 1993.

Bailey, Harry A., Jr. *Negro Politics in America*. Columbus, Ohio: Charles E. Merrill Books, 1967.

Baker, Houston A., Jr. *Singers of Daybreak: Studies in Black American Literature*. Washington, D. C.: Howard University Press, 1974.

———. *The Journey Back: Issues in Black Literature and Criticism*. Chicago: University of Chicago Press, 1980.

———. *Blues Ideology, and Afro-American Literature: A Vernacular Theory*. Chicago: University of Chicago Press, 1984.

———. *Modernism and the Harlem Renaissance*. Chicago: University of Chicago Press, 1987. Reprint, 1989.

Barlow, William. *Looking up at Down: The Emergence of Blues Culture*. Philadelphia: Temple University Press, 1989.

Basie, William "Count." *Good Morning Blues: The Autobiography of Count Basie, as told to Albert Murray*. London: William Heinemann, 1986. Reprint, London: Paladin Books, 1987.

Bastin, Bruce. *Crying for the Carolines*. London: Studio Vista, 1971.

———. *Red River Blues: The Blues Tradition in the Southeast*. Basingstoke, Hampshire, England: MacMillan Press, 1986.

———. *Never Sell a Copyright: Joe Davis and his Role in the New York Music Scene 1916–1978*. Chigwell, Essex, England: Storyville Publications, 1990.

Bell, Bernard W. *The Afro-American Novel and Its Tradition*. Amherst, Mass.: University of Massachusetts Press, 1987.

Blum, John Morton. *V Was for Victory: Politics and American Culture During World War II*. San Diego, Calif: Harcourt Brace Jovanovich, 1976.

Bradford, Perry. *Born with the Blues: His Own Story*. New York: Oak Publications, 1965.

Brogan, Hugh. *Longman History of the United States of America*. London: Longman, 1985. Reprint, London: Book Club Associates, 1993.

Broonzy, William, and Yannick Bruynoghe. *Big Bill Blues: Big Bill Broonzy's Story*. London: Cassell & Co., 1955. Reprint, New York: Oak Publications, 1964.

Broughton, Viv. *Black Gospel: An Illustrated History of the Gospel Sound*. Poole, Dorset, England: Blandford Press, 1985.

Bruin, Leo W. *Malvina My Sweet Woman: The Story of Big Joe Williams*. Utrecht, The Netherlands: Oldie Blues, 1974.

Buhite, Russell D., and David W. Levy, eds. *F.D.R.'s Fireside Chats*. University of Oklahoma Press, 1992. Reprint, Harmondsworth, Middlesex, England: Penguin Books, 1993.

Bunche, Ralph J. *The Political Status of the Negro in the Age of FDR*. Chicago: University of Chicago Press, 1973.

Burns, James MacGregor. *Roosevelt: The Lion and the Fox*. London: Secker & Harburg, 1956.

———. *Roosevelt: The Soldier of Freedom 1940–1945*. London: Weidenfeld & Nicolson, 1971.

Calt, Stephen. *I'd Rather Be the Devil: Skip James and the Blues*. New York: Da Capo Press, 1994.

Calt, Stephen, and Gayle Wardlow. *King of the Delta Blues: The Life and Music of Charlie Patton*. Newton, N. J.: Rock Chapel Press, 1988.

Carter, Dan T. *Scottsboro: A Tragedy of the American South*. London: Oxford University Press, 1969. Reprint, Oxford, 1971.

Chafe, William H. *The Unfinished Journey: America Since World War II*. Oxford: Oxford University Press, 1986. Reprint, New York, 1991.

Charters, Samuel B. *The Country Blues*. New York: Rhinehart, 1959. Reprint, New York: Da Capo Press, 1977.

———. *The Poetry of The Blues*. New York: Oak Publications, 1963. Reprint, New York: Avon Books, 1970.

———. *The Bluesmen*. New York: Oak Publications, 1967.

———. *The Legacy of the Blues: A Glimpse into the Art and the Lives of Twelve Great Bluesmen*. New York: Da Capo Press, 1977.

———. *Sweet as the Showers of Rain: The Bluesmen, Volume II*. New York: Oak Publications, 1977.

Chilton, John. *Who's Who of Jazz: Storyville to Swingstreet.* London: Bloomsbury Bookshop, 1972. Reprint, London: MacMillan, 1985.

————. *Let The Good Times Roll: The Story of Louis Jordan and His Music.* London: Quartet Books, 1992.

Cobb, James C., ed. *The New Deal and the South.* Jackson, Mississippi: University Press of Mississippi, 1984.

————. *The Most Southern Place on Earth: The Mississippi Delta and the Roots of Regional Identity.* New York: Oxford University Press, 1992.

Cohn, Lawrence, ed. *Nothing but the Blues: The Music and the Musicians.* New York: Abbeville Press, 1993.

Coit, Margaret L. *Mr. Baruch.* Cambridge, Mass.: Houghton Mifflin Company, 1957.

Collier, Peter, with David Horowitz. *The Roosevelts: An American Saga.* New York: Simon & Schuster, 1994.

Congdon, Don. *The Thirties: A Time to Remember.* New York: Simon & Schuster, 1962.

Cook, Blanche Wiesen. *Eleanor Roosevelt: Volume One, 1884–1933.* New York: Viking Penguin, 1992. Reprint, Harmondsworth, Middlesex, England: Penguin Books, 1993.

Coolidge, Calvin. *The Autobiography of Calvin Coolidge.* London: Chatto & Windus, 1929.

Courlander, Harold. *Negro Folk Music, U. S. A.* New York: Columbia University Press, 1963.

Cowley, John. *Carnival, Canboulay and Calypso: Traditions in the Making.* Cambridge: Cambridge University Press, 1996

Cullen, Countee. *My Soul's High Song: The Collected Writings of Countee Cullen, Voice of the Harlem Renaissance.* New York: Anchor Books, 1991.

Daniel, Pete. *Deep'n As It Come: The 1927 Mississippi River Flood.* New York: Oxford University Press, 1977.

Daniels, Roger. *The Bonus March: An Episode of the Great Depression.* Westport, Conn.: Greenwood Publishing, 1971.

Davis, John P., ed. *The American Negro Reference Book.* Englewood Cliffs, N. J.: Prentice Hall, 1966.

Davis, Kenneth S. *FDR: The New Deal Years, 1933–1937.* New York: Random House, 1986.

————. *FDR: Into the Storm, 1937–1940.* New York: Random House, 1993.

Dixon, R. M. W., and J. Godrich. *Recording the Blues.* London: Studio Vista, 1970.

————. *Blues & Gospel Records 1902–1943.* 3rd ed. Chigwell, Essex: Storyville Publications, 1982.

Dixon, Willie, and Don Snowden. *I Am the Blues: The Willie Dixon Story.* London: Quartet Books, 1989.

Dulles, Foster Rhea. *The American Red Cross: A History*. New York: Harper and Brothers, 1950.

Ellison, Mary. *Extensions of the Blues*. New York: Riverrun Press, 1989.

————. *Lyrical Protest: Black Music's Struggle Against Discrimination*. New York: Praeger, 1989.

Evans, David. *Tommy Johnson*. London: Studio Vista, 1971.

————. *Big Road Blues: Tradition and Creativity in the Folk Blues*. Berkeley, Calif.: University of California Press, 1982.

Fahey, John. *Charley Patton*. London: Studio Vista, 1970.

Ferris, William, Jr. *Blues from the Delta*. London: Studio Vista, 1970.

Frazier, E. Franklin. *The Negro Church in America*. New York: Schocken Books, 1964.

Freedman, Russell. *Franklin Delano Roosevelt*. New York: Clarion Books, 1990.

Freidel, Frank. *Franklin D. Roosevelt and the New Deal: An Inaugural Lecture*. Oxford: Oxford University Press, 1956.

Gallup, George, H. *The Gallup Poll: Public Opinion 1935–1971, Volume One, 1935–1948*. New York: Random House, 1972.

Garon, Paul. *The Devil's Son-in-Law: The Story of Peetie Wheatstraw and His Songs*. London: Studio Vista, 1971.

————. *Blues and the Poetic Spirit*. London: Eddison Bluesbooks, 1975.

Garon, Paul, and Beth Garon. *Woman with Guitar: Memphis Minnie's Blues*. New York: Da Capo Press, 1992.

Gates, Henry Louis, Jr. *Black Literature and Literary Theory*. New York: Methuen, 1984.

————. *Figures in Black: Words, Signs, and the "Racial" Self*. New York: Oxford University Press, 1987.

————. *The Signifying Monkey: A Theory of Afro-American Literary Criticism*. New York: Oxford University Press, 1988.

Gatewood, Willard B., Jr. *Theodore Roosevelt and the Art of Controversy*. Baton Rouge, La.: Louisiana State University Press, 1970.

George, Nelson. *The Death of Rhythm & Blues*. New York: Random House, 1988.

Goodman, James. *Stories of Scottsboro*. New York: Random House, 1994.

Goodwin, Doris Kearns. *No Ordinary Time: Franklin and Eleanor Roosevelt: The Home Front in World War II*. New York: Simon & Schuster, 1994.

Goreau, Laurraine. *Just Mahalia, Baby: The Mahalia Jackson Story*. Waco, Tex., 1975. Reprint, Gretna, La.: Pelican Publishing Company, 1984.

Graham, Otis L., ed. *Franklin D. Roosevelt: His Life and Times: An Encyclopedic View*. Boston, Mass.: G. K. Hall, 1985.

Green, Archie. *Only a Miner: Studies in Recorded Coal-Miner Songs*. Urbana, Ill.: University of Illinois Press, 1972.

Green, Stanley. *Ring Bells! Sing Songs! Broadway Musicals of the 1930's*. New York: Galahad Books, 1971.

Groom, Bob. *The Blues Revival*. London: Studio Vista, 1971.

Gunther, John. *Roosevelt in Retrospect*. New York: Harper, 1950.

Hacker, Andrew. *Two Nations: Black and White, Separate, Hostile, Unequal*. New York: Charles Scribner's Sons, 1992.

Harlan, Louis R. *Booker T. Washington: The Making of a Black Leader*. New York: Oxford University Press, 1972.

Harris, Michael. W. *The Rise of Gospel Blues: The Music of Thomas Andrew Dorsey in the Urban Church*. New York: Oxford University Press, 1992.

Harris, Sheldon. *Blues Who's Who: A Biographical Dictionary of Blues Singers*. New Rochelle, N. Y.: Arlington House, 1979. Reprint, New York: Da Capo Press, 1989.

Harrison, Daphne Duval. *Black Pearls: Blues Queens of the 1920s*. New Brunswick, N. J.: Rutgers University Press, 1988.

Haskins, Jim. *Nat King Cole: The Man and his Music*. London: Robson Books, 1986.

Haskins, Jim, and Mitgang, N. R. *Mr. Bojangles: The Biography of Bill Robinson*. New York: Morrow, 1988.

Havelock, Eric A. *The Muse Learns to Write: Reflections on Orality and Literacy from Antiquity to the Present*. New Haven: Yale University Press, 1986.

Heilbut, Anthony. *The Gospel Sound: Good News and Bad Times*. New York: Garden City, 1971. Reprint, New York, Limelight Edition, 1985.

Herzstein, Robert Edwin. *Roosevelt & Hitler: Prelude to War*. New York: Paragon House, 1989.

Himes, Chester B. *If He Hollers Let Him Go*. 1945. Reprint, London: Pluto Press, 1986.

Hoover, Herbert C. *The Memoirs of Herbert Hoover: The Great Depression, 1929–1941*. New York: The MacMillan Company, 1952. Reprint, 1965.

Howard, Donald S. *The WPA and Federal Relief Policy*. New York: Russell Sage Foundation, 1943.

Jackson, Bruce. *Wake Up Dead Man: Afro-American Worksongs from Texas Prisons*. Cambridge, Mass.: Harvard University Press, 1972.

———. *Get Your Ass in the Water and Swim Like Me: Narrative Poetry from Black Oral Tradition*. Cambridge, Mass.: Harvard University Press, 1974.

Johnson, James Weldon. *Along this Way: The Autobiography of James Weldon Johnson*. New York: Viking Penguin, 1933. Reprint, Harmondsworth, Middlesex, England: Penguin Books, 1990.

Kimball, Warren F. *The Juggler: Franklin Roosevelt as Wartime Statesman.* Princeton, N. J.: Princeton University Press, 1991.

Kirby, John B. *Black Americans in the Roosevelt Era: Liberalism and Race.* Knoxville, Tenn.: University of Tennessee Press, 1980. Reprint, 1992.

Kirk, Elise K. *Music at the White House: A History of the American Spirit.* Urbana, Ill.: University of Illinois Press, 1986.

Lammers, A. "Franklin D. Roosevelt: De Rechters en de Democraten 1936–1938." Ph. D. diss., Meppel, The Netherlands, 1977.

———. *God Bless America: Zegeningen en Beproevingen van de Verenigde Staten.* Meppel, The Netherlands: Balans, 1987.

———. *Franklin Delano Roosevelt: Koning van Amerika.* Amsterdam, The Netherlands: Balans, 1992.

Lash, Joseph P. *Eleanor and Franklin: The Story of their Relationship Based on Eleanor Roosevelt's Private Papers.* New York: W. W. Norton & Company, 1971.

Laughton, Robert, and Cedric J. Hayes. *Gospel Records, 1943 to 1969: A Black Music Discography.* London: Record Information Services, 1992.

Leadbitter, Mike, ed. *Nothing but the Blues.* London: Hannover Books, 1971.

Leadbitter, Mike, and Neil Slaven. *Blues Records 1943–1970, Volume One—A to K.* London: Hannover Books, 1987.

Leadbitter, Mike, Neil Slaven, and Leslie Fancourt. *Blues Records 1943–1970, Volume Two—L to Z.* London: Record Information Services, 1994.

Leuchtenburg, William E. *Franklin D. Roosevelt and the New Deal, 1932–1940.* New York: Harper & Row, 1963.

———. *In the Shadow of FDR: From Harry Truman to Ronald Reagan.* Ithaca, N. Y.: Cornell University Press, 1983. Reprint, 1989.

Levine, Lawrence W. *Black Culture and Black Consciousness: Afro-American Folk Thought from Slavery to Freedom.* Oxford, England: Oxford University Press, 1977. Reprint, New York, 1980.

———. *The Unpredictable Past: Explorations in American Cultural History.* New York: Oxford University Press, 1993.

Lieb, Sandra. *Mother of the Blues: A Study of Ma Rainey.* Amherst, Mass.: University of Massachusetts Press, 1981.

Lippman, Theo, Jr. *The Squire of Warm Springs: F. D. R. in Georgia, 1924–1945.* New York: Simon & Schuster, 1977.

Lisio, Donald J. *The President and Protest: Hoover, Conspiracy, and the Bonus Riot.* Columbia, Mo.: University of Missouri Press, 1974.

———. *Hoover, Blacks and Lily-Whites: A Study of Southern Strategies.* Chapel Hill, N. C.: University of North Carolina Press, 1985.

Little, Arthur W. *To the Rhine: The Story of New York's Colored Volunteers*. New York: Covici Friede Publishers, 1936.

Lomax, Alan. *The Land Where the Blues Began*. London: Methuen, 1993.

Lomax, John A., and Alan Lomax. *Our Singing Country: A Second Volume of American Ballads and Folk Songs*. New York: The MacMillan Company, 1949.

Lorenz, Wolfgang. *Bluebird Blues: The Blues of John Lee "Sonny Boy" Williamson*. Bonn, Germany: Moonshine Books, 1986.

Lornell, Kip. *Happy in the Service of the Lord: Afro-American Gospel Quartets in Memphis*. Chicago: University of Illinois Press, 1988.

———. *Virginia's Blues, Country & Gospel Records 1902–1943: An Annotated Discography*. Lexington, Ky.: University of Kentucky Press, 1989.

MacArthur, Douglas. *Reminiscences*. New York: McGraw-Hill, 1964.

MacKenzie, Compton. *Mr. Roosevelt*. London: George G. Harrap & Co., 1943.

Macleod, R. R. *Yazoo 1–20*. Edinburgh, Scotland: Pat, 1988.

———. *Yazoo 21–83*. Edinburgh: Pat, 1992.

———. *Document Blues—1*. Edinburgh: Pat, 1994.

———. *Document Blues—2*. Edinburgh: Pat, 1995.

———. *Document Blues—3*. Edinburgh: Pat, 1996.

Mahony, Dan. *Columbia 13/14000-D Series: A Numerical Listing*. Highland Park, N. J.: Walter C. Allen, 1961.

Malone, Bill C. *Country Music, USA*. 2nd ed. Austin, University of Texas Press, 1987.

McCullough, David. *Truman*. New York: Simon & Schuster, 1992.

McElvaine, Robert S. *The Great Depression: America, 1929–1941*. New York: Times Books, 1984.

McJimsey, George. *Harry Hopkins: Ally of the Poor and Defender of Democracy*. Cambridge, Mass.: Harvard University Press, 1987.

McMillen, Neil R. *Dark Journey: Black Mississippians in the Age of Jim Crow*. Urbana, Ill.: University of Illinois Press, 1989. Reprint, 1990.

Miller, Merle. *Plain Speaking: An Oral Biography of Harry S. Truman*. New York: Berkley Publishing Corporation, 1974.

Miller, Nathan. *F.D.R.: An Intimate History*. Lanham, Md.: Madison Books, 1983.

———. *Theodore Roosevelt: A Life*. New York: William Morrow & Co., 1992.

Moore, Dave. *Brown Skin Gal: The Story of Barbecue Bob*. Ter Aar, The Netherlands: Agram Blues, 1976.

Moran, Lord (Charles Wilson). *Winston Churchill: The Struggle for Survival, 1940–1965*. London: Houghton Mifflin, 1966.

Morgan, Ted. *FDR: A Biography*. New York: Simon and Schuster, 1985.

Mullen, Robert W. *Blacks in America's Wars: The Shift in Attitudes from the Revolutionary War to Vietnam*. New York: Anchor Foundation, 1973. Reprint, 1990.

Murray, Albert. *Stomping the Blues*. London: Paladin, 1976.

Myrdal, Gunnar. *An American Dilemma: The Negro Problem and Modern Democracy*. New York: Harper and Row, 1944.

Napier, Simon, ed. *Backwoods Blues*. Bexhill on Sea, England: Blues Unlimited, 1968.

Oakley, Giles. *The Devil's Music: A History of the Blues*. London: BBC, 1976.

Odum, Howard W., and Guy B. Johnson. *The Negro and his Songs: A Study of Typical Negro Songs in the South*. Chapel Hill, N. C.: University of North Carolina Press, 1925. Reprint, Hatboro, Pa.: Folklore Associates, 1972.

————. *Negro Workaday Songs*. Chapel Hill, N. C.: University of North Carolina Press, 1926.

Oliver, Paul. *Bessie Smith*. London: Cassell, 1959.

————. *Blues Fell This Morning: Meaning in the Blues*. London: Cassell, 1960. Reprint, Cambridge: Cambridge University Press, 1991.

————. *Conversation with the Blues*. London: Cassell, 1967.

————. *The Story of the Blues*. London: Barrie and Jenkins, 1969.

————. *Screening the Blues: Aspects of the Blues Tradition*. London: Cassell & Co., 1968. Reprint as *The Blues Tradition: A Fascinating Study of the Richest Vein of Black Folk Music in America*. New York: Oak Publications, 1970.

————. *Savannah Syncopators: African Retentions in the Blues*. London: Studio Vista, 1970.

————. *Songsters & Saints: Vocal Traditions on Race Records*. Cambridge: Cambridge University Press, England, 1984.

————. *Blues off the Record: Thirty Years of Blues Commentary*. Tunbridge Wells, England: Baton Press, 1984. Reprint, New York: Da Capo Press, 1988.

————, ed. *The Blackwell Guide to Blues Records*. Cambridge, England: Blackwell, 1989.

Olsson, Bengt. *Memphis Blues*. London: Studio Vista, 1970.

Oster, Harry. *Living Country Blues*. Detroit: Folklore Associates, 1969.

Ottenheimer, Harriet J. *Cousin Joe: Blues from New Orleans*. Chicago: University of Chicago Press, 1987.

Palmer, Robert. *Deep Blues*. New York: Viking Press, 1981.

Paris, Mike, and Chris Comber. *Jimmie the Kid: The Life of Jimmie Rodgers*. London: Eddison Bluesbooks, 1977.

Pemberton, William E. *Harry S. Truman: Fair Dealer & Cold Warrior*. Boston: Twayne Publishers, 1989.

Perkins, Frances. *The Roosevelt I Knew*. London: The Viking Press, 1946.

Ploski, Harry A., and Ernest Kaiser. *The Negro Almanac*. New York: Wiley, 1971.

Pratt, Ray. *Rhythm and Resistance: Explorations in the Political Uses of Popular Music*. New York: Praeger, 1990.

Ramsey, Frederic, Jr. *Been Here and Gone*. New Brunswick, N. J.: Rutgers University Press, 1960. Reprint, 1969.

Raper, Arthur F. *Preface to Peasantry*. Chapel Hill, N. C.: University of North Carolina Press, 1936.

Ratner, Sidney. *Taxation and Democracy in America*. New York: Wiley, 1967. Reprint, New York: Octagon Books, 1980.

Robinson, Edgar Eugene, and Vaughan Davis Bornet. *Herbert Hoover, President of the United States*. Stanford, California: Stanford University Press, 1975.

Roosevelt, Eleanor. *This I Remember*. New York: Harper & Brothers, 1949.

———. *The Autobiography of Eleanor Roosevelt*. New York: Da Capo Press, 1992.

Roosevelt, Theodore. *Autobiography*. New York: Da Capo Press, 1985.

Rosenberg, Bruce. *The Art of the American Folk Preacher*. New York: Oxford University Press, 1970.

Rowe, Mike. *Chicago Breakdown*. London: Eddison Bluesbooks, 1973.

Russell, Frances. *President Harding: His Life and Times 1865–1923*. London: Eyre & Spottiswoode, 1969.

Russell, Ross. *Bird Lives! The High Life and Hard Times of Charlie "Yardbird" Parker*. London: Charterhouse, 1973. Reprint, 1988.

Russell, Tony. *Blacks, Whites and Blues*. London: Studio Vista, 1970.

Rust, Brian. *The Victor Master Book, Volume 2 (1925–1936)*. Hatch End, Middlesex, England: self-published. Reprint, Highland Park, N. J.: Walter C. Allen, 1974.

———. *Jazz Records, 1897–1942, Volume 1*. New York: Arlington House, 1978.

———. *Jazz Records, 1897–1942, Volume 2*. New York: Arlington House, 1978.

Sackheim, Eric. *The Blues Line: A Collection of Blues Lyrics from Leadbelly to Muddy Waters*. Japan: Grossman Publishers, 1969. Reprint, New York: Schirmer Books, 1975.

Sacré, Robert, ed. *The Voice of the Delta: Charley Patton and the Mississippi Blues Traditions. Influences and Comparisons*. Liège, Belgium: Presses Universitaires de Liège, 1987.

———. *Les Negro Spirituals et les Gospel Songs*. Paris: Presses Universitaires de France, 1993.

Sanjek, Russell, and David Sanjek. *American Popular Music Business in the 20th Century*. Oxford, England: Oxford University Press, 1991.

Schlesinger, Arthur M. *The Age of Roosevelt: The Coming of the New Deal*. Cambridge, Mass.: Houghton Mifflin Company, 1958.

Schulte Nordholt, J. W. *Het Volk dat in Duisternis Wandelt: De Geschiedenis van de Negers in Amerika*. Arnhem, The Netherlands: Van Loghum Slaterus, 1956. Reprint, 1957.

————. *Woodrow Wilson: Een Leven voor de Wereldvrede*. Amsterdam: Meulenhoff, 1990. Reprint, in an English translation, as *Woodrow Wilson: A Life for World Peace*. Oxford, England: University of California Press, 1991.

Shaw, Arnold. *Honkers and Shouters: The Golden Years of Rhythm and Blues*. New York: Collier Books, 1978. Reprint, New York, MacMillan, 1986.

Sherwood, Robert E. *Roosevelt and Hopkins: An Intimate History*. New York: Harper & Brothers, 1948.

Shoumatoff, Elizabeth. *F.D.R.'s Unfinished Portrait*. Pittsburgh, Pa.: University of Pittsburgh Press, 1990.

Silvester, Peter. *A Left Hand Like God: A Study of Boogie-Woogie*. London: Quartet Books, 1988.

Sitkoff, Harvard. *A New Deal for Blacks: The Emergence of Civil Rights as a National Issue: Volume I, The Depression Decade*. New York: Oxford University Press, 1978. Reprint, Oxford, England: Oxford University Press, 1981.

Smith, Gene. *The Shattered Dream: Herbert Hoover and the Great Depression*. New York: William Morrow & Company, 1970.

Southern, Eileen. *The Music of Black Americans: A History*. New York: W. W. Norton & Co, 1971.

Spragens, William C. *Popular Images of American Presidents*. New York: Greenwood Press, 1988.

Sterling, Christopher H., and John M. Kittross. *Stay Tuned: A Concise History of American Broadcasting*. Belmont, Calif.: Wadsworth Publishing Company, 1978.

Sterner, Richard. *The Negro's Share: A Study of Income, Consumption, Housing and Public Assistance*. New York: Harper and Brothers, 1943.

Stewart-Baxter, Derrick. *Ma Rainey and the Classic Blues Singers*. London: Studio Vista, 1970.

Taft, Michael. *Blues Lyric Poetry: A Concordance*. New York: Garland Publishing, 1983.

Titon, Jeff Todd. *Early Downhome Blues: A Musical and Cultural Analysis*. Urbana, Ill.: University of Illinois Press, 1977. Reprint, 1979.

Townley, Eric. *Tell Your Story: A Dictionary of Jazz and Blues Recordings 1917–1950*. Chigwell, Essex, England: Storyville Publications, 1976.

————. *Tell Your Story No. 2: A Dictionary of Mainstream Jazz and Blues Recordings 1951– 1975*. Chigwell, Essex, England: Storyville Publications, 1987.

Tracy, Steven C. *Going to Cincinnati: A History of the Blues in the Queen City*. Chicago, Ill.: University of Illinois Press, 1993.

Traum, Happy. *Guitar Styles of Brownie McGhee*. New York: Oak Publications, 1971.

Truman, Margaret. *Harry S. Truman*. New York: William Morrow & Company, 1973.

Tugwell, Rexford G. *The Democratic Roosevelt: A Biography of Franklin D. Roosevelt*. New York: Doubleday, 1957.

Tully, Grace. *FDR, My Boss*. New York: Charles Scribner's Sons, 1949.

Vreede, Max E. *Paramount 12000/13000 Series*. London: Storyville Publications, 1971.

Washington, Booker T. *Up From Slavery: An Autobiography*. New York: Bantam, 1956.

Washington, Joseph R., Jr. *Black Sects and Cults*. New York: Anchor Press, Doubleday & Company, 1972.

Waters, W. W. and William White. *B. E. F.: The Whole Story of the Bonus Army*. New York: John Day Company, 1933.

Weiss, Nancy J. *Farewell to the Party of Lincoln: Black Politics in the Age of FDR*. Princeton, N. J.: Princeton University Press, 1983.

Wentworth, Harold, and Stuart Berg Flexner. *Dictionary of American Slang*. New York: Simon & Schuster, 1960.

White, Graham, and John Maze. *Harold Ickes of the New Deal: His Public Life and Public Career*. Cambridge, Mass.: Harvard University Press, 1985.

Whittle, Tyler. *The Last Kaiser: A Biography of William II, German Emperor and King of Prussia*. London, 1977.

Winfield, Betty Houchin. *FDR and the News Media*. Chicago: University of Illinois Press, 1990. Reprint, New York: Columbia University Press, 1994.

Wolfe, Charles, and Kip Lornell. *The Life and Legend of Leadbelly*. New York: Harper Collins, 1992.

Wolters, Raymond. *Negroes and the Great Depression: The Problem of Economic Recovery*. Westport, Conn.: Greenwood Publishing Corporation, 1970.

Woodruff, Nan Elizabeth. *As Rare as Rain: Federal Relief in the Great Southern Drought*. Urbana and Chicago: University of Illinois Press, 1985.

Zur Heide, Karl Gert. *Deep South Piano: The Story of Little Brother Montgomery*. London: Studio Vista, 1970.

Articles

Abbott, Lynn, and Doug Seroff. "America's Blue Yodel." *Musical Traditions* 11 (1993): 5.

Bastin, Bruce. "Fort Valley Blues." *Blues Unlimited* 111 (December 1974/January 1975): part 1; 112 (March/April 1975): part 2; 113 (July/August 1975): part 3.

Bethune, Mary McLeod. "My Secret Talks with FDR." *Ebony* (April 1949): 43–51.

Bogert, Brenda. Sleeve notes to *Clifford Hayes & the Louisville Jug Bands, Volume 4, 1929–1931*. RST JPCD 1504-2, Vienna, Austria (1994).

Bogert, Pen. Sleeve notes for Bill Gaither, *Complete Recorded Works in Chronological Order, Volume 1*. Document DOCD 5251, Austria (1994).

Casey, Ralph D. "Republican Propaganda in the 1936 Campaign." *Public Opinion Quarterly* 1 (April 1937): 35.

Chalmers, Allan K. "Scottsboro Boys." In *The Thirties: A Time to Remember*, edited by Don Congdon, 172. New York: Simon and Schuster, 1962.

Charters, Samuel B. Notes to Lonnie Johnson, *The Complete Folkways Recordings*. Smithsonian Folkways SFCD 40067.

Cowley, John. Unpublished notes prepared for *I'm in the Highway Man*. Flyright FLYLP 542, Great Britain (1980).

———. "Shack Bullies and Levee Contractors: Black Protest Songs & Oral History." *Juke Blues*, parts 1 and 2 (December 1985): 6–12; part 4 (spring 1986): 9–15.

Evans, David. "The Bubba Brown Story." *Blues World* 21 (October 1968): 9.

———. "Bubba Brown: Folk Poet." *Mississippi Folklore Register* 7, no. 1 (spring 1973): 15–31.

———. "The Toast in Context." *Journal of American Folklore* 90 (1977): 129–48.

Garon, Paul. "Peetie's Brother, an Interview with Sam Bunch." *Living Blues* 7 (winter 1971–72): 15.

Garraty, J. A. "The New Deal, National Socialism, and the Great Depression." *American Historical Review* 78, no. 4 (1973): 907–44.

Groom, Bob. "Blues Forum." No. 172, *Blues World* 28 (March 1970): 12.

———. "Tiger in the Night." *Blues & Rhythm* 66 (January 1992): 12–15.

———. Sleeve notes to Walter Roland, *Complete Recorded Works in Chronological Order—Volume 2, 1934–35*. Document DOCD 5145, Austria (1993).

Hall, Bob, and Richard Noblett. "A Handful of Keys: A Man Trying to Get Away—Charlie Spand." *Blues Unlimited* 117 (January/February 1977): 22–23.

Harrah-Conforth, Bruce. Sleeve notes for *Nobody Knows My Name: Blues from South Carolina and Georgia*. Heritage HTLP 304, Great Britain (1984).

Harris, Sheldon. "Obituary for Viola Wells." *Living Blues* 64 (March/April 1985): 70.

Heilbut, Tony. Sleeve notes for "The Gospel Sound." CBS LP 67234.

Jones, Tad. "Professor Longhair Interview." *Living Blues* 26 (March/April 1976): 20.

Kent, Don. "Marshall Owens Obituary." *Living Blues* 26 (March/April 1976): 7.

Leadbitter, Mike. "A Memory of 'Forest City Joe.'" *Blues Unlimited* 112 (March/April 1975): 9.

Lotz, Rainer E. Sleeve notes to *Charlie and His Orchestra: German Propaganda Swing 1941–1942*. Harlequin HQCD 03.

Lowry, Pete. "Questions & Answers # 25." *Living Blues* 16 (spring 1974): 45.

McDuffie, Elizabeth. "FDR Was My Boss." *Ebony* (April 1952): 73–74, 81.

Morgan, Roberta. "Social Implications and the Human Side." *The Journal of the Birmingham Historical Society* 1, no. 1 (January 1960) 14–15.

O'Neal, Jim. Sleeve notes to *Okeh Chicago Blues*, Epic EGLP 37318 (c. 1983).

———. "BluEsoterica." *Living Blues* 114 (April 1994): 128.

Oliver, Paul. "Sales Tax on It: Race Records in the New Deal Years." In *Nothing Else to Fear: New Perspectives on America in the Thirties*, edited by Stephen W. Baskerville and Ralph Willett. Manchester, England: Manchester University Press, 1985.

Rijn, Guido van. "Denomination Blues." *The International Conference on African-American Music and Literature: Religion Versus Secularity in African American Cultural Traditions*. Liège University, Belgium (24–26 October 1991), to be published.

———. "De President Blues: Het Beeld van Amerikaanse Presidenten in de Blues." In *The Pursuit of Happiness en de Paradox van de Vrijheid*, edited by Hans Bak, 120–22. Nijmegen, The Netherlands: Nijmegen Universiteitsdrukkerij, 1994.

———. "Jesus is a President Too: Actuele Blues en Gospel Songs over de Moord op John F. Kennedy." In *Amerikanisten: Werk in Uitvoering*. Groningen, The Netherlands: Groningen Universiteitsdrukkerij, 1995.

Rijn, Guido van, and Hans Vergeer. Sleeve notes for Charley Jordan, *It Ain't Clean*. Agram Blues ABLP 2002, The Netherlands (1978).

———. Sleeve notes for Walter Vinson, *Rats Been on My Cheese*. Agram Blues ABLP 2003, The Netherlands (1978).

———. Sleeve notes for Lucille Bogan, *Women Won't Need No Men*. Agram Blues ABLP 2005, The Netherlands (1979).

———. Sleeve notes for Joe Pullum, *Black Gal*. Agram Blues ABLP 2012, The Netherlands (13 February 1986).

Roosevelt, Eleanor. "Some of My Best Friends Are Negro." *Ebony* (February 1953): 23.

Rowe, Mike. "Review of *Bluebird Blues* by Wolfgang Lorenz." *Blues Unlimited* 148/9 (winter 1987): 56.

Russell, Tony. Sleeve notes to Cecil Gant, *Rock Little Baby*, Flyright LP 4710 (1974).

Rye, Howard. In Tony Burke and Dave Penny's "Big Band Blues: Feedback & Updates." *Blues & Rhythm* 6 (February 1985): 40.

Seroff, Doug. "The Original Fisk Jubilee Singers and the Spiritual Tradition." *Keskidee* 2 (1990): 9.

Sheatsley, Paul B. "O.P.A." *Blues Unlimited* 91 (May 1972): 20.

Sidey, Hugh. "Where's His Wheelchair?" *Time* (29 May 1995): 55.

Summers, Keith. Review of *Religious Recordings from Black New Orleans*. 504 LP 20, *Keskidee* 3 (summer 1993): 57.

Ward, Geoffrey C. "Douglas MacArthur: An American Soldier." *National Geographic* 181, no. 3 (March 1992): 54–83.

Wardlow, Gayle Dean. "Gress Barnett Interview." *78 Quarterly* 5 (1990): 95.

Wilson, James Q. "Two Negro Politicians: An Interpretation." In *Negro Politics in America*, edited by Harry A. Bailey, 152–59. Columbus, Ohio: Charles E. Merrill Books, 1967.

Wolfe, Charles. "Where the Blues Is At: A Survey of Recent Research." *Popular Music and Society* 1 (1971–72): 153.

Young, Frank A. "Brown America Takes the Air: The Story of the First Negro Fliers in the United States Air Corps." *Chicago Defender* (13 June 1942): 23.

DISCOGRAPHY

Page	Artist	Title	Date	Record
087	Armstrong, Louis & Mills Brothers	W.P.A.	4/10/40	Decca 3151
128	Big Bill Broonzy	My Big Money	1/29/37	ARC 7-11-67
139	Big Bill Broonzy	Unemployment Stomp	3/30/38	Vocalion 04378
144	Big Bill Broonzy	That Number of Mine (Number 158)	12/17/40	OKeh 06080
022	Black Billy Sunday	This Old World's in a Hell of a Fix	1/?/31	Par. 13052
162	Blackwell, Willie "61"	Junian's, A Jap's Girl Christmas for His Santa Claus	7/16/42	LofC unissued
010	Blake, Arthur "Blind"	He's in the Jailhouse Now	11/?/27	Par. 12565
045	Bogan, Lucille	Red Cross Man	7/17/33	Banner 33072
183	Booze, Wee Bea	War Rationin' Papa	3/27/42	Decca 8621
077	Brewer, Annie	Roosevelt Blues	3/11/37	LofC unissued
196	Brown, Charles & Johnny McNeil	End O'War Blues	3/?/45	Exclusive 205
049	Brown, John Henry "Bubba"	The Red Cross Store	6/9/67	Unissued
004	Cannon, Gus	Can You Blame the Colored Man	11/?/27	Par. 12571
171	Clayton, Peter J. "Doctor"	'41 Blues	7/1/41	OKeh 06375
151	Clayton, Peter J. "Doctor"	Pearl Harbor Blues	3/27/42	BlueBird B9003
091	Cox, Ida	Pink Slip Blues	10/31/39	Vocalion 05258
063	Darby, Blind Teddy	Meat and Bread Blues (Relief Blues)	3/25/35	Vocalion 02988
061	Davis, Walter	Red Cross Blues	8/2/33	BlueBird B5143
061	Davis, Walter	Red Cross Blues—Part 2	12/11/33	BlueBird B5305
091	Dupree, "Champion" Jack	Warehouse Man Blues	6/13/40	OKeh 05656
195	Dupree, "Champion" Jack	F.D.R. Blues	4/18/45	Joe Davis 5102
204	Dupree, "Champion" Jack	God Bless Our New President!	4/18/45	Joe Davis 5102
152	Dupree, "Champion" Jack	Pearl Harbour Blues	9/28/60	Unissued
122	Easton, Amos "Bumble Bee Slim"	When I Get My Money (I Mean That Bonus)	3/11/36	Vocalion 03221
126	Edgewater Crows	No Bonus Blues	7/15/36	Melotone 7-01-62
170	Edwards, Frank	We Got to Get Together	5/28/41	OKeh 06363
103	Estes, "Sleepy" John	Government Money	8/2/37	Decca 7414
186	Ezell, Buster "Buzz"	Obey Your Ration Laws (A)	8/1/43	LofC unissued
176	Ezell, Buster "Buzz"	Roosevelt and Hitler	8/1/43	LofC unissued
141	Ezell, Buster "Buzz"	Soldier Boy Blues	8/1/43	LofC unissued
041	Fitzgerald, Ella & Chick Webb	F. D. R. Jones	10/6/38	Decca 2105
145	Five Breezes	My Buddy Blues	11/15/40	BlueBird B8614
169	Florida Kid	Hitler Blues	11/7/40	BlueBird B8589
143	Fuller, "Blind Boy"	When You Are Gone	6/19/40	OKeh 05756
141	Gaither, Bill	Changing Blues	9/14/39	Decca 7659
140	Gaither, Bill	Army Bound Blues	9/13/39	Decca 7647
141	Gaither, Bill	Uncle Sam Called the Roll	1/24/41	OKeh 06092
020	Gates, Rev. J. M.	These Hard Times Are Tight Like That	12/12/30	OKeh 8850
070	Gates, Rev. J. M.	No Bread Line In Heaven	8/1/34	BlueBird B5600
097	Gates, Rev. J. M.	President Roosevelt Is Everybody's Friend	8/1/34	BlueBird B5600
172	Gates, Rev. J. M.	Hitler and Hell	10/2/41	BlueBird B8851
174	Golden Gate Quartet	Stalin Wasn't Stallin'	3/5/43	OKeh 6712
107	Gordon, Jimmie	Don't Take Away My P.W.A.	10/2/36	Decca 7230
112	Harlem Hamfats	Sales Tax on It	8/14/36	Decca 7206

Reissue	Composer credit	Location	State	Birth
Classics CD 615	Jesse Stone	New York City	NY	LA
Document DOCD 5127		Chicago	ILL	MISS
Document DOCD 5129	Broomzy	Chicago	ILL	MISS
Document DOCD 5132	Broonzy	Chicago	ILL	MISS
Wolf WSELP 136	McPherson	Grafton	WIS	
Flyright FLYLP 541	xxx		ARK	
Document DOCD 5025	Miller and Williams	Chicago	ILL	FLA
Blues Doc. BDCD 6037		New York City	NY	MISS
Wolf WBJCD 007		New York City	NY	MD
		Montgomery	ALA	
	Johnnie McNeil	Los Angeles	CAL	TEX
		Los Angeles	CAL	MISS
Document DOCD 5032		Chicago	ILL	MISS
Document DOCD 5179	Cleighton	Chicago	ILL	GA
Document DOCD 5179	Joe Clayton	Chicago	ILL	GA
Affinity AFSCD 1015	Grainger	New York City	NY	GA
Blues Doc. BDCD6042		Chicago	ILL	KY
Document DOCD 5281	W. Davis	Chicago	ILL	MISS
Document DOCD 5281	W. Davis	Chicago	ILL	MISS
Columbia CKCD 52834-2	Dupree	Chicago	ILL	LA
Columbia CKCD 52834-2	Joe Davis	New York City	NY	LA
Red Pepper RPLP 701	Joe Davis	New York City	NY	LA
Magpie PYCD 53		Herstmonceux	England	LA
Document DOCD 5266	Amos Easton	Chicago	ILL	GA
	xxx	Hattiesburg	MISS	
Document DOCD 5426	F. Edwards	Chicago	ILL	GA
Document DOCD 5015	Estes-Nixon	New York City	NY	TENN
		Fort Valley	GA	
		Fort Valley	GA	
		Fort Valley	GA	
Classics CD 518	Rome	New York City	NY	VA
Document DOCD 5444	Eugene Gilmore	Chicago	ILL	
Document DOCD 5427	Ernest Blunt	Chicago	ILL	ARK
Document DOCD 5096	xxx	New York City	NY	KY
Document DOCD 5254	Hill	Chicago	ILL	KY
Document DOCD 5254	Gaither	Chicago	ILL	KY
Document DOCD 5255	Gaither	Chicago	ILL	KY
Document DOCD 5483	xxx	Atlanta	GA	
Document DOCD 5483		Atlanta	GA	
Document DOCD 5484		Atlanta	GA	
	xxx	Atlanta	GA	
Document DOCD 5475	W. Johnson	New York City	NY	
Story of Blues CD 3518-2	Mills-Gordon	Chicago	ILL	
Document DOCD 5271	McCoy	Chicago	ILL	

Page	Artist	Title	Date	Record
019	Hicks, Robert "Barbecue Bob"	We Sure Got Hard Times	4/18/30	Col. 14558-D
014	Hill, Bertha "Chippie"	Hard Time Blues	10/16/28	Vocalion 1264
063	Hollins, Tony	Stamp Blues	6/3/41	OKeh 06351
164	House, Son	American Defense (This War Will Last You For Years)	7/17/42	LofC unissued
197	Jackson, Otis	Tell Me Why You Like Roosevelt—Part 1	9/?/49	Gotham 626
198	Jackson, Otis	Tell Me Why You Like Roosevelt—Part 2	9/?/49	Gotham 626
028	Jenkins, Hezekiah	The Panic Is On	1/16/31	Col. 14585-D
007	Johnson, Blind Willie	When the War Was On	12/11/29	Col. 14545-D
119	Johnson, Lil	That Bonus Done Gone Thru	2/12/36	ARC 6-05-52
109	Johnson, Lonnie	Four-O-Three Blues	11/2/39	BlueBird B8338
103	Jones, Lemuel	Po' Farmer	5/31/36	LofC unissued
025	Jordan, Charley	Starvation Blues	1/6/31	Vocalion 1627
129	Jordan, Charley	Look What a Shape I'm In (Bonus Blues)	11/2/37	Decca 7455
187	Jordan, Louis	You Can't Get That No More	3/15/44	Decca 8668
184	Jordan, Louis	Ration Blues	10/4/42	Decca 8654
191	Jordan, Louis	The Infantry Blues	8/?/43	AFRS Jubilee 41
067	Kelly, Jack	R.F.C. Blues	8/1/33	Banner 32857
066	Kelly, Jack	President Blues (President Roosevelt Blues)	8/2/33	Banner 32857
055	Ledbetter, Huddie "Leadbelly"	Red Cross Sto'	2/13/35	LofC unissued
135	Ledbetter, Huddie "Leadbelly"	Scottsboro Boys	12/26/38	LofC unissued
057	Ledbetter, Huddie "Leadbelly"	The Red Cross Store Blues	6/15/40	BlueBird B8709
057	Ledbetter, Huddie "Leadbelly"	Red Cross Sto'	8/23/40	LofC unissued
168	Ledbetter, Huddie "Leadbelly"	The Roosevelt Song	8/23/40	LofC unissued
136	Ledbetter, Huddie "Leadbelly"	The Scottsboro Boys	8/23/40	LofC unissued
150	Ledbetter, Huddie "Leadbelly"	Dear Mr. President & President Roosevelt	1/20/42	LofC unissued
173	Ledbetter, Huddie "Leadbelly"	Mr. Hitler	1/20/42	LofC unissued
076	Martin, Carl	Let's Have a New Deal	9/4/35	Decca 7114
123	Martin, Carl	I'm Gonna Have My Fun (When I Get My Bonus)	3/24/36	Champion 50074
194	McCain, James "Jack of All Trades"	Good Mr. Roosevelt	1/?/45	Chicago 103
106	McCoy, Charlie	Charity Blues	8/13/34	Decca 7046
060	McDowell, Mississippi Fred	Red Cross Store	3/8/69	Red Lightnin' LP 0053
017	McGhee, Brownie	The Red Cross Store	5/?/42	LofC unissued
083	McKenzie, Billie	That Man on the W.P.A.	11/4/36	Vocalion 03385
096	Memphis Minnie	Sylvester and His Mule Blues	1/10/35	Decca 7084
154	Millinder, Lucius "Lucky"	We're Gonna Have to Slap the Dirty Little Jap	2/18/42	Decca 4261
111	Mississippi Sheiks	Sales Tax	3/27/34	BlueBird B5453
075	Mississippi Sheiks	I Can't Go Wrong	1/19/35	BlueBird B5881
017	Moss, Buddy	Chesterfield	6/10/66	Biograph BLP 12019
114	Piano Red	The Sales Tax Boogie	5/10/52	Victor 20-4766
062	Pittman, Samson	Welfare Blues	10/16/38	LofC unissued
117	Pullum, Joe	Black Gal What Makes Your Head So Hard?	4/3/34	BlueBird B5459

Reissue	Composer credit	Location	State	Birth
Document DOCD 5048	xxx	Atlanta	GA	GA
Document DOCD 5330		Chicago	ILL	SC
Document DOCD 5270		Chicago	ILL	MISS
Travelin' Man CD 02	House	Robinsonville	MISS	MISS
Krazy Kat KKLP 7417	Jackson	Philadelphia	PA	
Krazy Kat KKLP 7417	Jackson	Philadelphia	PA	
Document DOCD 5481	xxx	New York City	NY	
Columbia CKCD 52835-2	xxx	New Orleans	LA	TEX
Document DOCD 5307	Lil Johnson	Chicago	ILL	
Blues Documents BDCD 6024	L. Johnson	Chicago	ILL	LA
Blues Ridge Institute BRLP 001		Richmond	VA	
Document DOCD 5097		Chicago	ILL	ARK
Document DOCD 5099		Chicago	ILL	ARK
Juke Box Lil JBLP 602	Louis Jordan-Sam Theard	New York City	NY	ARK
Decca BM 03545	L. Jordan-A. Cosby-C. Clark	Los Angeles	CAL	ARK
Natasha NICD 4025		Hollywood	FLA	ARK
Blues Documents BDCD 6005		New York City	NY	MISS
Blues Documents BDCD 6005		New York City	NY	MISS
Document DOCD 5444		Wilton	CONN	LA
Document DLP 609		New York City	NY	LA
Document DOCD 5226	xxx	New York City	NY	LA
Document DLP 610		Washington	DC	LA
Document DLP 612		Washington	DC	LA
Document DLP 612		Washington	DC	LA
		New York City	NY	LA
		New York City	NY	LA
Document DOCD 5229	Carl Martin	Chicago	ILL	VA
Document DOCD 5229	Carl Martin	Chicago	ILL	VA
Document DOCD 5411		Chicago	ILL	
Blues Documents BDCD 6019		Chicago	ILL	MISS
	xxx	London	England	TENN
Document DOCD 5230		Washington	DC	TENN
Document DOCD 5295		Chicago	ILL	
Blues Documents BDCD 6008	McCoy	Chicago	ILL	LA
Classics CD 712	Bob Miller	New York City	NY	ALA
Document DOCD 5086		San Antonio	TEX	
Document DOCD 5086		New Orleans	LA	
	Moss	Washington	DC	GA
Bear Family 15658-4	Willie Perryman	Atlanta	GA	GA
Laurie LCD 7002	xxx	Detroit	MICH	ARK
Document DOCD 5393	J. Pullem	San Antonio	TEX	

Page	Artist	Title	Date	Record
069	Pullum, Joe	CWA Blues	4/3/34	BlueBird B5534
122	Pullum, Joe	Bonus Blues	2/25/36	BlueBird B6372
118	Red Nelson	When the Soldiers Get Their Bonus (Even if It Don't Last Long)	2/6/36	Decca 7155
102	Red Nelson	Relief Blues	10/11/37	BlueBird B7265
047	Roland, Walter	Red Cross Blues	7/17/33	Banner 32822
051	Roland, Walter	Red Cross Blues No. 2	7/17/33	Banner 33121
072	Roland, Walter	C.W.A. Blues	7/30/34	Banner 33136
052	Scott, Sonny	Red Cross Blues	7/18/33	Vocalion 25012
052	Scott, Sonny	Red Cross Blues No. 2	7/20/33	Vocalion 02614
155	Selah Jubilee Singers	Wasn't That an Awful Time at Pearl Harbor	5/20/42	Decca 7896
050	Shaw, Thomas	Richard Nixon's Welfare Blues	?/?/71	Advent LP 2801
024	Short, J. D. "Joe Stone"	It's Hard Time	8/2/33	BlueBird B5169
187	Sorter-McCoy, Ann	Tell It to the O.P.A.	?/?/45	Chicago 100
157	Soul Stirrers	Pearl Harbor—Part 1	6/2/47	Aladdin 2025
158	Soul Stirrers	Pearl Harbor—Part 2	6/2/47	Aladdin 2025
026	Spand, Charlie	Hard Time Blues	9/?/31	Par. 13112
147	Sykes, Roosevelt	Training Camp Blues	11/21/41	Okeh 6709
026	Tampa Red	Depression Blues	10/24/31	Vocalion 1656
126	Taylor, Rev. R. H.	The Bonus Have Found the Stingy Mens Out	7/21/36	Melotone 6-11-64
125	Thomas, Earl	Bonus Men	7/7/36	Decca 7221
014	Thomas, Willard "Ramblin'"	No Job Blues	2/?/28	Par. 12609
180	Unidentified Man	Hitler Toast	8/4/42	LofC unissued
096	Washboard Sam	CCC Blues	12/16/38	BlueBird B7993
048	Washboard Trio (Mobile Washboard Band)	Red Cross Blues	7/17/41	LofC unissued
081	Weldon, Will "Casey Bill"	W.P.A. Blues	2/12/36	Vocalion 03186
084	Weldon, Will "Casey Bill"	Casey Bill's New W.P.A.	10/20/37	Vocalion 03930
120	Wheatstraw, Peetie	When I Get My Bonus (Things Will Be Coming My Way)	2/18/36	Decca 7159
083	Wheatstraw, Peetie	Working on the Project	3/30/37	Decca 7311
085	Wheatstraw, Peetie	New Working on the Project	11/2/37	Decca 7379
085	Wheatstraw, Peetie	304 Blues (Lost My Job on the Project)	4/1/38	Decca 7453
068	White, Josh	Low Cotton	8/15/33	Banner 32858
094	White, Josh	Bad Housing Blues	?/?/41	Key 515
149	White, Josh	Defense Factory Blues	?/?/41	Key 516
148	White, Josh	Uncle Sam Says	?/?/41	Key 514
073	Williams, Big Joe	Providence Help the Poor People	2/25/35	BlueBird B5930
189	Williams, Big Joe	His Spirit Lives On	?/?/45	Chicago 103
159	Williams, Blind Connie	Oh, What a Time	5/5/61	Test. TLP 2225
189	Williams, Henry "Rubberlegs"	4-F Blues	1/?/45	Continental C6020
084	Williamson, Sonny Boy	Project Highway	11/11/37	BlueBird B7302
142	Williamson, Sonny Boy	War Time Blues	5/17/40	BlueBird B8580
053	Williamson, Sonny Boy	Welfare Store Blues	5/17/40	BlueBird B8580
179	Williamson, Sonny Boy	Check Up on My Baby	12/14/44	BlueBird 34-0722
165	Williamson, Sonny Boy	We Got to Win	7/2/45	Victor unissued

Reissue	Composer credit	Location	State	Birth
Document DOCD 5393	xxx	San Antonio	TEX	
Document DOCD 5394	xxx	San Antonio	TEX	
Blues Documents BDCD 6006		Chicago	ILL	MISS
Old Tramp OTCD 06		Aurora	ILL	MISS
Document DOCD 5144	xxx	New York City	NY	
Document DOCD 5144	xxx	New York City	NY	
Document DOCD 5145	xxx	New York City	NY	
Document DOCD 5450		New York City	NY	
Document DOCD 5450		New York City	NY	
Document DOCD 5500	Ruth-Ford-Townsley	New York City	NY	
	xxx	Manhattan Beach	CAL	TEX
Document DOCD 5147		Chicago	ILL	MISS
	Leroy Allen	Chicago	ILL	
Imperial LMLP 94007	xxx	Chicago	ILL	
Imperial LMLP 94007				
Document DOCD 5108	Spand-Lamoore	Grafton	WIS	
Document DOCD 5122	Sykes	Chicago	ILL	ARK
Document DOCD 5076		Chicago	ILL	GA
	xxx	Hattiesburg	MISS	
Blues Documents BDLP 2052		Chicago	ILL	
Document DOCD 5107	xxx	Chicago	ILL	LA
		Sherard	MISS	
Document 5173	Robert Brown	Aurora	ILL	ARK
Travelin' Man TMCD 09		Selma	ALA	
Document DOCD 5217		Chicago	ILL	ARK
Document DOCD 5219		Chicago	ILL	ARK
Document DOCD 5243	Bunch	New York City	NY	TENN
Document DOCD 5245	Jordan	Chicago	ILL	TENN
Document DOCD 5245	Jordan	Chicago	ILL	TENN
Document DOCD 5245	Jordan	New York City	NY	TENN
Document DOCD 5194	xxx	New York City	NY	SC
Document DOCD 5405	Cuney-White	New York City	NY	SC
Document DOCD 5405	Cuney-White	New York City	NY	SC
Document DOCD 5405	Cuney-White	New York City	NY	SC
Blues Documents BDCD 6003		Chicago	ILL	MISS
Blues Documents BDCD 6004		Chicago	ILL	MISS
Testament OTCD 2024	xxx	Philadelphia	PA	FLA
Black and Blue BBLP 33008	R. Williams	New York City	NY	
Document DOCD 5055		Aurora	ILL	TENN
Document DOCD 5057	Sonny Boy Williamson	Chicago	ILL	TENN
Document DOCD 5057		Chicago	ILL	TENN
Document DOCD 5058	Sonny Boy Williamson	Chicago	ILL	TENN
Document DOCD 5058		Chicago	ILL	TENN

SONG INDEX

ARTIST INDEX

GENERAL INDEX